SOMEWHERE, A BOY AND A BEAR

SOMEWHERE,
A BOY
AND A BEAR

A Biography of A. A. Milne
and Winnie-the-Pooh

GYLES BRANDRETH

MICHAEL  JOSEPH

PENGUIN BOOKS

UK | USA | Canada | Ireland | Australia
India | New Zealand | South Africa

Penguin Books is part of the Penguin Random House group of companies
whose addresses can be found at global.penguinrandomhouse.com

Penguin Books, Penguin Random House UK,
One Embassy Gardens, 8 Viaduct Gardens, London SW11 7BW

penguin.co.uk

Penguin
Random House
UK

First published 2025
005

Cover illustration by J. H. Dowd.
Jacket design © Penguin Books Ltd 2025

Set in Imprint MT by Couper Street Type Co.
Printed and bound in Great Britain by Clays Ltd, Elcograf S.p.A.

The authorized representative in the EEA is Penguin Random House Ireland,
Morrison Chambers, 32 Nassau Street, Dublin D02 YH68

A CIP catalogue record for this book is available from the British Library

HARDBACK ISBN: 978-0-241-58254-1

Penguin Random House is committed to a sustainable future
for our business, our readers and our planet. This book is made from
Forest Stewardship Council® certified paper.

'Let a man live to be a hundred, his first twenty years will be the greater part of his life. In those years the man was made.'

– J. V. Milne (1845–1932)

'Whatever subject an author chooses or has chosen for him, he reveals no secret but the secret of himself.'

– A. A. Milne (1882–1956)

'For us, to whom our childhood has meant so much, the journey back is short, the coming and going easy.'

– C. R. Milne (1920–96)

Contents

The Characters

Alan Alexander Milne – who created the world of Winnie-the-Pooh and wrote four of the most successful children's books in the history of publishing – thought of himself principally as a playwright. Each of his forty plays begins with a list of characters. Here is ours.

In England and America

JOHN VINE MILNE and his wife, MARIA
Their three sons:
BARRY, KEN, ALAN
And their three wives:
CONNIE, MAUD, DAPHNE
And their children, most notably Alan and Daphne's only son:
CHRISTOPHER ROBIN,
known within the family first as Billy, then as Moon, then
    simply as Christopher
And Christopher's nanny, OLIVE RAND
And Christopher's wife, LESLEY, and their only daughter:
CLARE
Together with an assortment of relations, family friends and
    acquaintances, maids, cooks, gardeners, teachers, mentors,
    editors, journalists, agents, publishers, illustrators, notably
    E. H. Shepard, and writers of distinction, including:
H. G. WELLS, J. M. BARRIE, P. G. WODEHOUSE

Plus military men, theatrical producers, actors, actresses, and
some world-famous figures, among them:
QUEEN ELIZABETH II and WALT DISNEY

In the Forest and the One Hundred Acre Wood

WINNIE-THE-POOH
'A Bear of Very Little Brain'

CHRISTOPHER ROBIN
'Winnie-the-Pooh went round to his friend Christopher
Robin, who lived behind a green door in another part of
the Forest.'

PIGLET
'The Piglet lived in a very grand house in the middle of a
beech tree . . . "It is because you are a very small animal
that you will be Useful in the adventure before us."'

RABBIT
'"Rabbit's clever," said Pooh thoughtfully. "Yes," said Piglet.
"Rabbit's clever." "And he has Brain." "Yes," said Piglet.
"Rabbit has Brain." There was a long silence. "I suppose,"
said Pooh, "that's why he never understands anything."'

EEYORE
'The old grey donkey, Eeyore, stood by himself in a thistly
corner of the Forest, his front feet well apart, his head on
one side, and thought about things. Sometimes he thought
sadly to himself, "Why?"'

OWL
'Owl lived at The Chestnuts, an old-world residence of great
charm, which was grander than anybody else's . . . "And
if somebody knows anything about anything . . . it's Owl
who knows something about something."'

KANGA AND BABY ROO

'Nobody seemed to know where they came from, but they were in the Forest: Kanga and Baby Roo.'

TIGGER

'"Do Tiggers like honey?" "They like everything," said Tigger cheerfully.'

Together with an assortment of bees, beetles, Heffalumps, hedgehogs, Woozles, and all Rabbit's friends and relations

Prologue

in which we are introduced to the author of this book
and his lifelong interest in the world of A. A. Milne

A. A. Milne, Christopher Robin, Winnie-the-Pooh, and me

'Pooh, promise you won't forget about me, ever. Not even
    when I'm a hundred.'
Pooh thought for a little.
'How old shall *I* be then?'
'Ninety-nine.'
Pooh nodded.
'I promise, he said.

The House at Pooh Corner

24 December 2024: Jamaica

This feels like the right day for starting this book. Today,
officially, is the ninety-ninth birthday of Winnie-the-Pooh.
At least, today is the ninety-ninth anniversary of Pooh's first
appearance in print.

On 24 December 1925, the London *Evening News* –
according to its masthead, 'London's predominant evening
journal' boasting 'The largest evening net sale in the world'
– ran a banner headline right across the top of its front page:

A CHILDREN'S STORY BY A. A. MILNE

There were other, smaller headlines on the front page. It was going to be a 'Christmas without snow' in London, though 'great storms' were sweeping over Derbyshire; 'Lord Cobham's Mansion', Hagley Hall, was engulfed by fire, with 'priceless art treasures' threatened; there was trouble in China, a financial scandal in the City, and an amusing account of Sir Harry Lauder, the popular Scottish singer and comedian, missing his train home to Glasgow. But the main event was the arrival of Winnie-the-Pooh:

> A new story for children, 'Winnie-the-Pooh', about Christopher Robin and his Teddy Bear, written by Mr A. A. Milne specially for 'The Evening News' appears tonight on page 7.
>
> It will be broadcast from all stations by Mr Donald Calthrop, as part of the Christmas Day wireless programmes at 7.45 p.m. tomorrow.

These were the early days of radio (the British Broadcasting Company was founded in 1922) and this was big stuff. A. A. Milne was a famous writer: columnist, novelist and playwright. And Donald Calthrop was a major British film star: he appeared in more than sixty films between 1916 and 1940, including five directed by Alfred Hitchcock.

Christopher Robin and his bear had already made a brief appearance in a poem by A. A. Milne called 'Teddy Bear' published in the magazine *Punch* earlier in the year and included in Milne's first collection of children's verses published that November, but it was on page 7 of the *Evening News* that Christmas Eve that the 'Bear of Very Little Brain' was introduced to us properly and by name:

Here is Edward Bear, coming downstairs now, bump, bump, bump, on the back of his head, behind Christopher Robin. It is, as far as he knows, the only way of coming downstairs, but sometimes he feels that there really is another way, if only he could stop bumping for a moment and think of it. And then he feels that perhaps there isn't. Anyhow, here he is at the bottom, and ready to be introduced to you. Winnie-the-Pooh.

This, then, Pooh's birthday, is the right day on which to begin my book – and where I am standing now, notebook in hand, is the right place, I reckon, to begin writing it.

I am in the parish of Clarendon on the island of Jamaica in the Caribbean Sea. It is an enchanted place. There are blue skies above and I am in a forest of flowering trees: dogwood and logwood and fiddlewood, wild ackee and yellow sanders. There are mango and papaya groves nearby and along the track through the woodland golden dewdrops, crape jasmine and hibiscus. This is the place where A. A. Milne's father, J. V. Milne, was born.

This is a book about a boy and a bear, but it is also a book about fathers and sons, about the effects of parents on their children, about the nature of childhood itself – about the magic and the mystery and the importance of childhood.

The notion – and the reality – of childhood has evolved across the centuries, of course. Once upon a time children were viewed simply as small adults and, unless they came from wealthy families, as necessary (and cheap) contributors to the workforce. (They still are in some parts of the world today.) At university, for a time, I studied French and philosophy and I remember reading John Locke and Jean-Jacques Rousseau and learning that our modern notion of childhood – a time of innocence and playfulness, of discovery and learning, of carefree adventure within safe boundaries – began during the Age of Enlightenment in the seventeenth and eighteenth centuries and the Romantic period that followed. I read Rousseau's famous 1762 novel, *Emile: or On Education*, where he defines childhood as the enchanted place where a child can live freely for a few, brief years before having to encounter the dangers and difficulties of adulthood.

Rousseau would have loved the wild Jamaican wood where I am standing now. Rousseau believed in the essential beauty and goodness of nature. 'Everything is good as it comes from the hands of the Maker of the world,' he said, 'but degenerates once it gets into the hands of Man.' Famously, he also said: 'The world of reality has its limits; the world of imagination is boundless.'

In the mid-1840s, when J. V. Milne was born in Clarendon, the son of missionary parents, there were very few children's books to feed a child's imagination. There were instructional religious tracts aimed at children, but not a lot besides. The first nursery rhyme collection to be printed was *Tommy Thumb's Song Book*, published a century before. Hans Christian Andersen's first collection of *Fairy Tales Told for Children* appeared in the mid-1830s. But the golden age of children's literature was yet to be: *The Water Babies* by Charles Kingsley appeared in 1862, *Alice's Adventures in Wonderland* by Lewis Carroll in 1865, Louisa M. Alcott's *Little Women* in 1868.

Today, the parish of Clarendon is famous as the birthplace of the singer Millie Small, who had a huge hit with 'My Girl Lollipop' in 1964, and of Davina Bennett, 'Miss Universe' in 2017. Doreen Lawrence (Baroness Lawrence of Clarendon), the British campaigner for social justice, was born here. Her teenage son Stephen, who was murdered in Eltham in London in 1993, is buried here.

The story of the Milne family that I am going to recount in the pages that follow contains no brutal or horrific murders, but it does contain tragedy, disappointment and heartache, betrayal, dishonesty, and moments of despair. There is joy, too, of course, a good deal of joy, because there is Winnie-the-Pooh, and you wouldn't be reading this book at all if it wasn't for Winnie-the-Pooh.

Lines Written by a Bear of Very Little Brain

On Monday, when the sun is hot
I wonder to myself a lot:
'Now is it true, or is it not,
'That what is which and which is what?'

On Tuesday, when it hails and snows,
The feeling on me grows and grows
That hardly anybody knows
If those are these or these are those.

On Wednesday, when the sky is blue,
And I have nothing else to do,
I sometimes wonder if it's true
That who is what and what is who.

On Thursday, when it starts to freeze
And hoar-frost twinkles on the trees,
How very readily one sees
That these are whose—but whose are these?

On Friday—

Winnie-the-Pooh

Today in Clarendon right now the sun is hot. It's 31 degrees and feels like 36 degrees. There was a shower earlier and thunderstorms are threatened for later. This is an enchanted place, but with changeable weather and – I have just seen a huge spider scuttling through the undergrowth – more complicated than it seems on the surface. This is the right place to start.

5 January 2025: New York

I am now in New York, and it is bitterly cold. I have come to meet Winnie-the-Pooh. Yes, the original Winnie-the-Pooh, the real Christopher Robin's very own teddy bear. He has been living here in the United States since not long after the Second World War. He is here because his proper owner, Christopher Robin, had had enough of him and because the man who made him world-famous, A. A. Milne, was weary beyond words of being forever associated with the Bear of Little Brain.

Milne was a playwright, and probably his most success-ful play, *Mr Pim Passes By*, opened in London, at the New Theatre (now the Noël Coward), on this day, 5 January, in 1920. It was a huge hit (with Leslie Howard, one of the future stars of *Gone with the Wind*, among the leads), trans-ferring to the London Garrick Theatre and then to the Play-house, running for 246 performances in all. The play opened in New York, at the 910-seater Garrick Theater on West 35th Street, on 28 February 1921 and ran for 124 performances. It was revived in New York, in London, in Australia, and per-formed by repertory companies and by amateurs for years. In 1921 it was turned into a silent movie and later produced several times by the BBC on both radio and TV.

Milne was a hot ticket on Broadway in the 1920s. Quite a few of his plays opened here before they opened in London. *The Great Broxopp* arrived at the Punch and Judy Theater on West 49th Street in November 1921, eighteen months before it opened in London. *The Dover Road* (another of Milne's most successful plays) opened at the New Bijou Theater on West 45th in December 1921, six months before its London premiere. *The Lucky One* ('I used to think it was my best play; well, I suppose it was once') was presented by the Theater Guild at the Garrick Theater in New York in November 1922 when it could not find a London producer. *Michael and Mary* arrived in New York in 1929, at the Charles Hopkins Theater (the Punch and Judy Theater renamed), before it opened in London in 1930. *The Ivory Door* arrived at the Charles Hopkins Theater in 1927 and in London in 1929. For a decade and more Milne was a Broadway fixture: *The Truth about Blayds* (Booth Theater, 1922); *The Man in the Bowler Hat* (Belasco, 1924); *Ariadne, or Business First* (Garrick, 1925); *Meet the Prince* (Lyceum, 1929); *Give Me Yesterday* (Charles Hopkins Theater, 1931); *Other People's Lives* (Charles Hopkins, 1932).

Most of the Broadway theatres where Milne's plays enjoyed their first success – the Garrick, the Bijou, the Charles Hopkins – have long since disappeared, demolished to make way for office blocks and high-rise hotels. Most of Milne's plays are just distant memories, too. All anyone in New York now knows of A. A. Milne is that he's the guy who created Winnie-the-Pooh.

6 January 2025: New York

Twelfth Night. It's snowing in New York. Clutching my notebook in very cold hands (it's minus 1 degree here and feels like minus 3), I am walking down Fifth Avenue – past St Patrick's Cathedral, past Saks Fifth Avenue, past the Rockefeller Plaza, where the Christmas tree is still all lit up, past the Dyson store . . . St Patrick, Saks, Rockefeller, Dyson – these are all names to reckon with, like Winnie-the-Pooh.

I am on my way to the New York Public Library on Fifth Avenue and 42nd Street. This is where the original Winnie-the-Pooh now lives. That's clear from the posters outside the library. It's clear from the posters inside the library. Pooh's image is everywhere. He is in the elevators. He is outside the toilets. He is in the coffee shop.

With my wife, Michèle, I have come to see the official 'Treasures of the New York Public Library', and Christopher Robin's very own Winnie-the-Pooh is here – alongside the Guttenberg Bible, a Shakespeare First Folio, and a fair copy of the 1776 Declaration of Independence in Thomas Jefferson's own hand. The library boasts 56 million items, some going back four thousand years, but among its treasures Pooh has pride of place. It also has Virginia Woolf's walking stick on display: it was found lying on the bank of the river Ouse in East Sussex where, aged fifty-nine, the writer took her own life on 28 March 1941; they also have a letter to Vita Sackville-West from Leonard Woolf telling her he assumed Virginia was dead; her body was not recovered until 18 April. They have Charles Dickens's desk from Gadshill Place, his house in Rochester in Kent, with the date on the perpetual calendar set at Tuesday 9 June, unchanged since the day he died in 1870. And they have Winnie-the-Pooh: the original Winnie-the-Pooh, the bear Christopher Robin was given on his first birthday on 21 August 1921, the most famous bear in literature, and, thanks to the merchandising (a soft toy bear sells better than a soft toy mouse), the most profitable character in the Walt Disney catalogue.

Never mind how the New York Public Library acquired Virginia Woolf's walking stick and Charles Dickens's desk: how did they get Pooh? And Piglet and Tigger and Eeyore and Kanga, too. (Where's Roo? He's missing. That's a mystery I will need to unravel.)

I have to say the animals look to be in beautiful condition – much fresher than when I last saw them here in New York thirty years ago. They were in the library's children's department then, in nothing like so grand a case, and certainly not as dazzlingly displayed and spotlit as they are now. I remember that Pooh in particular looked a bit dishevelled. Now he looks . . . well, not as good as new, but exactly as he appears in the famous photographs taken of him with Christopher Robin and A. A. Milne in 1926, when Pooh was five and Christopher Robin was six. Methuen, the London publishers of *Winnie-the-Pooh*, commissioned the photographs from Howard Coster, who went on to take portraits of most of the great literary and theatrical figures of the day, from Arnold Bennett and E. M. Forster to Laurence Olivier and Vivien Leigh. Tuft by tuft, Pooh has been restored by the New York Public Library at great expense and with appropriate sensitivity and skill.

The Coster photographs are now in the National Portrait Gallery in London. Why isn't Pooh in London, too? That's where he comes from. He is a British-made teddy bear, bought from the famous department store, Harrods of Knightsbridge, as a present for Christopher Robin for his first birthday. London is where Christopher was born. Why on earth are Pooh and Co. living in Manhattan?

Years ago, in the late 1980s, I tried to get them back to Britain. With my wife, Michèle, I had opened a Teddy Bear Museum in Stratford-upon-Avon – birthplace, we claimed, of William Shakesbear, author of *MacBear*, *King Bear* and *The Merry Bears of Windsor*. Because the teddy bear owes his name to the twenty-sixth American president, Theodore 'Teddy' Roosevelt, the then US ambassador to the UK launched the museum for us, and because the bears in our collection have pedigree (they include the first Paddington Bear to feature on television, given to me personally by Michael Bond, and, given to me personally by Jim Henson, what the Muppets' creator told me was 'the original Fozzie Bear'*), I had hopes that the real Winnie-the-Pooh might be able to come to the museum for a brief English vacation.

I approached the New York Public Library about the possibility. 'No way,' I was told. 'No way whatsoever. We own Pooh. Pooh stays here.' In the late 1990s, Gwyneth Dunwoody, a British Member of Parliament, on a trip to New York, saw Pooh and his little stuffed companions and decided they 'look very unhappy indeed'. She announced a campaign to bring Pooh and his pals back to their native country. 'We're going to keep him here and keep him safe,' countered New York's pugnacious Mayor Rudolph W. Giuliani, arriving at Pooh's glass case in the library with a no-nonsense statement ready for the cameras and an appealing, appeasing jar of honey for Pooh.

'This is to show his friends in England that he's being fed well and he enjoys New York cuisine,' Giuliani told the watching world. 'I think Winnie-the-Pooh is an example of

---

* Years later, when he heard about it, Frank Oz (the original voice of Fozzie) could not believe it – or bear it.

the very best in immigration,' the mayor continued, warming to his theme. 'He's very, very proud of his background and heritage, but now he's found a new land and he's found a better life for himself here.'

'Does he have a green card?' called out one of the reporters in the crowd. According to the man from the *Los Angeles Times*, "The mayor leaned to the case and whispered "Hey, Winnie, ya got a green card?" Then the mayor went on to argue that Pooh had three times as much chance of being stolen in London than in New York, due to Manhattan's plummeting robbery rate.'

Today, almost thirty years on, thanks to an introduction from the most recent US ambassador to the UK, I am meeting Dr Tony Marx, President of the New York Public Library, and his senior team. They are all very charming – and very protective of their bear. Millions visit the Treasures of the Library exhibition every year – and the exhibit they most want to see is Winnie-the-Pooh.

'Can I tell you a story?' asks Dr Marx, sixty-six, urbane and handsome, formerly the head of Amherst College in Massachusetts, President and CEO of the New York Public Library since 2011. 'I don't get many phone calls. Everyone gets in touch by email nowadays. So a few years back when my assistant said, "You're wanted on the telephone," I was surprised. They said, "It's Number Ten Downing Street." I took the call.

'I picked up the phone and a voice asked, "Is that Dr Marx?" I said, "Is that Ten Downing Street?" The voice replied, "Actually, no. I'm calling from the White House – the call was just patched through the Downing Street switchboard. I'm at the White House. The British Prime Minister – it was David Cameron – is meeting with the President

– Barack Obama – right now. They're in the Oval Office – and they are talking about Winnie-the-Pooh. It seems you have Winnie-the-Pooh . . ."

"'Well, yes, we do," I said.

"'And, at the end of their meeting, in their joint press conference, the President and the Prime Minister want to announce that they've agreed that Winnie-the-Pooh is returning to England."

"'That would be a matter for the library's trustees," I said.

"'You don't understand – the President and the Prime Minister are meeting right now. They are in the Oval Office waiting."

"'Well, I'm sorry," I said.

"'You don't understand," he repeated, "I'm speaking on behalf of the President of the United States and—"

"'You don't understand," I interrupted, "I am the President of the New York Public Library – and the answer is 'no'."

"'You don't understand," he continued, "I have a Prime Minister who needs to make a statement any minute now – and back home he has an election to win.'"

The President and the Prime Minister made their end-of-visit statement without reference to Winnie-the-Pooh.

When Dr Marx has finished telling his story, he smiles.

I smile, too. 'Yes,' I say, 'Winnie-the-Pooh is the literary world's Elgin Marbles.'

'Let's not mention the Elgin Marbles,' says Dr Marx, quickly.

It's clear the New York Public Library's trustees have always been fearful that if Pooh ever got home to England, it might be tricky to get him back to the US again.

How come he's in America in the first place?

'Well,' says Dr Marx, 'I always understood that Christopher Robin didn't want him. That he felt Pooh and the stories had infantilized him and ruined his life. That he and his father fell out over Pooh.'

One of Dr Marx's colleagues interrupts. Dr Julie Golia, Curator of Manuscripts, says 'That's sort of part of the story, but it's more complicated than that.' The toy animals lived with the Milne family until 1947, when, at the suggestion of Milne's American publisher, E. P. Dutton, they were sent to the United States on an extended promotional book tour. They never came home. For forty years they were on show at Dutton's offices on Park Avenue, until Dutton was absorbed into the Penguin publishing group and the Milne menagerie was donated to the New York Public Library.

Iris Weinshall, the library's beady-eyed Chief Operating Officer, CFO and Treasurer, now speaks for the first time. 'I have heard,' she says softly, 'that the reason no senior British royal has been to New York in recent years is that they won't come until Pooh is allowed to go back to England.'

'I'm sure that can't be true,' I say, quickly, adding at once: 'But we would love to have Pooh back sometime, if only for a brief vacation . . . and 2026 is coming up. It's the centenary of the publication of *Winnie-the-Pooh* and the centenary of the birth of one of Pooh's earliest admirers, Queen Elizabeth II . . .'

'And 2026 is the 250th anniversary of the Declaration of Independence,' chips in Dr Brent Reidy, six foot seven inches (at least), and Andrew W. Mellon Director of Research Libraries.

I explain to my new friends that I am a trustee of the Queen's Reading Room, Queen Camilla's charity promoting the joy of reading, and that I know that Her Majesty would be happy to welcome Pooh to Buckingham Palace or Windsor Castle and look after him if he could be spared for a centenary celebration back in his home country.

'Pooh is priceless,' says Dr Marx. 'The insurance, the security, the transportation – it'd be expensive. And we'd need to have something equally priceless in exchange to have on show here while he's away – maybe something in the royal archives connected with 1776 or a crown or something. They must have a few spare crowns around the place. Pooh belongs to our crown jewels, you know.'

He is smiling.

'Let's see what we can do,' I say. Where presidents and prime ministers have failed, I am thinking it would be gratifying to succeed.

Later . . .

I have just had an email from Dr Marx: 'Lovely to meet you and Michèle. Excited to see how this progresses and hopeful we can make it all come out great! Yours, Tony.'

Fingers crossed.

10 January 2025: Austin, Texas

I am enjoying the notice on the door of the locker where I am storing my computer and notebooks. It reads:

ATTENTION
Storage of handguns
is not allowed in
these lockers

I am in Texas. At the University of Texas. I have been here for a week – an invaluable week – in Austin, the state capital, working in the library of the Harry Ransom Center, where they have a Guttenberg Bible (of course) and *three* copies of Shakespeare's First Folio (this *is* Texas) and have somehow also managed to collect the papers of – wait for it! – D. H. Lawrence, T. E. Lawrence, T. S. Eliot, James Joyce, John Steinbeck, Lewis Carroll, Kazuo Ishiguro, Harry Houdini and Robert de Niro, to name just a few. I am here because they specialize in the papers of twentieth-century playwrights, among them George Bernard Shaw, Samuel Beckett, Arthur Miller, Tennessee Williams, Tom Stoppard – and A. A. Milne.

There are ten boxes of Milne material – a treasure trove, but also a challenge. Alan Milne's handwriting is small and spidery and not easy to decipher. But the library has let me photograph anything and everything I want, so I can pore over it all at leisure and in detail in the weeks to come. There are the original manuscripts of poems and stories, novels and plays, on most of which is a note to the typing agency requesting 'One typed copy and two carbons by the end of the week if possible.' Milne's wife Daphne's handwriting is larger, rounder and clearer. She sometimes transcribed to her husband's dictation and regularly acted as his secretary, replying to fan mail under the assumed name of 'Celia Brice'.

From these boxes – and the half-dozen boxes, also here, of the working papers of Ann Thwaite, whose magisterial biography of Milne appeared in 1990 – I am realizing that I have to be careful not to accept too readily the Daphne I saw depicted in the 2017 film, *Goodbye Christopher Robin*, or the Daphne I was told about by Christopher Robin's wife, Lesley. I met first met Lesley with Christopher in the early 1980s and interviewed her again after Christopher's death. Lesley was openly hostile towards her mother-in-law.

This is going to be a complicated family story (I suppose most family stories are), but there is plenty in these boxes to help me understand it – not least wonderful letters between Alan and the key figure in his life, his older brother Ken. There are delightful childhood letters of Alan's, too, and reflections on childhood from the vantage point of later years, including intriguing observations on the importance of children's literature that appeals both to the young child and to the adult who may be reading out loud to the little one: 'It is torture to read anything aloud with which we ourselves are bored.'

There is plenty here to remind me that Milne was a very funny man. Delving into the first of the boxes on Day One of my time here, I found the 'Opening Chorus' of what seems to be a musical revue: 'How I Loathe Everybody'.

I hate the gentleman goggling there . . .
With the plastered hair . . .
And the skull that's bare . . .

I hate the woman with scarlet lips . . .
And the one that skips . . .
To reduce her hips . . .

I hate the fellow with shoulders high . . .
And the roving eye . . .
And the made-up tie . . .

I hate the girl with the close-cropped head . . .
And the eyebrows dead . . .
And the nails too red.

How I loathe everybody
Everybody, everybody

How I loathe everybody,
Everybody! Ugh!

The world is full of ghastly men,
And ghastly women too.

There is plenty, too, on A. A. Milne's preoccupation with war and the horrors of war. The creator of the world of Winnie-the-Pooh is a complex character, but, above all else, a beautiful writer (I have read all six of his significant novels in recent weeks: they are a joy to read and comfortably stand the test of time) and a writer conscious of his own worth. There is much detailed business correspondence in the boxes, mostly with Albert Curtis Brown (1866–1945), Milne's principal literary agent – including a postcard to Curtis Brown dated 12 June 1918 that should induce a sense of fellow-feeling with every author:

Cheque received safely. Many thanks.
– A. A. Milne

Astonishingly, I found there are letters from me in these boxes. This is because in the 1980s I wrote a stage show called *Now We Are Sixty*. It was a play (produced at the Arts Theatre, Cambridge, and directed by James Roose-Evans, whose papers are also here in Austin) telling the story of the Milne family – with music by Harold Fraser-Simson (1872–1944), who composed the music for Milne's songs and poems in the 1920s, and new music by Julian Slade (1930–2006), a friend of mine, a lovely man, best remembered as the composer of London's longest-running musical of the 1950s, *Salad Days*. Julian was a friend of Christopher Robin, and it was through Julian, and through writing *Now We Are Sixty*, that I got to know Christopher, and because Christopher

– reticent with strangers and naturally a private person – knew, liked and trusted Julian, that Christopher allowed me into his world. We got on well. I think I amused him. He let me visit him at his home in Devon. He introduced me to his wife and daughter. I think he trusted me. He told me that in the play I had got his father 'about right'.

Because I keep a diary, I can tell you that I first met Christopher Milne on Tuesday 15 December 1981. I was thirty-three and a bit Tigger-like. He was sixty-one, spindly, slightly bent, with owlish glasses, though recognizably Christopher Robin. He had a charming mischievous glint in his eye. Julian Slade and I travelled down to Devon to meet him. I arrived expecting to find him reluctant to talk about either Winnie-the-Pooh or his parents. Not so. His manner was gentle, but he was immediately forthcoming. 'We must talk about Pooh,' he said straight away. 'It's been something of a love–hate relationship down the years, but it's all right now. Believe it or not, I can now look at those four books without flinching. I'm quite fond of them really.'

Those four books, published between 1924 and 1928 – the two Pooh books and the two collections of nursery verses: 70,000 words in all, a tiny fraction of A. A. Milne's lifetime's output – dominated Christopher's whole life.

On the day we arrived here in Austin, our host, Dr Eric Colleary, Cline Curator of Theater and Performing Arts, took us to his office, where he let us see and touch a few pages of the original manuscript of the last of those four books, *The House at Pooh Corner*. It was a special moment in a special place – for Dr Colleary, clearly, an enchanted place. The office was in the basement of the building, I think. (It was difficult to tell: reaching it, we came in and out of elevators, along dark corridors and passageways, with lighting that came on and off as we passed.) When we reached it, the room had the feel of a stage set: it was windowless and, for reasons not explained, was laid out as a reproduction of the office of John Foster Dulles, President Eisenhower's Secretary of State. The Milne manuscript – and a rough sketch by Ernest Shepard of a dust-jacket illustration of Piglet and Eeyore, apparently never used – were laid out on Dulles's desk for us.

As well as the Milne treasures, Eric was keen for us to see Evelyn Waugh's desk in the room next door – and magic tricks belonging to Houdini – and, knowing of my interest in Arthur Conan Doyle as well as A. A. Milne, the manuscript of *The Scandal in Bohemia*. It was on top of a box that contained the last will and testament of Lord Byron. (I found A. A. Milne's all-important will in one of the Milne boxes later in the week.) 'And you love Oscar Wilde, too, don't you?' said Eric. 'You're President of the Oscar Wilde Society, aren't you?' 'I am,' I replied. 'Then you've got to see this – it's the original manuscript of Wilde's *Salomé*.'

Talk of Wilde led to talk of *The Importance of Being Earnest*, which led to talk of Dame Edith Evans and her celebrated portrayal of Lady Bracknell ('*A haaaandbag!*'), which led to Eric taking us through the book stacks (they have a million books on site) towards the shelves containing A. A. Milne's own library (donated by Daphne after her husband's death), via a vast room full of stage and movie costumes (including those worn by Vivien Leigh, Clark Gable, Leslie Howard and others in *Gone with the Wind*) to see clothes worn by Edith Evans and to be told a story I had not heard before. According to Eric, the young Maggie Smith learned an invaluable lesson from Dame Edith when they worked together in the 1960s. Dame Edith told Maggie,

'If you don't know what a line means, say it as though it's a little bit naughty.'

It has been an extraordinary week. We did not see much of Texas. In fact, we did not see any of Texas beyond the university campus. From 9 a.m. to 5 p.m. every day, we sat in the library, immersed in the life and times of A. A. Milne. Last night, in the restaurant in the campus hotel, our young server asked me why we had come to Austin. I told her. 'That's great,' she said, 'then you'll be coming back in April.'

'In April?'

'For Eeyore's birthday. In Austin, we always have a big party on the last Saturday in April to celebrate Eeyore's birthday.'

The young server had no idea that Milne's papers are stored in Austin, but she knew that Eeyore was a gloomy character, and a friend of Winnie-the-Pooh, and that he needed cheering up. 'Look at the world,' she said. 'We all need cheering up.'

Eeyore's Birthday Party began in 1963 as a spring picnic in the park organized by students and faculty from the university. It was named in honour of Eeyore because of the story in Chapter Six of *Winnie-the-Pooh* in which Eeyore is at his gloomiest:

> Eeyore, the old grey donkey, stood by the side of the stream, and looked at himself in the water.
>
> 'Pathetic,' he said. 'That's what it is. Pathetic.'

It is Eeyore's birthday and he assumes nobody either knows nor cares.

Over the years, according to our young server, Austin's Birthday Party for Eeyore has grown into a huge family fun day out, with thousands attending. The original event was held on campus at Eastwoods Park and featured a single trash-can loaded with ice and cans of beer and lemonade, honey sandwiches, a maypole and a real-life flower-bedecked donkey. Apparently, in the early days the party had a distinctly 'hippie vibe'. It still does to an extent, with large drum circles featuring hundreds of drummers and dancers as part of the entertainment. Today, alongside the music and the costume parades and the carnival games and food stalls, they still have a live donkey. And in Eastwoods Park there is now a commemorative sculpture in bronze of a slumped and seated donkey. The sculpture is called 'And He Was Sad'.

'If anybody wants to clap,' said Eeyore when he had read this, 'now is the time to do it.'

They all clapped.

'Thank you,' said Eeyore. 'Unexpected and gratifying, if a little lacking in Smack.'

The House at Pooh Corner

---

12 January 2025: Mid-Atlantic

I am flying home to London. I have just been watching *Goodbye Christopher Robin* on the plane. I have seen it before. It's a well-made movie, directed by Simon Curtis, with Domhnall Gleeson as Alan, Margot Robbie as Daphne, and Kelly Macdonald as Olive Rand, Christopher Robin's nanny, but it's a movie, not a documentary, and there is a lot in it that isn't quite right and some of it that is quite wrong. Alan coming out of the 1914–18 war suffering from long-term post-traumatic stress disorder is certainly overplayed, and making the illustrator, Ernest Shepard (played by Stephen Campbell Moore), Alan's closest friend is a major mistake.

Ernest Howard Shepard (1879–1976) was a wonderful artist and book illustrator, and, of course, his drawings for all four of Milne's children's books now feel 'definitive', but he and A. A. Milne were never close. When Winnie-the-Pooh made his first appearance in the *Evening News* the illustrator was not Shepard but another regular contributor to *Punch* magazine, James H. Dowd (1884–1956).

E. H. Shepard got the Milne book assignment at the suggestion of E. V. Lucas (1868–1938), who was on the staff of *Punch* from 1904 onwards, and, from 1908, also a reader for the publishing company Methuen & Co. He became the chairman of the company in 1924, the year in which Methuen published *When We Were Very Young*. A. A. Milne had sent his children's verses to Lucas at Methuen to see what he made of them: Lucas immediately recognized their potential, both for *Punch* and as a book, and, at *Punch* one day, asked Shepard to produce some initial sketches to see if Milne might like them.

Milne had a history of *not* liking Shepard's work. More than once in the past, he had said to *Punch*'s art editor, 'What on earth do you see in this man? He's perfectly hopeless.' This time he rather liked Shepard's drawings, and, over time, he came to like them very much, gratefully acknowledging their contribution to his books' success and suggesting Shepard have a share of the royalties – a quite unusual arrangement for the period. Later, in a copy of *Winnie-the-Pooh*, he inscribed this tribute to his collaborator:

When I am gone,
Let Shepard decorate my tomb,
And put (if there is room)
Two pictures on the stone:

Piglet from page a hundred and eleven,
And Pooh and Piglet walking (157) . . .
And Peter, thinking that they are my own,
Will welcome me to Heaven.

E. H. Shepard was Milne's colleague, not his boon companion. Milne invited Shepard to his house in Chelsea to meet Christopher Robin and his toys, and took him on a walk through Ashdown Forest in East Sussex so that Shepard could see exactly where the stories were set, but theirs was always a working relationship – and if Milne wasn't happy with a Shepard drawing he didn't hesitate to say so.

This very week, as it happens, an auction house is selling a batch of Shepard drawings and Milne correspondence. It features illustrations from some early spin-off merchandise – *The Christopher Robin Birthday Book*, 1930 – with a note from Milne to the publisher telling him that Shepard 'must do new drawings for April and September as the originals are very poor'. The drawings will all sell for thousands, come what may. Shepard's Milne-related work achieves astonishing prices at auction. His original illustrated map of the Hundred Acre Wood, which features in the opening pages of *Winnie-the-Pooh*, sold for £430,000 ($600,000) at Sotheby's in London in 2018, setting a world record for a book illustration.

The partnership was valuable to them both, but neither author nor illustrator pretended there was any special intimacy between them. Each was grateful to the other, but both had quite different world views (Milne had a horror of war; Shepard had won an MC in 1917) and full and contrasting creative lives before and after Pooh. In time, Shepard, like Milne, came to tire of what he called 'that silly old bear' because it so overshadowed the rest of his work.

E. H. Shepard wrote two autobiographies, but said of Milne, 'I never knew him intimately.' He found him 'rather a cagey man' who didn't give much away. With A. A. Milne, he said, 'It was difficult to get beyond the facade.'

That's the challenge. Can I get beyond the facade? I hope so.

16 January 2025: Windsor Castle

In 1981, Christopher Milne told me that now he was sixty he had made his peace with his father's four children's books – the books that had made 'Christopher Robin' world famous. He enjoyed the Pooh stories unreservedly, and the poems, too, with one notable exception. To the end of his days, he could not stand the verse that first introduced the world to the little boy called Christopher Robin, the poem called 'Vespers' that begins:

> Little Boy kneels at the foot of the bed,
> Droops on the little hands little gold head.
> Hush! Hush! Whisper who dares!
> Christopher Robin is saying his prayers.

A. A. Milne lamented in his autobiography that the poem was mostly misunderstood and sentimentalized by readers who took it to be about a darling child dutifully saying his prayers when, in fact, it's about a real little boy who isn't saying his prayers because 'his thoughts are engaged with other, more exciting matters'.

Christopher Milne came to hate the poem because it was turned into a song, with music by H. Fraser-Simson, and the song became very popular. Christopher recorded a version

of it himself when he was seven and, among the many commercial recordings, two of the most popular were sung by
Gracie Fields and Vera Lynn. The actor Norman Shelley
(the voice of *Children's Hour* on the radio in Britain in the
1950s) recited it to an organ accompaniment at A. A. Milne's
funeral. Aled Jones sang it as Christopher Robin in my play,
Now We Are Sixty, in 1986.

To me, Christopher called it 'that wretched poem . . . the
bane of my life'. When he came to write his own childhood
memoir, Christopher considered the poem carefully 'for the
first time in my life' and realized it wasn't as soppy as Vera
Lynn had made it sound. In fact, it wasn't sentimental at
all; it was mildly cynical. But as a boy, especially when he
was in his teens at boarding school, and later when he joined
the army, the poem brought him 'toe-curling, fist-clenching,
lip-biting embarrassment'. At Stowe, his public school, the
other boys teased him mercilessly, he remembered, mocking
and taunting him, playing the Vera Lynn record endlessly –
until he took the record and 'broke it into a hundred pieces
and scattered it in a distant field'.

I am in the Royal Library at Windsor Castle looking at
the first-ever edition of 'that wretched poem', 'Vespers'. It's
an edition of one, not printed, but written in A. A. Milne's
own hand and bound in vellum. It is one of the 595 miniature books created for the Library of Queen Mary's Dolls'
House in the early 1920s.

Queen Mary was the wife of King George V. The dolls'
house was the idea of Queen Mary's childhood friend and
first cousin by marriage, Princess Marie Louise, one of
Queen Victoria's granddaughters. The princess had seen the
Queen furnishing a dolls' house to sell to raise funds for the

London Hospital and, knowing how Queen Mary loved all things miniature, decided to create a special dolls' house as a gift for her. The great architect Sir Edwin Lutyens (who designed the Cenotaph in Whitehall and so much besides) agreed to design the dolls' house to a scale of 1:12 (one inch to one foot), and a wide assortment of artists and model makers contributed the contents and fittings. The carpets, curtains and furnishings are all copies of the originals from Windsor Castle. The bathrooms are fully plumbed with piped, running water, and include a flushable lavatory with miniature toilet paper.

One hundred and seventy-six of the books in the miniature library are manuscripts, contributed by the leading literary lights of the day – including three of the authors A. A. Milne admired most: Thomas Hardy, Rudyard Kipling and J. M. Barrie. (Of those asked, only George Bernard Shaw declined the invitation to contribute something.) Milne's poem arrived with a simple compliment slip dated 10 October 1922.

Milne recalled writing the poem, as a distraction, 'while at work on a play'. When he had 'wasted a morning' on it, he gave it to his wife, Daphne, 'as one might give a photograph or a valentine, telling her that if she liked to get it published anywhere she could stick to the money'. She sent it to *Vanity Fair* in New York and was delighted to receive fifty dollars for it. In due course, according to Milne, she 'collected one forty-fourth of all the royalties of *When We Were Very Young*, together with her share of various musical and subsidiary rights'. With 'decorations' by E. H. Shepard, the poem was reproduced and framed and hung in thousands of nurseries across America and the British empire. Alan did not begrudge his gift to Daphne, but he did point out that it was certainly 'the most expensive present I had ever given her'.

'Vespers' came to Windsor in October 1922. Milne included the poem as the final poem in *When We Were Very Young*, published in November 1924, with a note on the Contents page explaining '"Vespers," being in the library of the Queen's Dolls' House, is printed here by special permission.' In fact, no permission was required, but it was understandable that Milne and his publishers wanted to make mention of the royal connection.

There is a copy of *When We Were Very Young* here in the Royal Collection. It is not the very first edition, but the sixth printing of the first edition (the book was a runaway success) and, intriguingly, it was given to Princess Elizabeth, later Queen Elizabeth II, as a wedding present in November 1947, signed 'with every good wish, Cyril Ebor'. 'Ebor' is the abbreviation of the Latin *Eboracum*, an early Latin name for York. Cyril Garbett was the Archbishop of York who preached the sermon at the twenty-one-year-old Princess Elizabeth's marriage to the Duke of Edinburgh. It is a charming but unexpected gift, unless the archbishop knew that Milne was a favourite author of the young Elizabeth – or was anticipating that a young bride might soon be a young mother and here was a suitable first book for a royal nursery. Princess Elizabeth was married on 20 November 1947. Her son, Prince Charles (now King Charles III), was born a year later, on 14 November 1948.

Many years later, around the time of her golden jubilee in 2002, when I was writing a biography of the Duke of Edinburgh, Elizabeth II told me that Winnie-the-Pooh had been 'a lifelong favourite' with her, long before Paddington Bear came onto the scene.* She remembered that A. A. Milne and the composer H. Fraser-Simson had written to her parents, then the Duke and Duchess of York, to ask if they might dedicate a book of the songs of Winnie-the-Pooh to her. 'It was the first book ever dedicated to me, which is rather nice,' she said, beaming.

The book, *The Hums of Pooh*, is here at Windsor now. Published in 1929, with 'lyrics by Pooh' and an 'additional lyric by Eeyore', the score is accompanied by little jokes. One song, for example, is to be performed 'With movement, but not too much because of his tub.' In 1928, the Yorks, who later became King George VI and Queen Elizabeth, visited the Ashtead Pottery works in Surrey and were presented with some examples of early Milne merchandise. Here in the Royal Library, alongside their Shakespeare First Folio (acquired by George IV when Prince of Wales) and their Shakespeare Second Folio (annotated by Charles I while imprisoned at Windsor Castle during the English Civil Wars),† it is good to see a Winnie-the-Pooh tea-plate, sugar bowl, mug and teapot.

---

* In the same conversation the Queen also told me she had a soft spot for Rupert Bear, the cartoon-strip character created for the *Daily Express* in 1920. She remembered reading the Rupert annuals when she was a girl. She told me that Prince Charles loved Rupert, too. I told her that Rupert aficionados claim that Rupert isn't a bear at all: he is a boy with a bear's head. 'That can't be right,' she said, 'Surely not.' 'Well,' I said, 'if you look at the pictures, you'll see he's got fingers on his hands and very human-looking feet.' 'I'm sorry you told me that,' she said. 'Some things are best left unknown, don't you think?'

† This was before Charles I was put on trial for High Treason and executed in 1649. Inside the Folio you can see in the King's hand the Latin phrase *Dum spiro spero*, meaning 'While I breathe, I hope.'

18 January 2025: London SW3

More than fifty years ago, when my wife, Michèle, was a very young television reporter, she was sent to St Ives in Cornwall to interview the great English sculptor and artist Dame Barbara Hepworth. This was not long before Hepworth died in an accidental fire at her studio on 20 May 1975 at the age of seventy-two. Michèle asked Hepworth where the ideas for her work came from. Hepworth said: 'Perhaps what one wants to say is formed in childhood and the rest of one's life is spent trying to say it.'

It seems a childhood lasts a lifetime. Michèle will tell you, with a wan smile, that I have never left mine. I hope that's not entirely true, but certainly my childhood (my very happy childhood) is still very vivid to me. Every day, something – a sight, a sound, a taste, a smell, a random recollection – takes me back to it. Of course, when we were very young there were shadows as well as sunshine: sad days, bad days, times when I was bullied at school or felt misunderstood at home. But everything I have done in my working life – as a writer, as a broadcaster, in politics, in the theatre – and the kind of person I am, alone or with others, and as a husband and father and grandfather – I can trace back to the first ten or fifteen years of my life.

I am what my childhood made me. For good or ill, most of us are. And the children's books of A. A. Milne were very much part of my childhood. My parents read them to me. My mother, especially, loved the poems, and she and I would recite them together out loud. I still know a good number of them by heart. When I was six or seven and joined the Cub Scouts, I took part in the Christmas Gang Show and made my first appearance on a stage, dressed in a nurse's uniform, playing the part of 'Alice' in a fully choreographed version of 'They're changing guards at Buckingham Palace'.

I am writing this in a coffee shop on the King's Road in Chelsea. It is just around the corner from Mallord Street, SW3, A. A. Milne's London home during the most creative years of his life, from 1919 until the beginning of the Second World War. It is the house where Christopher Robin was born. This is the part of London where I was brought up, too. These are the streets where I rode my tricycle as a small boy and skipped along making sure I kept in the squares on the pavement and never trod on the lines.

> Whenever I walk in a London street,
> I'm ever so careful to watch my feet;
> And I keep in the squares,
> And the masses of bears,
> Who wait at the corners all ready to eat
> The sillies who tread on the lines of the street,
> Go back to their lairs,
> And I say to them, 'Bears,
> Just look how I'm walking in all of the squares!'
> *Now We Are Six*

We lived first in Lower Sloane Street and then in Oakley Street, a five-minute walk from where I am sitting now. One of our neighbours in Oakley Street was a lovely actor called Richard Goolden (1895–1981). He was bent and rather gnome-like when I knew him. He told me that he had played more than five hundred parts in his long career, but that his three favourite roles by a long way had been created by just two authors: William Shakespeare and A. A. Milne. Goolden had loved playing the Fool in *King Lear*, but even more so, he told me, he loved playing the title role in *Mr Pim Passes By* and Mole in *Toad of Toad Hall*, A. A. Milne's stage adaption of Kenneth Grahame's *Wind in the Willows*. Richard Goolden played Mole almost every year from 1930 until the end of the 1970s.

As a small boy I saw *Toad of Toad Hall* almost every Christmas. I was a lucky child. My parents took me to the theatre a lot. *Peter Pan* by J. M. Barrie (A. A. Milne's favourite play) was another regular Christmas treat – as was *Where the Rainbow Ends*, for fifty years, from 1911, a seasonal favourite that told the story of two girls and two boys and their pet lion, who travelled the world by magic carpet, guarded by St George, England's patron saint, dressed as a knight in shining armour, ever ready to protect the children from the dragon of evil. As I remember, most of the action was set in 'Rainbow Land', home to talking animals, mythic beasts and a kind-hearted white witch.

Now I am on this trip down memory lane, I am realizing, quite suddenly, that where I am sitting now is exactly opposite the site of the old Chelsea Palace Theatre, built as a music hall in 1903, demolished to make way for Heal's department store in 1966. It was at the Chelsea Palace Theatre that I fell in love for the first time. It was Christmas 1955 and I was taken to the Chelsea Palace to see *Alice Through the Looking-Glass*. I fell for Alice at first sight – the moment she came onto the stage. I fell in love with her immediately. Completely. Comprehensively. Alice was played by Juliet Mills. I was seven; she had just turned fourteen.

Through the Looking-Glass, Wonderland, Rainbow Land, Neverland, down by the riverbank, the One Hundred Acre Wood – these were the imaginary enchanted places of my early childhood. They still are enchanted places to me, but I don't sentimentalize them. Falling for Alice was thrilling, but disconcerting, too.

I recall reading an interview with the contemporary American novelist Nicole Krauss in which she said that because her mother was English her 'early world' had been the worlds of A. A. Milne, Kenneth Grahame and Lewis Carroll, among others, and how she admired them because 'none of these writers thought it necessary to protect children from darkness'. On the contrary, 'they guided their readers right toward it'. I was struck by Krauss's observation that 'This gives one an enormous sense of being respected as a child. Not just of being trusted to handle things as they are, but to be accepted as not entirely good. To be recognized as having darkness within oneself, too. I don't think I've trusted any author since who doesn't address me with that assumption.'

A little later in my childhood, when I was nine or ten, I began to discover Shakespeare. First, I was taken to see *A Midsummer Night's Dream*, where wonderful (magical, romantic, hilarious) things happen in 'a wood near Athens'. Then, at school when I was about eleven, I was cast as Rosalind in *As You Like It* and spent a happy summer term in the Forest of Arden exploring a play that's got the lot: adventure, excitement, danger, laughter, romance – and cross-dressing. (I did not appreciate it then, but I love the play all the more now that I realize that, centrally, it is about forgiveness and reconciliation, too.)

There is a pathway, I think, that leads directly from the Forest of Arden and 'the wood near Athens' to Ashdown Forest and the Hundred Acre Wood. It is very much an English pathway, but it seems to have a universal appeal. A. A. Milne's children's books have been global bestsellers for a hundred years. *Winnie-the-Pooh* has been translated into more than eighty languages, including Esperanto and Latin. In France they call him Winnie l'Ourson; in Poland he's Kubuś Puchatek; in Japan he's Kuma no Pooh-san.

Today, 18 January, is International Winnie-the-Pooh Day, because today marks the birthday of A. A. Milne.

I want to know more about Milne – I want to get beneath the facade – because I am intrigued by how he knows so much about us. In the Forest and the One Hundred Acre Wood he has created an enchanted place that felt totally real to me as a child (and feels real to me still), and then he peopled it with a boy and a bear and an unlikely assortment of animals, each of whom has a very distinct personality. I believe it is because we recognize them – and we recognize ourselves and people we know in them – that his children's books are among the most successful children's books of all time.

Whatever you are like, you can find yourself in the pages of *Winnie-the-Pooh* and *The House at Pooh Corner*. I am one of life's Tiggers. If you know me, you will know that. And sometimes, you might find me quite annoying.

> 'Tigger's getting so Bouncy nowadays that it's time we taught him a lesson. Don't you think so, Piglet?'
>
> Piglet said that Tigger was very Bouncy, and that if they could think of a way of unbouncing him, it would be a Very Good Idea.

But, of course, there is more to me than Tigger. You won't know it, but there are days when I am not bouncy at all, days when I am cowed and frightened.

> '*Hush!*' said Eeyore in a terrible voice to all Rabbit's friends-and-relations, and 'Hush!' they said hastily to

each other all down the line, until it got to the last one of all. And the last and smallest friend-and-relation was so upset to find that the whole Expotition was saying 'Hush!' to *him*, that he buried himself head downwards in a crack in the ground, and stayed there for two days until the danger was over, and then went home in a great hurry, and lived quietly with his Aunt ever-afterwards. His name was Alexander Beetle.

Alan Alexander Milne was born a long time ago – on this day, 18 January, in 1882 – but we are reading him still because he was a beautiful writer with uncanny access to the secrets of the human heart.

Chapter One

in which we first meet the parents and
grandparents of A. A. Milne

A childhood lasts a lifetime

If a childhood lasts a lifetime, John Vine Milne was a fortunate man. He was born in Jamaica, to missionary parents, and imbued with sunshine and missionary zeal from a very young age. He led a good life, doing good work. He was a good man – according to A. A. Milne, his third child and youngest son, 'the best man I have ever known . . . the most truly good, the most completely to be trusted, the most incapable of wrong'.

Alan Alexander Milne, and his older brothers David Barrett Milne, known as Barry, and Kenneth John Milne, known as Ken, saw their father as an almost God-like figure. 'He differed from our conception of God,' said Alan, 'only because he was shy, which one imagined God not to be, and was funny, which one knew God was not.'

JV, as John Vine Milne was generally known, was a God-fearing man, with a straightforward, uncomplicated faith, the eldest son of a clergyman and the grandson of an Aberdeenshire stonemason.

Or not, as the case may be. Grandfather Milne had possibly been a freemason, but had he been a stonemason, too? When it came to the detail of the Milne family history,

Alan was a bit hazy. JV was probably born in 1845 (or a little earlier; he was alive by then, for sure; and there is a death certificate to show he died in 1932), but whether his missionary father was a Presbyterian minister, as Alan maintained in his autobiography, or a Congregational minister, as his wedding certificate suggests, is difficult to establish. His name was definitely William Milne (1815–74) and he was certainly a Christian missionary in the West Indies – though not to be confused with another, more celebrated, missionary by the name of William Milne (1785–1822) who did his missionary work in China and may or may not have been a distant kinsman of our missionary Milne.

Alan wasn't sure his grandfather had been a stone-mason, and if he had been, whether he had been a craftsman who wielded a chisel and a hammer or an entrepreneur who owned a quarry. Alan was clear that there had once been some money in the family, but equally clear that there wasn't much evidence of it in his day. 'A second cousin of Father's died intestate in 1892,' he recalled, leaving £30,000, the equivalent, in today's money, of something approaching £5 million. 'Unfortunately,' according to Alan, 'she also left thirty second-cousins.' A first cousin of Alan's father died at around the same time, leaving, 'more characteristically', three silver teaspoons, two of which went to JV and the third to his younger brother.

When telling stories about his family, and writing his autobiography, A. A. Milne focused, understandably, on the heroic and the eccentric. His paternal grandmother had an uncle who had served as one of Nelson's captains at the Battle of Trafalgar and is commemorated with a monument in Bath Abbey. His paternal grandfather, William Milne, married a fellow missionary in Jamaica, fathering the first of their ten children there, before returning to England, giving up the ministry and starting a school – the first of a dozen schools he founded around the country. None of the schools prospered and six of his children died, but William Milne had a faith that was profound: 'The Lord giveth and the Lord taketh away, blessed be the name of the Lord.' The children who died in infancy were going to a better place, and what was money for but to give to the poor – or to secure new pews for the chapel?

Alan said of Grandfather Milne, 'He was the world's most unworldly muddler . . . neither sanctimonious nor fanatical. He just believed quite simply that nothing which happened in this world mattered to a good man; to a man, that is, who believed in God and would return to Him.'

Alan felt for Grandmother Milne. She had been a young missionary herself. Also born in Jamaica, she was christened Harriet Newell Barrett in honour of Harriet Newell (1793–1812), the first American missionary to die overseas in the service of the Lord and a heroine and role model to many young Christian women following the posthumous publication of her journals. Harriet Barrett (1820–78) married William Milne in Jamaica in 1843 and accepted her lot in life with Christian fortitude. It was not easy living with a man who never earned more than £80 a year, bearing his ten children and bringing up the four who survived virtually single-handed and in such a way as made them feel both loved and truly to be living their best life.

Only one female character features in the Winnie-the-Pooh stories: Roo's loving, caring, calm, dutiful, devoted mother, Kanga. A conscientious housekeeper and a protective parent, she is wise and kindly, but firm and forthright, too. She is a single mother, as Harriet Milne became in her widowhood. Is

Kanga based on A. A. Milne's grandmother Harriet? Milne, of course, would have pooh-poohed the idea (if you'll forgive the phrase); he did not personally know his grandparents (they died before he was born, so all he knew of them was what his father told him), but there is no doubt that the similarities between the character of Kanga and the long-suffering, good-hearted, traditional-minded Grandma Milne are striking.

While Harriet and Kanga are comparable, old-fashioned, reassuring mother figures, JV cannot for a moment be mistaken for Roo. For those who like playing this game, JV is not Roo: he is Owl. He has to be Owl because JV became a schoolmaster, and JV, like Owl, 'knew everything', though, according to Alan, 'even if Father knew everything, he knew most of it wrong.'

'. . . if anyone knows anything about anything,' says Pooh when we first meet Owl in *Winnie-the-Pooh,* 'it's Owl who knows something about something . . . or my name's not Winnie-the-Pooh . . . Which it is . . . So there you are.'

Owl, of course, knows much of everything wrong: 'for Owl, wise though he was in many ways, able to read and write and spell his own name WOL, yet somehow went all to pieces over delicate words like MEASLES and BUTTEREDTOAST.'

The truth is Owl cannot spell; Owl cannot read. Owl thinks himself very knowledgeable, when he isn't. He uses long words unnecessarily and believes himself to be always in the right. When he sneezes, he denies it:

'I *didn't* sneeze.'

'Yes, you did, Owl.'

'Excuse me, Pooh, I didn't. You can't sneeze without knowing it.'

Owl is obstinate, pretentious, pedantic. Owl has no sense of humour and rarely, if ever, admits to being in the wrong. JV was nothing like Owl. JV could laugh at himself and made others laugh, too. A. A. Milne liked to tell the story of his father, the headmaster, reprimanding a boy for arriving late in the school dining room:

> 'Henry,' says my father, 'you're late again.'
>
> 'Yes, sir. Please, sir, it wasn't my fault—'
>
> 'No excuses, Henry. You must put your chair away and stand.'
>
> So Henry eats his first course standing.
>
> 'All right, Henry, you may take your chair now.'
>
> 'Yes, sir, thank you, sir. Please, sir, Matron sent me upstairs for her spectacles just as I was coming in.'
>
> Awed silence. 'Sucks for JV,' the boys are thinking, 'he'll have to apologize.' The younger assistant masters look up anxiously. Do schoolmasters ever apologize? Isn't it bad for discipline?
>
> 'Then in that case,' says my father, wishing to get it quite clear, 'it wasn't your fault you were late?'
>
> 'Please, sir, no, sir.'
>
> 'Oh!' (Everybody is waiting.) 'Oh, well, then, you'd better take two chairs.'
>
> And everybody laughs and is happy.

When William Milne, missionary and unworldly muddler, died in 1874, John Vine Milne was in his late twenties and working for his Bachelor of Arts degree at London University. JV had long wanted to be a teacher – and a different kind of teacher – but it took him time to achieve his goal because his family, while wholly respectable, was always pressed for money and he needed to contribute what he could to the household's expenses. According to his son Alan, JV worked variously as a clerk in the counting-house of a biscuit factory and an apprentice in an engineering firm, but his 'over-mastering concern' was with education – his own and that of others. 'After twelve hours in the engineering shop,' reported Alan, 'he would walk back to his room, spend an hour getting clean, and then settle down to the real work of the day, the achievement of a degree.'

He achieved his degree and soon discovered, said his son, 'that he really had the gift of teaching for which he had longed, and with it the gift of preserving discipline among boys bigger, and little younger, than himself.' His build was slight; his manner was mild; he wore pince-nez; to add to his authority, he grew a beard. Alan reckoned his father had both a sense of humour and courage, qualities essential for a successful schoolmaster. J. V. Milne also had something we don't necessarily expect from a Victorian schoolmaster: a love of his work and of his charges. 'Without affection, the schoolroom is a hard, forbidding place,' he said. 'With love, it becomes the next best place to home.'

JV believed in a God of love. At one of the schools where he taught early on in his career, the headmaster one Sunday preached a fire-and-brimstone sermon to the boys, warning them that they were destined for an eternity in Hell unless they pulled up their socks and concentrated in class. JV was given permission to preach to the boys the following Sunday and told them there was no such place as Hell and no such thing as Everlasting Fire, but encouraged them to work all the same because work was worthwhile and working hard now meant you wouldn't have to work so hard later. After delivering his sermon, he offered the headmaster his resignation, but the headmaster wouldn't have it. JV was too good a teacher to lose.

JV taught in a number of schools before he arrived at the establishment that changed his life. In 1874, he was teaching at a school in Braintree in Essex and looking for advancement. He applied for two posts, each offering £100 salary a year. One was to be a private tutor to a family in Tottenham. The other was to be assistant master at a boys' school at Wellington in Shropshire. He was offered both. He opted to move away from London. 'It was,' said his son Alan, more than sixty years later, 'the decisive moment of his life.' 'And,' he added, 'of mine. For at Wellington, Shropshire, he met my mother.'

'Loving is misery for women always,' is one of the haunting lines from Thomas Hardy's first major literary success, *Far from the Madding Crowd*, published that same year, 1874. Sarah Maria Heginbotham had been unlucky in love and, apparently, was wary of romantic entanglement because of past, unhappy experience. Originally from the High Peak in Derbyshire, she was now thirty-four, still unmarried, and earning a modest living keeping a 'School for Young Ladies' not far from the boys' school where JV was appointed assistant master.

JV and Sarah met at the musical soirées held at the girls' school on Thursday evenings during term-time. JV was musical. He played the flute. Sarah liked that. He was shy, but amusing. She liked that, too. He was gently droll, passionate about his work, serious about his faith, and quite quickly smitten. One Thursday evening, when the music was done and it was time to go home, he pressed a note into her hand, asking her to marry him.

He did not have the courage (or perhaps simply the confidence) to ask her to her face. Finding difficulty in openly expressing your feelings is a recurring theme in the story of the Milne family across several generations.

> 'I just said "Oh!"' said Piglet nervously. And so as to seem quite at ease he hummed Tiddely-pom once or twice in a what-shall-we-do-now kind of way.
>
> *The House at Pooh Corner*

By letter, Sarah Maria gave JV his answer. It was a firm but gentle 'no', and it continued to be 'no' on quite a regular basis for more than a year. Sarah Maria was wary of men. She had been hurt before. But JV was different. He persisted, as others had done, yet he did so shyly, charmingly, amusingly, with respect, affection, Christian courtesy and Christian fortitude. Their faith mattered to them both. Eventually, Sarah Maria said 'yes'. They were married in Buxton in Derbyshire, near her birthplace, on 27 August 1878. The groom was thirty-three. The bride was thirty-eight.

'All romances end at marriage,' said Thomas Hardy in *Far from the Madding Crowd*. Not so. John Vine and Sarah Maria Milne lived happily together until she died, aged eighty-one, in 1921 – the year after Christopher Robin was born. And theirs was a lifelong romance. A friend wrote to JV after Sarah Maria's death to express her delight in 'seeing what sweethearts you were to the very end'. Christopher Milne showed me the reply his grandfather had sent back: 'In my wife I had a wonderful gift.'

Chapter Two

in which we meet three brothers:
Barry, Ken and Alan Milne

A child's world

'One writes in a certain sort of way,' said A. A. Milne, 'because one is a certain sort of person; one is a certain sort of person because one has led a certain sort of life.'

Alan Milne's childhood was his enchanted place. It was where he was happiest. When he came to publish it in 1939, aged fifty-seven, he devoted more than half of his autobiography to his childhood years, and made no apology for doing so. 'When I read the biography of a well-known man,' he said crisply, 'I find that it is the first half of it which holds my attention.' He explained: 'I watch with fascinated surprise the baby, finger in mouth, grow into the politician, tongue in cheek; but I find nothing either fascinating or surprising in the discovery that the cynicism of the politician has matured into the pomposity of the Cabinet Minister. It was inevitable.'

It is inevitable, too, that we are especially intrigued by Milne's childhood. He is one of the most successful children's authors of all time. It is only because of his four children's books – amounting to less than 1 per cent of his lifetime's creative output – that you are reading this book now. The world he created – the enchanted place he made for

Christopher Robin and Winnie-the-Pooh to visit and play in – has touched the childhoods of millions of children. What was his own childhood like? How did it make him the certain sort of person who could write the certain kind of books he wrote?

JV and Sarah Maria were married in the summer of 1878 and within three and a half years all three of their sons had been born. Alan was the last to arrive, on 18 January 1882. We do not have a picture of him as a baby, finger in mouth. The first pictorial record we have of him is a family photograph taken in 1886: the four male members of the Milne family in their Sunday best, pictured close together, out of doors, with a fine brick wall as a backdrop. JV is seated in the centre, the forty-one-year-old pater familias, bearded and bespectacled, watchchain across his waistcoat, holding hands with his two older sons, who are perched on either side of him. Alan, aged four, is seated on a pouffe by his father's knees, looking knowingly at the camera. Everyone in the picture has a serious demeanour.

All three little boys in the photograph look like little girls to us, of course, because that was the fashion of the era. Their thick hair falls down to their shoulders. Alan's is blond and curly. He looks very like the five-year-old boy in the famous painting by Sir John Everett Millais, titled 'A Child's World' and first exhibited at the Grosvenor Gallery in that same year, 1886. The painting of Millais's grandson blowing bubbles was bought by Thomas J. Barratt, the managing director of A. & F. Pears, and used for many years to advertise the company's bars of soap. The older Milne boys look a tad tougher than Millais's cherubic grandson, but all the children are dressed in similar outfits, with full lace ruffs around their necks. It was the look made famous by Little Lord Fauntleroy, the eponymous hero of Frances Hodgson Burnett's bestselling novel, also published in that same year, 1886. Fauntleroy and Burnett were as internationally successful in their day as Pooh and Milne were in his and Harry Potter and J. K. Rowling became in ours. For a generation from 1886, every small boy whose parents could afford one was in possession of what became known as a Fauntleroy suit.

It wasn't a look that Alan Milne much liked – which is odd when you think how he allowed his own son, Christopher Robin, to be dressed when he was a four-year-old in the early 1920s. As a boy and a man of his time, Milne probably accepted that how a young child is dressed was in the gift of the child's mother.

Sarah Maria, or Maria as she was mostly known to family and friends, was a devoted mother. In another family portrait, she looks quite stolid, serious and matronly. She was traditional in her outlook, occasionally tiresome, as mothers can be, always anxious for her brood, as the best mothers are. (Was she, in fact, the model for Kanga?) Given his awareness of the privilege and enchantment of his childhood, Alan Milne was almost patronizingly dismissive of her in his autobiography. He admitted that he knew really nothing of her background. He thought she might have been a farmer's daughter, but he wasn't sure. Clearly, he never asked her. It was part of the family creed, he said, 'that Papa knew everything, and Mama knew nothing'. By which he meant that his father was the one with 'Knowledge' and his mother was not. 'Once, at dinner,' he recalled, 'when Father was telling us proudly, as if partly responsible for it, that Light travelled at the rate of 150,000 miles a second, our awed silence was broken by Mother's simple announcement from the other end of the dinner table: "I don't believe it." What the answer to that is I don't know, nor did Father ever discover it.'

Alan loved both his parents, but not unreservedly. As an adult, he looked back at them and recognized their limitations. He said he was probably happier with his mother than his father. Why? 'She didn't argue; she didn't drive the moral home. She was simple; she was wise; she was affectionate. She was restfully aloof.'

And she was good at what she did. Indeed, she was the best at what she did: no one could cook, or dust, or mend, or make a bed, or wash clothes or put on bandages better than she. 'She was unemotional,' said her son, 'she was common-sensible. Nothing upset her.' (Yes, she must have been the model for Kanga.) While JV was prey to anxiety, on public occasions 'twittering like a sparrow with nervousness', Maria Milne was always calm under pressure.

When he was in his late fifties, in 1939, Alan said of his mother: 'I don't think I ever really knew her.' He was thirty-nine when she died in 1921. Did he try to get to know her, either as a boy or as a man? It seems not. 'When I was a child,' he said, 'I neither experienced, nor felt the need of, that mother-love of which one reads so much, and over which I am supposed (so mistakenly) to have sentimentalized.'

A. A. Milne took a pride in being hard-headed and dispassionate when talking about his feelings for his parents. They gave him the secure childhood in which he revelled, and for which he was grateful, but he would not let that blind him to their imperfections and to the nature of his relationship with each of them. 'Certainly as a child I gave my heart to my father,' he said. 'If he were there, all was well; if he were away, I asked Mama when he was coming back.' But with adolescence, as we shall see, came a parting – an 'inevitable parting', as Alan saw it. His father he knew, and understood, and loved, and lost. His mother, he never really knew, but, over time, he was more at ease with her because her company was uncomplicated. She was, as he said, 'restfully aloof'. He never lost her because he never felt that close to her.

In his autobiography, he writes of his parents almost as if they are characters in one of his plays – or even characters in somebody else's play. They are central to his life, inevitably, but not for long and not profoundly so. It's different with his brother, Ken. Ken is the only whole-hearted, full-blooded, uncompromised and uncompromising relationship of his childhood. Perhaps, even of his life. Often surrounded by people – at home, at school, at university, in editorial offices, in the army, in the theatre, playing cricket, at his club – Alan remained a sort of loner all his life. Funny and gregarious in company, he always held something back. As a writer, he was an observer and, as many of the best observers are, he was an outsider even when he was in the middle of the room.

'My father's heart remained buttoned-up all through his life,' said Christopher Milne.

'Can you help unbutton it for me?' I asked him.

'No,' he laughed. 'I wouldn't begin to try. I couldn't begin to try. I'm not sure how well I knew him. I'm not sure how well he knew me.'

His whole life long, Alan Milne seemed to keep those closest to him slightly at bay. The only exception to that rule was, for a few, short years, maybe a dozen, his son, Christopher (Christopher acknowledged that), and always, from start to finish, from beginning to end, without question, doubt or a moment's equivocation, his brother Ken.

Alan and Ken were brothers, but they were more than that. They were true friends, just as Christopher Robin and

Winnie-the-Pooh are true friends. For a time, as we shall see, the two of them merge into one.

Before we get to brother Ken, let's get brother Barry out of the way. It won't take long. Quite early on in life, Alan seems to have decided that his oldest brother, Barry, was a bad hat. Why? It's difficult to say. Maybe he simply did not like the look of him. Consider the family portrait of the three boys pictured with their father in 1886. Does Barry, aged seven, look just a touch more sinister than Ken, aged six, and Alan, aged four? It could be that he does. 'Sinister' was a word A. A. Milne used to describe his brother Barry.

Christopher Milne likened his uncle Barry to Mephistopheles. In the 1980s, Christopher showed me an old photograph he had only recently come across. The picture dated from around 1900 and showed the three Milne brothers side by side: Alan, Christopher's father, and Barry and Ken, his two uncles. The picture startled Christopher because he had not seen an image of his father as a young man before and he had not known what either of his uncles had looked like. Uncle Ken had died when Christopher was still a boy and Uncle Barry was never mentioned. He knew his aunts: Maud, who had been married to Ken, and Connie, who had been married to Barry. His aunts he knew and liked, but his uncles he considered something of a mystery – until he found this photograph, when everything, he said, had suddenly become clear.

In the middle of the photograph, seated in a chair (he was the eldest brother) is Barry, dressed in a Norfolk jacket and knickerbockers. On either side of him stand his younger siblings, dressed quite differently, in dark suits with stiff white collars, and looking quite different, too. 'Disturbingly different,' said Christopher. 'Can these really be brothers?'

he wondered. Dark-haired Barry appeared so different from fair-haired Alan and Ken.

Later, reflecting on that portrait of the three brothers, Christopher said: 'You can see at a glance that Barry is Mephistopheles and that inside himself he is chuckling "Ho, ho, ho!" And Ken is St George and inside himself he is laughing "Ha, ha, ha!"' But Alan? 'Alan is different. Alan is difficult. He is clearly Ken's man: dressed like Ken, looking like Ken, on Ken's side and on the side of the angels. But Alan doesn't wear his heart on his sleeve as the others do. Alan's heart is firmly buttoned up inside his jacket, and only the merest hint of it can be seen dancing in his eyes, flickering in the corners of his mouth.'

I asked Christopher about the root cause of Alan's animosity towards Barry. 'I couldn't say,' he replied, shaking his head. It was not that he would not say; he could not say. 'I simply don't know. They were just quite different, I suppose. How different you can see just by looking at them.'

Sigmund Freud, whose *Psychopathology of Everyday Life* was published around the same time that the tell-tale photograph of the Milne brothers was taken, would doubtless have been less tentative. As Freud liked to say, 'If it's not one thing, it's your mother.'

Maria Milne was fondest of her eldest son and, understandably, Alan might not have liked that. It is not uncommon for mothers to feel a special attachment to their firstborn, and according to Freud, 'A man who has been the indisputable favourite of his mother keeps for life the feeling of a conqueror.'

As you will recall, Alan was adamant that as a child he 'neither experienced, nor felt the need of, that mother-love of which one reads so much,' that mother-love which, according to Freud's younger colleague and friend Carl Jung, 'is one of the most moving and unforgettable memories of our lives, the mysterious root of all growth and change; the love that means homecoming, shelter, and the long silence from which everything begins and in which everything ends.'

The adult A. A. Milne was familiar with Jung's *Archetypes of the Collective Unconscious*, published in 1934. The boy Alan Milne claimed neither to have experienced nor needed mother-love. Barry took it as of right. Conqueror Barry took much as of right.

When the Milne brothers were little, they had a nanny/nursemaid/governess by the name of Beatrice Edwards, known as Bee. She was devoted, pretty and loving, and all three small boys wanted to marry her. As the eldest, Barry claimed her as his own – and she did not demur. She had two charming sisters, Trot and Molly, and she assured Ken and Alan that they could marry them. But Alan wanted Bee. And Barry thwarted him.

Later in life, Barry continued to get the girls. When, as an adult, in real life, Barry married a pretty girl called Connie, Alan, in a brotherly way, became close to his sister-in-law and dedicated one of his poems to Barry and Connie's elder boy, John. But Barry, in Alan's eyes, was not a good husband. He was a ladies' man and not to be trusted.

When they were children, of course, Barry was the bigger boy, and if he did not bully his youngest brother, he certainly teased him. One of the games the children played when walking in the London streets was the one where you had to make sure, as you walked, that you did not tread on the lines between the squares on the pavement. Years later, of course, Alan wrote one of his most famous children's verses about it.

When Alan was little and playing the game, Barry teased him, telling him not to mind what might happen if he trod on the lines, because something much more frightening – something truly horrible – could come up from sewers through the grating in the gutter by the pavement's edge. According to Alan, Barry enjoyed taunting and terrifying his young brother.

Barry was older, taller and, arguably, more handsome than either Alan or Ken, but he wasn't cleverer. Far from it. Ken was bright, but Alan was brightest. Alan was conscientious, too. He liked schoolwork in a way that Barry never did. According to JV, Alan's enthusiasm for learning was, for a while, a matter of concern. 'He made such strides at school,' the proud father revealed years later, when his son had become well known, 'that his mother became anxious. "Something will have to be done to stop Alan," she used to say to me. "You know these promising children wear themselves out and end by being dull men."'

Alan did not wear himself out. Far from it. He thrived on hard work. When the three boys were at school together, Ken, sixteen months older than Alan, was in the class above him, but Barry, two and a half years Alan's senior, was in the same class as Alan – and Alan was top of the class (90 per cent in English, 90 per cent in arithmetic, 95 per cent in algebra). Barry can't have liked that.

Later, when Ken and Alan succeeded in gaining scholarships to Westminster School, not-so-bright Barry was sent to a boarding school in Derbyshire, run by a family friend JV had known since his schoolmastering days in Shropshire. At sixteen, Barry left school altogether and moved to Weymouth in Dorset to be articled to a local solicitor, William Bowles Barrett, an amateur botanist of some note and a kinsman of Barry's long-suffering grandmother, Harriet Barrett, and also, more distantly, of the poet, Elizabeth Barrett Browning. JV found his son the position and gave him, in instalments, £1,000 to cover the cost of his articles and living expenses and to help set him on his way. A thousand pounds was a considerable sum and, in due course, JV looked after Ken and Alan in similar fashion. He was a good father – and a generous one. Over time, Alan came to believe that Barry took advantage of his father's generosity, taking a substantial loan from him at one point and, ultimately, persuading his father to alter his will to Barry's considerable advantage.

Until the episode with the will, which did not occur until JV was in his mid-eighties, after the deaths of both Maria and Ken, Alan maintained superficially cordial relations with Barry, for the sake of the family. He was fond of his sister-in-law, Connie, and of her children, and did not wish to upset his parents, who, as parents will, doted on their firstborn, despite his failings (or even because of them). Alan viewed his elder brother as a womanizer and a spendthrift. Just because they were family, they did not need to be friends. 'Whoever heard,' he observed in *Four Days' Wonder*, the novel he wrote just after his father's death, 'of two frogs assuming a friendliness which they did not feel, simply because they had been eggs in the same spawn. Ridiculous.'

When Ken died of tuberculosis in 1929, aged only forty-eight, he had hoped to be buried beside his mother in the graveyard of the local church at Wivelsfield in Sussex, where his parents had been living at the time. He wasn't. Alan blamed his solicitor brother Barry for the bureaucratic confusion. Following Ken's death, JV needed a new will. Alan proposed a solicitor other than his brother for the task. Alan did not trust Barry and wanted to protect the interests of Ken's widow, Maud, and their children. In the event, JV was apparently content to let Barry look after the new will, which he did, and in the new will, the residue of JV's estate was left entirely to Barry. Alan never spoke to Barry again.

As ever, there are two sides to the story. Barry's son, John Milne (named after JV), a solicitor himself (and, later, an Anglican clergyman), was sure his father meant for the best and fulfilled his grandfather's wishes to the letter. John said his father, Barry, provided for his mother, Maud, and his siblings, and, of course, Alan and his family wanted for nothing because of the success of *Winnie-the-Pooh*. When I asked Christopher Robin about it, he gave me a wan smile and said, gently, 'Wills can bring out the worst in people, can't they? I don't like talking about money. Money always seems to lead to rows and unhappiness.' But he agreed: 'My father loved Ken – absolutely. And he had no time for Barry – no question of that.' Christopher recalled that his father, as a boy, had a happy fantasy that he and Ken would wake up one morning and discover that everybody else was dead. The two brothers, Ken and Alan, would have the world to themselves.

For A. A. Milne, his brother Barry meant nothing and his brother Ken meant everything. When Alan and Ken were boys, 'We were inseparable,' said Alan, 'sometimes, when fighting, so mixed up as to be indistinguishable.' This was a bromance a century before the word was coined: 'We never ceased to quarrel with each other, nor to feel the need of each other. Save for the fact that he hated cheese, we shared equally all belief, all knowledge, all ambition, all hope and all fear.'

Sometimes, on holiday, they were also obliged to share a bed. As a rule, A. A. Milne did not much like sharing a bed. (As we will discover, when he married, he and his wife happily kept separate bedrooms.) The only bed companion he ever tolerated was Ken: 'I wish to put it on record that my love for Ken, as his for me, survived six holiday weeks in the same bed; with a fight every morning, when one of us found that the tide of clothes had receded in the night, leaving him bare and beached.'

In time, Alan would prove academically more success-ful than Ken, and Alan's career as a writer, of course, was more illustrious (and profitable) than Ken's as a civil servant would be. From the start, Alan attributed his own success to Ken's age and example: 'When Ken did a thing I did it too, and this meant that I was always sixteen months ahead of him.' Was Ken jealous of his clever younger sibling? Never. 'A boy can do a great deal in sixteen months,' said Alan, 'but he cannot change his nature, and Ken had one advantage of me which he was to keep throughout his life. He was defin-itely – nicer . . . kinder, larger-hearted, more lovable, more tolerant, sweeter-tempered.'

Alan insisted that if you knew them both, you would have preferred Ken – and that was probably true. 'I might be better at work and games,' said Alan, 'even better-looking, for he had been dropped on his nose as a baby (or picked up by it, we never could decide which); but "poor old Ken" or "dear old Ken" had his private right of entry into every-body's heart.'

If you want to play that game, you can see clever old Alan as Christopher Robin and dear old Ken as funny old Pooh. In the enchanted place that was A. A. Milne's childhood, Ken was his boon companion and his one true friend. He was, I think, the love of his life. When Ken died, Alan could not bear to go to his funeral. He stood alone, at the edge of the graveyard, away from all the other mourners, looking on, in tears.

Chapter Three

in which we get to know Alan and Ken

Us two

Alan Alexander Milne was born on Wednesday 18 January 1882, just seven days before Virginia Woolf and a fortnight before James Joyce. In England in 1882, Victoria was still Queen (it was the forty-fifth year of her reign), Gladstone was prime minister (it was the second of his four terms in office) and that month *Young Folks* magazine published the final episode of what would become a favourite boyhood book for A. A. Milne: Robert Louis Stevenson's *Treasure Island*.

Immediately after his son's birth, J. V. Milne walked the one and a half miles from the family's home in Kilburn, north-west London, to Hampstead Town Hall and registered his blond and blue-eyed boy's names as Alexander Sydney. A few days later, he returned to the register office to re-register the names as Alan Alexander. Alexander was the fixed part of the mix because it was the name of JV's younger and favourite brother, Alexander Milne, always known within the family as Ackie.

A. A. Milne was born at Henley House on Mortimer Road in Kilburn. The road is now called Mortimer Crescent (it was always crescent-shaped) and Henley House has been demolished and replaced with a block of council flats. In 1882, in fact, Henley House comprised two substantial houses that had once been large family homes and had later been converted into a school – until 1878 'an unsuccessful school', according to A. A. Milne. 1878 was the year when his father acquired the school, buying the 'goodwill' for £100. The money was a gift from Mr Vine, JV's 'unofficial god-father', from whom he had also acquired his middle name, and it enabled JV, aged thirty-three, to realize his dream of creating his own school and running it along his own lines. The school, when the Milnes took it over, amounted to little more than 'twenty or thirty inky desks, and half-a-dozen inky boys whose parents had been too lazy to find a better school for them'.

With JV as the headmaster, Ackie as assistant master, and a small handful of other youthful teachers, Henley House was, as Alan described it in 1939, 'one of those private schools, then so common, now so unusual, for boys of all ages'. The start-up years were not easy. There was much scrimping and saving: 'Mama's sewing machine never stopped working. She made her own clothes, she made our clothes, she would have made Papa's clothes if she hadn't been so busy making the curtains.' She was also busy doing her best to curtail her husband's tendency to buy equipment for the school before they could afford it. But, between them, they managed. Year on year, they balanced the books, and the school's reputation grew. In its modest way, it prospered. With around eighty boys, a quarter of them boarders, the ages ranged from six to seventeen. Some of the younger children were being prepared for entry to the major public schools of the day (Winchester, Eton, Harrow and the like); most were there because their parents could not afford or did not aspire to the major public schools – or because the boys weren't academically up to it, like Alan's older brother Barry.

In England universal compulsory education was introduced for children aged five to ten in 1880. The school-leaving age increased to eleven in 1893, to twelve in 1899, to fourteen after the Great War in 1918, and to fifteen after the Second World War in 1947. There was no free secondary education in the 1880s, and too many of the small private schools that existed then were still very much in the mould of Dickens's Dotheboys Hall as depicted in *Nicholas Nickleby* at the end of the 1830s. Henley House was different. It was mainly a day school, for local middle-class boys. The boarders were the children of army officers, civil servants, diplomats and entrepreneurs serving in assorted corners of the British empire – lest we forget, at its height, around the time Christopher Robin was born in 1920, the largest empire the world had ever seen, covering around a quarter of earth's land surface and ruling over 450 million people.

Henley House was unusual, too, because, once the Milnes took it over, it became a school founded on kindness. There was corporal punishment, but it was used sparingly. Love was central to J. V. Milne's philosophy of education. He was determined to create a loving atmosphere in the classroom and to encourage his students to love their work. 'He was the best man I have ever known,' said his son, Alan, whenever he talked about his father.

I asked Alan's son, Christopher Robin, if he remembered his father talking about Henley House. 'Oh yes,' he said, 'Henley House was where he was happiest. He could describe it in minute detail.' Alan especially remembered the hallway on what was known as the 'Family Side' of the house. There was a wide staircase with solid banisters – ideal for sliding down – and on the wall to the side of the staircase the huge horns of a buffalo, with hanging over them a rope lasso and an impressive pair of Mexican cowboy spurs, a gift to JV from a grateful Mexican old boy of the school by the name of Nuñez. Alan explained to his boy Christopher that sliding down the banisters with the buffalo horns, lasso and spurs in your eye-line could sweep you away more powerfully than any Hollywood cowboy film ever could. As he put it in his autobiography, 'Every time one slid down the banisters, one slid through Kilburn into a romantic world of which one's imagination only was master.'

When I talked to Christopher about his father's 'enchanted places', he referred to them as both 'enchanted places' and 'safe spaces – where my father felt secure'. They included the cricket pitch, the golf course, the Garrick Club, the Five Hundred Acre Wood – more of all of which anon – and Henley House. Christopher talked about 'those enchanted places where the past will always be present' and told me that Henley House, where Alan and Ken played so happily together in the 1880s and early 1890s was the past that was always present with him.

Alan recalled all the rooms: the drawing-room (with the gas fire) that was only used when visitors came and was generally reckoned 'the most beautiful drawing-room in Kilburn'; the sitting-room (the family room where JV read out loud to his sons and Mrs Milne did her needlework and fine embroidery); the big schoolroom beyond (made from combining the equivalent drawing-room and sitting-room of the house on the School Side of Henley House) where, during the holidays, Ken and Alan played pirates, jumping from desk-top to desk-top until the day of the almighty crash when Alan fell between desks and JV, playfully, in later years, referred to the accident as 'the great crisis' of his life: 'At first we feared for his spine . . .'

Alan remembered the music room at the far end of the ground-floor passage on the Family Side where a visiting music master, a Mr Howard, came to teach Ken and Alan to sing and play the piano. They were poor music scholars – or perhaps Mr Howard was a poor teacher. Alan recalled that Mr Howard had been involved in the 1870 Franco-Prussian war (on the French side) and had a German bullet lodged in his head. Or was he confusing Mr Howard with the French master at Westminster School? Possibly not. Wasn't he the one who had the German bullet lodged in his backside? Christopher said his father's stories often varied – but the ones from his Henley House days were consistently suffused in nostalgic sunshine. Years later, he would call one of his books *Happy Days*. And another: *Those Were the Days*. Christopher told me he believed his father in later life probably looked back on the happiness of his childhood 'through rose-tinted spectacles' because, as the years went by, he found less and less contentment in the present. 'For as long as I knew him,' said Christopher of his father, nostalgia 'was the only emotion that he seemed to delight in both feeling and showing'. Christopher, as we shall see, came to believe in the vital importance of living in the present. 'Today, today is all we have,' he said. 'The past is gone and done with. Who knows what tomorrow will bring?'

Alan also kept with him all his life the tastes and smells of his childhood.

He looked up at his clock which had stopped at five minutes to eleven some weeks ago.

'Nearly eleven o'clock,' said Pooh happily. 'You're just in time for a little smackerel of something,' and he put his head into the cupboard.

The House at Pooh Corner

Alan remembered that at Henley House, beneath the drawing-room was the kitchen, 'where Davis the cook, and Hummerson, the butler, reigned'. As a boy, Alan assumed they were married, but eventually realized they weren't, 'which accounts for their having different names'. He was funny about them, and grateful to them, because they were the guardians of the kitchen and the delights it kept in store. One of the chief delights was stored outside the kitchen, by the kitchen door. It was a large bin of oatmeal and, on days when Alan and Ken were up with the lark and up to larks, they would steal a handful of the oatmeal before dawn and stick their tongues into it, 'thus keeping ourselves alive until the breakfast porridge'.

Alan and Ken put sugar on their porridge, as much as they could. (JV did not approve.) Alan, like Pooh, had a very sweet tooth. His idea of Heaven as a boy was the freedom of the local sweet shops: 'West End Lane where they had those particularly good marzipan potatoes, over the footbridge to the Finchley Road (jumbles), and then up Fitzjohn's Avenue to the Heath, stopping at that little shop on the right for ices, ices, ices . . .'

Late-Victorian London was the largest city in the world, but its population of four million was half the size it is today. And Kilburn, where the Milnes lived, was almost on the edge of the countryside. The streets were safer then. The motor car was not invented until 1886. At weekends and in the holidays, Ken and Alan were up at daybreak and roaming free. 'Even now,' recalled Alan almost fifty years later, 'I can recapture the authentic thrill of those early-morning raids on London, as we drove our hoops through little, blinded streets, clean and empty and unaware of us.'

Wherever I am, there's always Pooh,
There's always Pooh and Me.
Whatever I do, he wants to do,
'Where are you going today?' says Pooh:
'Well, that's very odd 'cos I was too.
Let's go together,' says Pooh, says he.
'Let's go together,' says Pooh.

A. A. Milne called that poem, written in the 1920s, 'Us two'. In the 1880s, 'Us two' – Ken and Alan – ran through the London streets, propelling their wooden hoops with wooden sticks, 'lured now into a remote world of tall, silent houses, pillared like temples, behind whose doors strange, unreal lives were lived', until at last they burst onto the Bayswater Road – three miles from home – and wondered if anyone had ever run before from Kilburn to Bayswater, 'and what Papa would say when we told him'. And then, 'back to breakfast, with pauses now for breath, and chatter, and challenges to each other, back to Davis' porridge, back to the most divine meal of the day, the only meal which could never be a disappointment'.

'Us two' as boys was the only time in A. A. Milne's life that would never be a disappointment – and, years later, in his forties, he re-created the magic of it on paper in the poems and stories he wrote for his own son – and for us – in the books that made him famous. They had hoops to roll and bicycles to ride on and footballs to kick. They played at being pirates on top of the desks in the big schoolroom. They played at being Mexican bandits with the lasso and silver spurs from the hallway. They played at being William Tell with the bow and arrow Ken had been given as a birthday present and an apple reluctantly supplied by Mrs Davis in the kitchen. They played at being Robin Hood and Will Scarlett – or was it Little John and Friar Tuck? – fighting with quarter-staffs in an imagined Sherwood Forest. They had real quarter-staffs: two bamboo poles, each twelve foot long, an interesting gift sent over by a family relation still resident in Jamaica.

'Pooh,' he said, 'where did you find that pole?'

Pooh looked at the pole in his hands.

'I just found it,' he said. 'I thought it ought to be useful. I just picked it up.'

'Pooh,' said Christopher Robin solemnly, 'the Expedition is over. You have found the North Pole!'

'Oh!' said Pooh.

Ken and Alan were great explorers. They never reached the North Pole, but they had fun on holiday in the woods around Limpsfield and Cobham in Surrey and on the beaches on the Isle of Thanet coastline in Kent, picnicking, swimming in the woodland ponds and in the sea, riding bicycles (at Stanford-in-the-Vale in Berkshire, riding a tandem tricycle), playing cricket, chasing butterflies, building sandcastles, visiting real castles, climbing up the steep circular stairway in the North Foreland lighthouse.

'The best of our life was lived in the summer holidays,' said Alan. The family rented a house away from London in July and August most years. They often went away at Easter, too. In 1884, when Alan was only two, they went to Shropshire, and Alan (according to the family legend which he encouraged) climbed on his own two feet, entirely unaided, to the top of the Wrekin, a hill four hundred metres high. A few years later, in 1890, when Alan was eight and Ken was ten, the pair became serious hikers and, according to Alan, strode, side by side and almost effortlessly, from Limpsfield in Surrey to the outskirts of Gravesend in Kent. That is almost twenty miles, so seems a bit unlikely, but Alan insisted it happened: 'If any other eight-year-old has walked nineteen miles in a day, carrying a knapsack, let him write to his local paper about it.' Ken remembered them walking from Limpsfield to Tandridge, which is ten miles, and still impressive.

These were Alan's happy days. Everything about them was golden. One summer, in Seaford in East Sussex, he had his hair cut and, gratefully, said goodbye to the Fauntleroy look. He had been appalled that Ken had been allowed to have his hair cut two years before. 'It shows how completely I had identified myself with him that I had always assumed our hair to be one and indivisible.'

Papa often featured in his happy summer holiday recollections. And Nanny Bee, too. Mama and Barry hardly at all. Ken, of course, is part of every story. When they stayed in Sevenoaks one year, Alan and Ken were adopted by a stray Gordon setter called Brownie: 'He was beautiful and faithful and loving, and with the possible exception of Papa, the most admirable character in the family. We took him back to Henley House. He was ours.'

The two boys were great 'collectors'. 'We "collected" everything,' said Alan. 'We collected "minerals". We bought a "geological hammer", whose head was like a chisel at one end and a marlinspike at the other.' With it, one Easter holiday they attacked the cliffs of Ramsgate on the Isle of Thanet in the hope of garnering ammonites, stalactites, stalagmites and fossilized remains of prehistoric animals. 'We got no more than a piece out of poor old Ken's leg,' admitted Alan, 'with the chisel end.' Their treasures were gathered together and kept in a drawer in a dressing-table and taken out each night and laid out on Ken's bed for inspection.

One day they decided to show their collection to the curator of London's celebrated Geological Museum. It is now part of the Natural History Museum in South Kensington. It was then located in Jermyn Street, off Piccadilly Circus. JV agreed the boys could go on their own, taking the bus to Oxford Circus, so long as they promised not to cross Piccadilly Circus without the assistance of a policeman. Those were the days when there was always a policeman on duty in Piccadilly Circus to direct the horse-drawn traffic. Happily, the policeman was in position and ready to help. Interestingly, as a reminder of how different London was a century and more ago, there was no traffic. Piccadilly Circus was entirely empty: 'We could have played leap-frog across it,' Alan remembered fondly, 'we could have stopped in the middle of the street and spread out our collection again.' He remembered, too, how surprised the Geological Museum curator was by the boys' visit, but how courteously he received them and how gratifying it was to find how impressed he seemed to be by the Milne collection, while pointing out that one treasured ammonite was in fact a dry old date-stone.

Both Alan and Ken were great readers. Alan claimed he could read before he was three and, since he also claimed that, except in the matter of the haircut, he always kept pace with Ken, who was sixteen months his senior, it is possible he could. JV liked to say that Alan's precocity as a reader showed he was 'Destined (under Providence) for Great Things'.

As well as reading for themselves, the boys loved to be read to by their father. John Bunyan's *The Pilgrim's Progress*, originally published in 1678 and considered by some as the first novel written in English, was a particular favourite. It combined Christian teaching with high adventure. There was a suitably moral tone to another Milne boyhood favourite: the stories featured in *Aunt Judy's Magazine*, a popular publication for children that ran from 1866 until 1885, and whose animal stories A. A. Milne later acknowledged had played their part in forming the writer who would one day create *Winnie-the-Pooh*. When he first saw Ernest Shepard's drawing of Pooh, the bear, standing on the branch of a tree outside Owl's house, he remembered all that *Reynard the Fox* and *Uncle Remus* and the Aunt Judy stories had meant to him as a boy.

The first of the nine *Uncle Remus* books was published in America in 1880, two years before Alan Milne was born. The books – essentially old African-American folk tales, compiled and retold by Joel Chandler Harris, a white journalist based in Atlanta, Georgia – became international bestsellers. (Bre'r Rabbit was the central figure in many of the stories and became a character as popular and famous in his day as Winnie-the-Pooh and Mickey Mouse would one day be. From the 1930s onwards, Enid Blyton published a series of Bre'r Rabbit books. Walt Disney's 1946 animation film *Song of the South* featured three Bre'r Rabbit stories.) Harris told the stories in the voice of Uncle Remus, a former slave, and tried to write using African-American dialect. Today he would be accused of white paternalism and cultural misappropriation. In his day he was acclaimed and touched the lives of countless children over two or three generations. Ezra Pound, born in 1885, and T. S. Eliot, born in 1888, corresponded in Uncle Remus-inspired dialect, referring to themselves as 'Brer Rabbit' and 'Old Possum', respectively. Theodore Roosevelt (the American president who gave his name to the teddy bear) said Harris's contribution to American literature would be treasured long after the names of most US presidents had been forgotten. A. A. Milne loved the Uncle Remus stories – for him *Uncle Remus* was 'a sacred book' – and there are strong echoes of Harris's narrative style and specific plot lines in the Winnie-the-Pooh books.

Another early literary influence on the precocious young Alan Milne was Robert Louis Stevenson. Of course, when he discovered it, Alan was gripped by *Treasure Island*, but before that he was introduced to *A Child's Garden of Verses*, published in 1885, when Alan was three.

> A child should always say what's true
> And speak when he is spoken to,
> And behave mannerly at table;
> At least as far as he is able.

Stevenson's wit and way with words charmed A. A. Milne as a child and influenced him later. When his own light verse started to appear in the pages of *Punch* magazine and, in the 1920s, when *When We Were Very Young* and *Now We Are Six* were published and critics compared Milne as a poet favourably with Stevenson (and with Lewis Carroll) he was mightily pleased. Milne took 'light verse' seriously and was infuriated by those who didn't. 'Light verse is not the output of poets at play,' he asserted, 'but of light-verse writers at the hardest and most severely technical work known to authorship.'

Alan Milne maintained a lifelong admiration for Robert Louis Stevenson. Milne was happy as a boy – happy in himself and by himself, happy as his father's son until about the age of twelve or thirteen, happy as Ken's brother always. As an adult he was not always happy, or emotionally engaged, as a husband or a father, but as a writer, alone in his study, he was at his most content, writing poems and stories, novels and plays. 'Fiction is to the grown man what play is to the child,' said Robert Louis Stevenson. 'It is there that he changes the atmosphere and tenor of his life.'

Chapter Four

in which Alan goes to school

Memories and dreams

'We all have our time machines, don't we. Those that
take us back are memories . . . And those that carry us
forward, are dreams.'

H. G. Wells

Herbert George Wells (1866–1946) was a good friend to the
Milne family over many years. They got to know him first in
the late 1880s, when, as a soon-to-be-qualified teacher, aged
twenty-two, he came to Henley House as the school's first
science master.

Wells went on, of course, to become world-famous, as an
author (four times nominated for the Nobel Prize for Literature), a novelist (*Kipps, The History of Mr Polly, Ann
Veronica*), 'the father of science fiction' (*The Time Machine,
The Invisible Man, The War of the Worlds* – 'the Shakespeare of science fiction' in Brian Aldiss's fine phrase), a
futurist (anticipating air travel, space travel, satellite television, the worldwide web and much more besides), an artist,
a socialist, a social reformer. His views on sex and marriage
– and his own private life: two marriages, one divorce, many
affairs, four children (in wedlock and out of it) – made him a

controversial and intriguing figure. To Alan Milne, 'HG' was 'a great writer, and a great friend'. Alan acknowledged that he was indebted to Wells for many things – including teaching him 'all the botany I never learnt' and providing wise counsel when he was starting out as a writer himself – but 'most of all for the affection which he always felt for my father'.

Wells admired JV hugely. 'Milne was a man who won my unstinted admiration and remained my friend throughout his life,' he wrote in his *Experiment in Autobiography* in 1934. He reckoned JV 'a really able teacher, keen to do his best for his boys and with a curious obstinate originality', adding, 'I learnt very much from him about discipline and management.' Wells liked Milne's approach to education: not formulaic learning by rote, but encouraging every child to become interested and enthusiastic about the subject in hand. Milne gave Wells one of his fundamental beliefs: 'What really matters is what you do with what you have.' JV wanted to bring out the best in each child in his charge. Young as Wells was at the time, he was aware that JV was constantly preoccupied with managing the school's finances, but admired the way the headmaster nonetheless 'watched his boys closely and would slacken, intensify or change their work, with a skilled apprehension of their idiosyncrasies. He would think of them at night. The boys had confidence in him and in us and I never knew a better-mannered school.'

Courtesy and kindness were the hallmarks of Henley House, which made the school so different from so many in late-Victorian England. JV was twenty-one years HG's senior, yet 'he was friendly and sympathetic with me from the outset.' Wells described Milne quite precisely: 'He was a little grey-clad extremely dolichocephalic man with glasses, a pointed nose and a small beard, rather shy in his manner;

he had a phantom lisp and there was a sort of confidential relationship between his head and his shoulders.' ('Dolicho-cephalic', meaning a long and narrow face, was doubtless a term Wells had picked up studying biology under the anthro-pologist T. H. Huxley at the Normal School of Science in South Kensington.)

Wells was struck by Milne's appearance, charmed by his manner, flattered by the headmaster's interest in sharing his educational ideas with the young science teacher, and amused by JV's idiosyncrasies – especially his enthusiasm for cycling. 'Every time I see an adult on a bicycle,' Wells said famously, 'I no longer despair for the future of the human race.' Once devoted to his tricycle, at around the time Wells arrived at Henley House JV had taken up bicycle-riding, recently made more comfortable by the Scottish veterinarian John Boyd Dunlop's 1887 invention of the pneumatic tyre. (The idea came to Dunlop when he wrapped a length of garden hose pipe around his son's metal bicycle wheel. In the early years, mending a puncture was a lengthy business. According to Alan, when his father got a puncture 'he wheeled his machine to the nearest station and went home by train').

Alan, who was only seven when Wells arrived at his father's school, later pronounced Wells 'not a great school-master': 'He was too clever and too impatient.' JV, who was forty-four at the time, was rather more admiring of Wells, who made a striking impression when he came for his job interview by turning up wearing a top hat – as Wells later described it, 'a symbol of complete practical submission to a whole world of social convention'. He was not wholly sub-missive, however. Milne offered him the job teaching science, mathematics, art and scripture for £60 a year. Wells declined to teach scripture because he said he could not teach a subject in which he did not believe. Milne liked him the more for that. As Wells reported: 'He liked my putting in that conscience clause at the risk of not getting a job I evidently wanted.'

J. V. Milne admired the young H. G. Wells, particularly 'his teaching of science, where his extensive reading and his power of expression enabled him to handle his subject in a manner at once exact and humorous'. Milne himself, though shy (sometimes awkwardly so, especially when encountering parents unexpectedly in the street: he could barely look them in the eye), was humorous and warmed to humorousness in others. He was grateful for the enthusiasm Wells aroused in his classes, and grateful, too, for the way the young science master took an active interest in all aspects of school life – except, of course, religious instruction. Wells was especially conscientious when it came to taking the boys on educational outings, examining the lithologic properties of the layers of rock on Primrose Hill or studying the wild animals at Regent's Park Zoo. 'Mr Wells, our science master, had long before promised us this treat if we wrote a good essay on Natural History,' Alan remembered. It seems Mr Wells was sufficiently tender-hearted that you got to go on the expedition even if the essay turned out not to be as good as hoped.

On the whole, A. A. Milne was good at essays. He was an attentive student, when the subject interested him, always sitting in the front row in class, usually (in spite of his own shyness in certain circumstances) among the first to put up his hand – 'Sir! Sir! Please sir!' – when he had a question to ask or an answer to give.

He was a bright child – quite as bright as Ken, and a lot brighter than Barry, as we know. Henley House was not Alan's first school. He started out in the kindergarten at Wykeham House, a school in Boundary Road, St John's Wood, a few streets away from Mortimer Road, Kilburn.

Once, in later life, as a middle-aged man, he retraced the little boy's daily walk to the kindergarten, remembering how he was taken to school by Bee. He recalled how Bee (Miss Beatrice Edwards), the Milne boys' nanny-cum-governess, had been his first true love – and how Barry had proposed to her and been accepted, and how he and Ken had been offered Bee's younger sisters as second and third best. Ken met Bee's pretty sister Trot when she visited Henley House. Ken duly proposed to her and was accepted. Alan never met Molly, but he was destined to marry her all the same – and on the walk to the kindergarten, passing along Priory Road, he considered each house in turn before deciding which one he and Molly would one day live in. He had seen a photograph of her. He knew that she was lovely, and he knew, too, that they would be very happy together in the house that was covered in virginia creeper and always appeared to catch the best of the sunshine. When he went back, fifty years later, he was pleased to find it was still the prettiest house in the road. He reckoned Molly would have liked it. 'Where is she now?' he wondered. 'Married, I suppose, to somebody else.'

There was often an idyllic, idealized, fairy-tale magic in the air when the middle-aged A. A. Milne looked back on his early childhood. Walking the half-mile from Henley House to Wykeham House, you crossed a railway bridge, 'and day and night,' Alan recalled, 'beneath that bridge, trains roared their romantic way to Scotland.' The kindergarten was run by a Miss Budd, who, to Alan, looked like the Duchess in *Alice's Adventures in Wonderland*, another of his favourite books. She was assisted by her younger sister, Miss Florence Budd, who played the piano for the nursery school's little morning assembly, when one of the children, either for good or bad behaviour (Alan never could remember which), was invited to choose the hymn. When it was his turn, Alan usually opted for 'All things bright and beautiful' because it was the one that came most instantly to mind, and he liked it.

> All things bright and beautiful,
> All creatures great and small,
> All things wise and wonderful,
> The Lord God made them all.

In late-Victorian England, everyone knew it and liked it – other than H. G. Wells and those of his disposition, of course. The words are by the Dublin-born poet Cecil Frances Alexander and were first published in her *Hymns for Little Children* of 1848. (She also gave us 'There is a green hill far away' and the Christmas carol 'Once in Royal David's city'.) The Misses Budd were comfortable with a verse that is often omitted when the hymn is sung nowadays:

> The rich man in his castle,
> The poor man at his gate,
> God made them, high or lowly,
> And ordered their estate.

The verse the Budds would not countenance, however, was this one:

> The tall trees in the greenwood,
> The meadows where we play,
> The rushes by the water,
> We gather every day.

Miss Budd insisted the verse be omitted because 'unfortunately it is not quite true of those of us gathered here today. We do *not* make a habit of gathering rushes.'

'Unimaginative Miss Budds,' thought Alan, aged six. 'I had gathered rushes and fallen into that stream a hundred times.'

A lot was happening in the life and mind of A. A. Milne between the ages of four and six, the age of the little boy we encounter in the four Christopher Robin books. In *Year In, Year Out*, a collection of favourite pieces published in 1952, when he was seventy, Milne suggested that this letter (now in one of the boxes in Austin, Texas), written from the kindergarten when he was two months shy of his fifth birthday, must have been the first letter he ever wrote:

96 Boundary Road
Nov 20th 1886

My dear Mama

We went to Hampstid Heft yestoday. We had a sanambil. We had piggy-backs.

I want some tools ples Mama

Lost of OOOOOOO O O OOO

OOO OO O OOOOO OO O OOOOOOOO
OO OO OO

You loving

Alan

There are plenty of echoes of the letter in Owl's distinctive spelling in *Winnie-the-Pooh*. Aged seventy, Milne explained that he had never liked collaboration and suggested that the letter showed he had spurned it even as a four-year-old. 'All around me,' he liked to think, 'were other little boys and girls writing to their dear mammas; asking their companions how to spell Hampstead Heath, or waiting glassy-eyed for some suggestion from the mistress as to what constituted "a letter". I just sailed ahead, tongue out, arms outspread. We had had a sanambil, and I had decided to be a carpenter. The family would expect to be told.

'If anybody else has ever had a sanambil, I should like him to get in touch with me. The word is clearly written, the "bil" heavily inked over; as if I had played with the idea of some other ending, but realised in time that this combination of letters was the most informative. Could I have meant a "scramble"? One from whose pen "piggy-backs" flowed so faultlessly would surely have made a better beginning of it. Well, we shall never know now; but I like to think of it as one of those pleasant Victorian games, now gone with so much else of those days, which was good.'

Aged four, in the writing stakes, Alan was flying solo. Aged seven, he left the kindergarten and joined his brothers at Henley House, where being the son of the headmaster does not appear to have caused him any embarrassment. He thrived at the school. According to his proud father, speaking in 1928 when his son had become famous, H. G. Wells had told JV that young Alan was especially strong in mathematics, indeed Wells 'predicted a brilliant career for him in this branch of learning'. We do not have any of A. A. Milne's end-of-term school reports from Henley House, but JV wrote a sketch of several of the boys for an issue of the school magazine. Without naming his son, this was his account of Alan as a pupil:

He does not like French – does not see that you prove anything when you have done. Thinks mathematics grand. He leaves his books about; loses his pen; can't imagine what he did with this, and where he put that, but is convinced that it is somewhere. Clears his brain when asked a question by spurting out some nonsense, and then immediately afterwards gives a sensible reply. Can speak 556 words per minute, and writes more in three minutes than his instructor can read in thirty. Finds this a very interesting world, and would like to learn physiology, botany, geology, astronomy and everything else. Wishes to make collections of beetles, bones, butterflies, etc, and cannot determine whether Algebra is better than football or Euclid than a sponge-cake.

As an adult, Alan reckoned that this report showed that as a boy he had been an enthusiast – and he gave his father the credit for that because his father was an enthusiast, too. 'And if I disliked French, and thought mathematics grand, it was because he, who could teach, taught me mathematics, and did not teach me French.'

The teaching at Henley House was good. Enthusiasm was encouraged and rewarded. Positivity was the order of the day. ('If you fell down yesterday, stand up today' – H. G. Wells.) In the summer of 1889, the Henley House school magazine recorded that a little boy had been asked 'how many things he had enjoyed that day'. This was his answer:

1. Hampstead Heath;
2. Spinning tops;
3. Dinner and breakfast and tea and was about to enjoy supper;

4. Getting clear of work;
5. Getting credit (for extra good work);
6. Geometry, and algebra, and grammar;
7. Preparation.

'Happy boy!' was the magazine's verdict on the answers. The boy, of course, was A. A. Milne, aged seven. Later, Milne would say 'Childhood is not the happiest time of one's life, but only to a child is pure happiness possible.'

The Pooh books are full of pure happiness – in a way that nothing else that Milne would write would be. That could be the single reason for their worldwide success. The children's books of A. A. Milne give you instant access to pure happiness. They are comfort reading from a man who as a boy loved spinning tops and comfort food: dinner and breakfast and tea and supper.

'. . . And we must all bring Provisions.'
'Bring what?'
'Things to eat.'
'Oh!' said Pooh happily. 'I thought you said Provisions. I'll go and tell them.' And he stomped off.

At Henley House, Barry Milne did not do so well academically, but Ken and Alan, stimulated by good teaching and, in Alan's case, a natural inclination to sustained endeavour, thrived. According to JV, when Alan had less to do he became 'mopy and listless'. He liked to be busy. He liked to be top of the class. He loved his brother Ken and admired him, but he wanted to do better than him, nonetheless. And he did.

In the summer of 1892, Ken, aged almost twelve, took the Westminster School scholarship exam – the 'Westminster

Challenge' – and failed. The following January, Ken had the chance to take the scholarship exam again: this time he succeeded. In the summer of 1893, Alan, aged eleven, took the Westminster Challenge, and succeeded at the first attempt.

JV told the readers of his school magazine, 'Scholarships are only gained by the cleverest of the clever, the *crème de la crème*.' His two younger sons were evidently just that – Ken delivering with a bit of a struggle, Alan, seemingly, with ease.

Alan, of course, worked hard and with determination. He wanted to succeed. Years later he reflected on the five-month lead-up to the Westminster scholarship exam: 'If ever in my life I said, "I can do it," I said it then.' Like Lewis Carroll, born fifty years to the week before him, A. A. Milne was a natural when it came to mathematics. Like Carroll, he was thoroughly at home with Euclid, algebra and ingenious numerical puzzles and conundra. Carroll might have had the edge over him when it came to Latin and Greek translation, but I imagine, as boys, both remarkable writers would have risen to the challenge in the General Paper when confronted (as Alan was in 1893) with questions like these:

- Trace carefully either the career of John the Baptist or Joshua's conquest of Palestine.
- Give a short account of Athens under Pericles.
- What do you know of the Mutilation of the Hermae, the Gerousia, the Olympic Games, the Helots, Ostracism?
- Explain fully Trade Winds, Land and Sea Breezes, Forced Draught, the Solar System, Centre of Gravity.

Alan was on his own, halfway up the gymnasium rope in the playground at Henley House, when the news of his success in the scholarship examination came through. His parents, he remembered, 'waved a telegram at me from the sitting-room window'. 'Good,' he thought to himself, 'now we are all right.'

His father told him that now he could 'do just as much or as little work' as he liked. JV meant that to apply to the rest of the summer term, of course. A. A. Milne decided it should apply to the rest of his life. From now on he would do what he wanted – no more and no less. That's why, years later, having written one successful murder mystery, he would write no more – however much his agent, his publishers, his readers might plead with him to do so. That is why he only wrote four children's books. From the age of twelve, he decided to live life his way. When he was twelve, everyone expected him to be what Lewis Carroll had been: a mathematician of distinction. Alan's teacher, H. G. Wells, predicted that in time he would go to Cambridge and achieve the highest overall marks among the students gaining first-class degrees in mathematics. It was not to be. At twelve, Alan said, not as an admission, but with a certain obstinate pride: 'I stopped working.' Why? Quite simply because 'I no longer thought mathematics grand.'

'What's twice eleven?' I said to Pooh.
  ('Twice what?' Said Pooh to Me.)

1893 was a year of change. H. G. Wells had moved on from Henley House and published his first work in 1893: a *Text-Book of Biology* in two volumes. J. V. Milne decided it was time to leave Henley House, too. For some years, according to Alan, he had been uneasy about Kilburn, sensing the neighbourhood was 'going down'. At the end of the year, at the end of Alan's first term at Westminster, the family moved from London to Westgate-on-Sea, not far from Margate on the Isle of Thanet on the north-east coast of Kent, a part of south-east England that from early Victorian times has abounded in boys' preparatory schools. (My father, born in 1910, went to one. I, born in 1948, went to another.) JV had come into a legacy of £1,000. He found a substantial house (old and long unlived-in), with seven acres of grounds, called Streete Court. The rent was £350 a year. He took it on and opened a new prep school of his own. It was a labour of love (and during the school holidays a home that Alan loved), but making it work, making it pay, was not easy. For a while, it did quite well, but it did not last.

'Nothing lasts really,' as Noël Coward (one of A. A. Milne's playwright rivals in the 1920s and 1930s) has a character say in *Brief Encounter*. 'Neither happiness nor despair. Not even life lasts very long.' Happiness when we are grown-up, according to one of Milne's characters, is always 'tainted with the knowledge that it will not last and the fear that one will have to pay for it'.

For A. A. Milne, childhood, the time – the only time – when 'pure happiness' is there to be had, came to an end when he turned twelve. Of course, there was happiness in his life later. Much happiness – though none of it lasted. 'Don't miss any happiness that is going,' he advised, 'or you'll find it gone.'

A. A. Milne's parents, like all good parents, had determined that there should be no favourites in their family. In practice, Alan knew, the affections are not so easily controlled: 'There was never any doubt that Barry was Mother's darling and that I was Father's.' At twelve, A. A. Milne began the lifelong process of saying goodbye. He began with his father.

Farewell, Papa, with your brave, shy heart and your funny little ways: with your humour and your wisdom and your never-failing goodness: from now on we shall begin to grow out of each other. I shall be impatient, but you will be patient with me; unloving but you will not cease to love me. 'Well,' you will tell yourself, 'it lasted until he was twelve; they grow up and resent our care for them, they form their own ideas, and think ours old-fashioned. It is natural. But oh, to have that little boy again, who I used to throw up to the sky, his face laughing down into mine—' And once, when he did this, his elbow, which he had put out at cricket, went out as he threw, and he had to catch me with one arm, and he told us the story, how often, and Ken and I would nudge each other, how often, and feel mocking and superior, as if we had never told a story more than once. But still, you had me until I was twelve, Papa, and if there was anything which you ever liked in me or of which you came to be proud, it was yours. Thank you, dear.

Chapter Five

in which Alan arrives at Westminster School

I do like a little bit of butter to my bread!

There were thirty-five Queen's Scholars out of 225 boys at Westminster when A. A. Milne arrived at the school in 1893. In his autobiography, Milne lets us know (in a suitably self-deprecating aside) that he was the youngest Queen's Scholar in the school's history.

And the school had – has – a long history. It descends from a charity school founded by Benedictine monks before 1066. In 1540, when Henry VIII ordered the dissolution of the monasteries he ensured the school's survival by royal charter. In 1560, Henry's daughter, Elizabeth I, re-founded the school with new statutes, including the establishment of the King's or Queen's Scholars. In late-Victorian England it was regarded as one of the 'great public schools', as scholastically challenging as Winchester, more gentlemanly and less hearty than Harrow. Westminster had played in the first public school cricket match against Charterhouse in 1794 and against Eton in 1796. It was a great school, whose alumni (known as 'Old Westminsters') included great men – Ben Jonson, George Herbert, John Dryden, John Locke, and Sir Christopher Wren among them. But J. V. Milne wanted his sons to go to Westminster, not because of its heritage, but because he reckoned it the right school for bright boys like Alan and Ken and he had great respect for the school's celebrated (and revered) headmaster, William Rutherford (1853–1907), a natural scientist turned Greek scholar who was appointed to the post when he was only thirty.

Overall, Alan Milne enjoyed his seven years at Westminster. If he was ambivalent about his time there, it was largely because of the food. He loathed the food – despised it: 'I cannot think of College meals without disgust and indignation,' he said with a shudder. At the start of the day, after an hour's schoolwork from seven to eight, breakfast was served – consisting of tea, and bread and butter. 'The bread was, to me,' Milne reflected forty years later, 'the dullest form of bread, the butter the one uneatable sort of butter; otherwise I should have liked it, for I like bread and butter.' Tea was tea, and Milne maintained he had never been fussy about tea – 'but the milk had been boiled, and great lumps of skin floated about on the top of it. It made me almost sick to look at that milk; it makes me almost sick now to remember it.'

The King's Breakfast

The King asked
The Queen, and
The Queen asked
The Dairymaid:
'Could we have some butter for
The Royal slice of bread?'
The Queen asked the Dairymaid,
The Dairymaid
Said, 'Certainly,
I'll go and tell

The cow
Now
Before she goes to bed.'

The Dairymaid
She curtsied,
And went and told
The Alderney:
'Don't forget the butter for
The Royal slice of bread.'
The Alderney
Said sleepily:
'You'd better tell
His Majesty
That many people nowadays
Like marmalade
Instead.'

The Dairymaid
Said, 'Fancy!'
And went to
Her Majesty.
She curtsied to the Queen, and
She turned a little red:
'Excuse me,
Your Majesty,
For taking of
The liberty,
But marmalade is tasty, if
It's very
Thickly
Spread.'

The Queen said
'Oh!':
And went to
His Majesty:
'Talking of the butter for
The royal slice of bread,
Many people
Think that
Marmalade
Is nicer.
Would you like to try a little
Marmalade
Instead?'

The King said,
'Bother!'
And then he said,
'Oh, deary me!'
The King sobbed, 'Oh, deary me!'
And went back to bed.
'Nobody,'
He whimpered,
'Could call me
A fussy man;
I only want
A little bit
Of butter for
My bread!'

The Queen said,
'There, there!'
And went to
The Dairymaid.

The Dairymaid
Said, 'There, there!'
And went to the shed.
The cow said,
'There, there!
I didn't really
Mean it;
Here's milk for his porringer,
And butter for his bread.'

The Queen took
The butter
And brought it to
His Majesty;
The King said,
'Butter, eh?'
And bounced out of bed.
'Nobody,' he said,
As he kissed her
Tenderly,
'Nobody,' he said,
As he slid down the banisters,
'Nobody,
My darling,
Could call me
A fussy man –
BUT
I do like a little bit of butter to my bread!'

When We Were Very Young

The evening meal was breakfast all over again, with the
addition of a few slabs of meat (cold) for anybody who wanted

them: 'Very few did.' The chief repast was lunch: meat (carved well in advance and brought to the right degree of tepidity in some sort of gas-cooker), boiled veg, and, as a treat, rhubarb, when in season. 'Not liking luke-warm slabs of beef (or rhubarb), I made no sort of contact with the midday meal,' said Milne, who recalled one terrible occasion when the headmaster came into the Hall and, observing the boy's lack of interest in the meat on offer, ordered a glass of 'milk' for him instead. 'I managed to get my lips to it without being sick,' Milne remembered, 'and prayed to Heaven that he should move away before the shameful catastrophe happened.' He did.

His abiding memory of his seven years at Westminster was the awfulness of the food. Boys could supplement breakfast and tea with cold food brought in or sent from home: sardines, tongues, potted meat, and jam. He found a 7lb tin of marmalade could help him through quite a lot of the tasteless bread. Even so, he was left with an inordinate craving for food: 'I lay awake every night thinking about food; I fell asleep and dreamed about food. In all my years at Westminster I never ceased to be hungry.'

There were other hardships to endure at Westminster in the 1890s. There were no baths in College. 'It was enough that it was built by Christopher Wren,' Milne observed tartly, adding: 'One cannot have everything; probably there are no baths at St Paul's Cathedral.' There was no hot water, either – just 'a shallow tin bath in which one could make cold splashing noises every morning'. According to Milne, 'These noises were about all that Juniors did towards keeping clean. After a muddy game of football in the afternoon, one had a quarter of an hour in which to get the mud off with cold water, and change back into a stiff white shirt, Eton collar and white bow-tie. If it was one's turn to shout "Rutherford's coming," one had five minutes less. It can be imagined how white and well-tied the ties were.'

If the Juniors didn't behave, sanctions could be imposed by older boys – including 'tanning'. The College captain assisted by three monitors would administer the 'justice' – two, four or six strokes of the cane on the backside: 'The "offence" and the names of victim and executioner are entered by the Captain in the Black Book.' The Junior could elect to appeal against the punishment to the headmaster, but he rarely did.

In later life, Alan Milne could not summon up any enthusiasm for the practice of tanning, but nor was he roused to an extreme of indignation at the thought of it. 'I don't suppose it did much harm, either to those that gave or those that took,' he said. 'It was not the actual pain, but the perpetual fear of it' which caused the hardship.

The headmaster would administer corporal punishment, too. If you failed to deliver in class (for example, by scoring less than twenty out of twenty-four in a class test) you would be 'sent up-School', which meant having to do schoolwork in the afternoon instead of playing games. Any boy sent up-School more than fifteen times a term risked being sent to the head for a 'handing' – sharp strokes administered across the hand by a birch. According to Milne, 'For a Queen's Scholar to be sent up-School even once a term was considered disgraceful.' The youngest Queen's Scholar in Westminster's history avoided this ignominy by the simple expedient of cheating.

When Milne's French master (remembered by his students chiefly for his long, luxuriant moustaches) dictated twenty-four questions, the boys wrote down their answers. That done, Milne remembered, 'we changed papers with the boy next to us, so that each boy was correcting somebody else's paper.' Inevitably, that which was supposed to prevent cheating made cheating more certain, because you were now doing it with an easy conscience on somebody else's behalf. Alan remembered the first time he cheated in this way: he did it on behalf of one Leonard Moon (the boys sat in class alphabetically). Moon was four years older than Milne and already something of a school hero because of his sporting prowess. He went on to become a double Blue at Cambridge, to play cricket for Middlesex, to score a century against the Australians, and to play football for the Corinthians. As Alan remembered him, he was extraordinarily handsome and charmingly modest – and he died of wounds suffered while fighting near Salonica in Greece during the First World War. The death was one of those that contributed to Alan Milne's conflicted views on pacifism and war. He never forgot him. Leonard Moon is buried in Karasouli Military Cemetery, Grave A189.

Back at Westminster, confronted with reading out the scores of the French test, could Milne let Moon (a hero on the playing field, but not so useful in the French depart-ment) go up-School and consequently forego an afternoon of football or cricket practice? Unthinkable. When Moon's name was read out, Milne said 'Twenty-one' firmly. And when Milne's name was read out, Moon said 'Twenty-two.'

At Westminster, College was the house for the Scholars. It had been since 1560. It still is. Today the school has 750 pupils (including girls in the Sixth Form), about a quarter of them boarders, and all divided between eleven houses, among the more recent being Liddell's (founded in 1956 and named after Henry Liddell, a former Westminster headmas-ter and the father of Alice Liddell, the inspiration for Lewis

Carroll's *Alice in Wonderland*), Purcell's (founded in 1981 and named after Henry Purcell, the composer and Westminster Abbey organist), and, most recently, Milne's, founded in 1997.

A. A. Milne was not only the youngest Queen's Scholar in Westminster's history, he was also the school's most generous benefactor. In his will, he bequeathed a one-quarter share of the copyright of *Winnie-the-Pooh* to the school, which remains the largest benefaction given to the school to this day. It is intriguing that he decided to give so much to Westminster, especially as he chose to send his own son, Christopher Robin, to a very different, much younger, less established, less 'establishment' public school: Stowe, founded in 1923 and only a decade old when Christopher Robin won a mathematics scholarship to secure a place there. One of the reasons Alan Milne gave for choosing Stowe for Christopher was that at Stowe, Milne felt, 'as, I suppose, at any good modern school', the rules of conduct are based on reason, not custom: 'No shock of apprehension clutches at the new boy's heart as he realises that he has turned up his right trouser leg instead of his left.'

Perhaps he left his money to Westminster because, as he approached the end of his life in the early years of Elizabeth II's reign, he sensed the school had changed since he was a schoolboy in the last years of Queen Victoria's reign. Or perhaps he left it in the hope his benefaction might help improve the food and provide hot running water in the showers. Probably he left it to Westminster because, overall, he was grateful for his time there and remembered it mostly with affection – just as he left a quarter of the children's book royalties to the Garrick Club, because he was grateful for his time there. (A. A. Milne died in 1956. In 2001, in a deal believed to be the biggest in British literary history, the Walt Disney organization bought out the rights to Winnie-the-Pooh for $350 million, providing Westminster School and the Garrick Club with around £60 million each. More on this in due course.)

There was plenty at Westminster that Alan Milne enjoyed: the cricket, the football (both on the pitch and, on Saturday nights, down the long stone corridor of College, played with a tennis ball, four or five a side), most of all the library. The library then, and books always, were safe havens for Alan Milne: 'It was wonderfully reassuring to feel through the darkest hours of school that David Copperfield or Becky Sharp or Mr Bennet was waiting for you round the corner, and that nothing could endanger the meeting.'

At Westminster, every day from 5.15 p.m. to 6.15 p.m., there was a sacrosanct hour, without responsibilities, without fagging duties, best of all without other people. You were alone and free: 'Nobody asked you what you were reading, or minded what you read, but the books were there, and you were there . . .'

He gave other recreations a go. He joined the school's Glee Soc. – briefly. In the spirit of the man about to be executed who was asked on the fateful morning if he had any last request and ventured, 'Well, what about learning the violin?', Alan said, 'What about learning to sing?' He claimed he couldn't sing, but was willing to try. He tried. The music master tried, too. Eventually, both gave up the struggle. He wasn't much better at art, though, again, he claimed he made the effort. At gymnastics he was more successful, and qualified for some competition or display, but was disheartened when he found on the night that he had turned up in white flannel shorts and everyone else was in long white flannel trousers. He decided he was happier 'up-Library'.

At Westminster in the 1890s, there was fagging and tanning and handing, the food was disgusting, and the bath-water was cold. But there was no outright bullying and, according to Alan, 'Big boys were not encouraged to take either a sadistic or a sentimental interest in smaller boys.' It was an offence, punishable by beating, for older boys and younger boys to go about together, and in the dormitories, Alan reported with approval, each boy slept in a separate 'and entirely sacred' cubicle.

Some of the school's traditions (everywhere seemed to have 'up' as a prefix: you went 'up-School', you played games 'up-Fields', you went for tuck at the provisions store known as 'up-Sutts') – some of the school slang (milk was 'bag', sugar was 'beggar', your jacket was called a 'shag') – Alan found unnecessary and irksome. And some of the privileges the boys enjoyed – being able to sit in the gallery of the House of Commons and observe proceedings; being able to promenade on the terrace of the Palace of Westminster overlooking the Thames – he quickly took for granted.

Of course, the best thing about Westminster was that Ken was there, too. Ken arrived at the school just six months before his younger brother did. Alan arrived as a Junior in the Upper Remove, the top form of the Lower School. In his third term he was promoted to the Under Fifth and found himself, aged twelve and a half, in a class of fourteen-year-olds. Alan was not remotely disconcerted. He was delighted, of course, because one of them was Ken.

The brothers were reunited and remained alongside one another at school for the next four years. You can view Ken and Alan as Christopher Robin and Pooh, or as Pooh and

Piglet: the relationship was always easy, always comfortable; they were mutually supportive and understood one another completely . . . 'they began to talk in a friendly way about this and that, and Piglet said, "If you see what I mean, Pooh," and Pooh said, "It's just what I think myself, Piglet," and Piglet said, "But, on the other hand, Pooh, we must remember," and Pooh said, "Quite true, Piglet, although I had forgotten it for the moment."'

Chapter Six

in which Alan gets a bad report –
and Ken gets a worse one

Ridiculously wrong

A. A. Milne had a lifelong contempt for critics – literary critics and drama critics in particular. In his final novel, *Chloe Marr*, published in 1946 when he was sixty-four, he has a character go to a first night at the theatre, choosing to sit in a box so that he can look down on the critics seated in the stalls: 'I like looking at the critics. They're so solemn and ugly.' Another character later in the same novel 'attributed his dislike of dramatic critics to the fact that the bloody fellers couldn't dress properly in the evenings'.

Milne's dislike of critics – his disdain for them – did not spring entirely from their unsatisfactory appearance, nor, I believe, was it caused by undue sensitivity on his part. It came from his conviction that, as a rule, he was right – he knew what he was doing – and the critics had nothing useful to contribute. He did not value their opinions. A fellow playwright and novelist, the American Irwin Shaw (1913–84), once advised all writers, in order to withstand criticism from without and compromise from within, to be vain about their work.

This lifelong antipathy towards criticism – combined with an obstinate determination to do it his way, whatever others might say or think – began at Westminster School in the summer of 1894, when Alan was twelve and got his first poor school report.

At the end of the spring term, the headmaster's verdict had been encouraging. A. A. Milne was 'Keen, intelligent and improving fast.' Dr Rutherford's assessment of K. J. Milne was relatively positive, too. According to Alan, 'Father, who took our reports seriously, being himself a headmaster, had his happiest holiday. We bicycled gaily up and down Kent.'

At the end of the summer term, the picture was not so rosy: 'I can't remember what Ken's next report said, but I know it must have been worse than mine, because it always was.' It was certainly worse than Alan's, and Alan's was bad enough. Dr Rutherford's assessment of Alan's performance that term was concise, to the point, and devastating: 'Has done ill, showing little or no ambition, even in mathematics.'

Alan was fiercely indignant: 'For (I would point out) I was twelve.' He was in the top mathematical set and in the term's exams had come top of that set. In the school as a whole there were only three boys who were better than him at maths, and they were maths specialists aged sixteen to eighteen. He was twelve, indignant and distressed. 'I can remember that report bursting into our happy summer holiday,' he recalled many years later, 'and Mother's anxiety at the sight of the envelope in case poor old Ken had got another bad one, and Ken's reassurance that his wouldn't be too bad, and my own certainty that mine would be so good that it would be good enough for the two of us . . . and then Father's stern, set face, as he began to read.'

In Alan's estimation, the report was wrong, 'ridiculously wrong'. But JV saw it differently. JV was a headmaster: 'Headmasters' reports *couldn't* be wrong. If Dr Rutherford said I had done ill, I had done ill.'

'Well,' reflected Alan a lifetime later, 'that was that.' That moment – that report: those eleven words – informed the rest of A. A. Milne's life. 'There seemed to be nothing left to work for. In my own subject I had beaten everybody I could beat; I was now permanently with Ken; and Father's happiness appeared to depend, not on my own efforts, but on an entirely haphazard interpretation of them. I stopped working.'

He did not stop working, of course. But he did stop working to satisfy the headmasters – and drama critics – of this world. He now worked for himself and for what mattered to him. And he worked, from that day onwards, at the pace and with the commitment of his choosing. Until that summer he had been 'just a clever little boy who could learn anything which an enthusiast taught him'. His school life had been 'a mixture of ambition and carelessness'; he was a boy who liked learning 'chiefly for the victories it brought him'. Now, 'there were neither enthusiasts nor victories in sight. Only Ken.' Only Ken, his one ally. And, in time, he would lose him, too.

In nostalgic retrospect, the holidays at Streete Court with Ken were always fun: reading together, riding their bicycles side by side, revelling in country walks (from a young age Alan loved flowers: annuals, perennials, climbers to ground cover, spring flowers to summer flowers, he knew all their names), collecting birds' eggs (nothing remarkable: blackbird, thrush, missel-thrush, starling, hedge-sparrow, housesparrow) and building a cabinet in which to display them. He was happy, too, at school, 'but only because I had to be at school, and must get therefore what happiness I could out of it.' He was especially happy at school when he and Ken received from their mother boxes of flowers to remind them of home. They brought with them, he said, 'a nostalgia almost unbearable', particularly 'those sprays of wisteria which lay, a little crushed, on the top of the box, and conveyed somehow all that I felt, but could not express, of Home and Beauty'.

Home and beauty in the holidays; school and duty during term-time. After two years, Latin, Greek and French could be set aside. Ken was just sixteen and Alan was fourteen: 'We sat together now, never to be separated, in the Mathematical Sixth.' This meant they occupied one corner of a classroom in which some more lowly mathematical set was being taught. 'Since we could not talk without disturbing the master-in-charge, we wrote letters to each other: long letters detailing our plans for the next holidays.' They added interest to the letters by omitting every other word, leaving blanks for the addressee to fill in. Sometimes they wrote in their own code, too. 'SWGUSIB?' would mean 'Shall we go up-Sutts in break?' – a question expecting the answer 'yes' and getting it. 'Ken would feel in his pockets and decide that, since we already owed Father 15/6, we might as well owe him sixteen shillings. We did.'

Work, conducted on these lines, was pleasant enough, according to Alan. 'Games of any kind we always enjoyed, even when they were compulsory.' Athletics, football, cricket – Alan was useful at all three. He was one of the school's fastest sprinters and, in his final year at Westminster, won the Open Challenge Cup for the long jump. On the soccer pitch, too, he was fast and effective: he played in the school First XI and for his college at Cambridge. As a cricketer, he maintained he was 'a taught batsman rather than a natural one' and not the fast bowler he might have liked to have been. Cricket, he said, was not the greatest game in the world to play, nor always the most exciting to watch, but it was, undoubtedly, in his view, and Ken's, 'the greatest to love'. So long as Ken lived, they shared a passion for cricket, spending the winter months counting the weeks until the next cricket season, spending happy hours selecting their own Test sides for England.

Intriguingly, while Alan admired Ken above all others, Alan was always fiercely competitive and determined to outdo his older, 'better' brother. 'All the rivalry between us came from me,' he acknowledged. 'As soon as we became competitors on anything like equal terms, I had to prove myself the better man of the two.' When Ken was batting better than Alan (which, often, he was: Ken scored a century once at school; Alan's finest hour was on the day he achieved thirty-nine runs), Alan confessed, 'I could bear to watch him no longer, but had to look away until he got out.' According to Alan, years later, Ken 'never knew this; he would never have suspected it of me, he could never show such ungenerous feeling himself.'

> Then Piglet saw what a Foolish Piglet he had been and he was so ashamed of himself that he ran straight off home and went to bed with a headache.
>
> *Winnie-the-Pooh*

Alan was ashamed of his envy of Ken's prowess on the cricket field, but, curiously, was happy to acknowledge that Ken was, without question, 'the writer of the family'. Perhaps Alan was content to make the concession because, ultimately, he had nothing to prove. It was Alan who became a world-famous author (plays on Broadway; bestsellers on four continents; books translated into more than eighty languages), and also, perhaps, because when they were both boys, it was true. Alan, according to Alan, was very far from being a 'born writer'. He was not like 'one of those lady novelists who had been scribbling away since she was six, nor the prospective dramatist who had seen his future mapped out from the age of four, when he was presented with a toy theatre as a birthday present'.

English language and literature did not feature on the curriculum at Westminster School in the 1890s. In his seven years as a Queen's Scholar, Alan was not required to write a single English essay. In his sixth year he joined the Literary Society, which, on Friday evenings, read the plays of Shakespeare in the company of the Master of the Queen's Scholars, the Revd Arthur Raynor, and his wife – who the boys assumed was a lady of delicate sensibility. To spare Mrs Raynor's blushes, as they read, the boys glanced ahead and did their best to omit the more outspoken passages. According to Alan, *Othello* was the play that presented the greatest challenges to auditors of a sensitive disposition. The boys did what they could to avoid words that might offend, but, in retrospect, Alan doubted if they ever quite deceived Mrs Raynor as to what was going on.

The only regular English language assignment required at Westminster was the one that obliged the boys to devote an hour every Sunday to penning a letter home. Since Ken and Alan had shared most of the same experiences during the week, they made a division of the available material – Ken, as it might be, taking the weather, and Alan the Saturday match. According to Alan, 'as we became older, we became more literary, sacrificing facts to the exploitation of our personalities and enlivening our letters with such scraps of quotable poetry as had lately come our way.' One Sunday Alan found a pretext to warn his father that there were more things in

Heaven and earth than were dreamed of in his philosophy – 'and he cannot have been more surprised than Mother was next Sunday, when I assured her that it was better to have loved and lost than never to have loved at all.' According to Alan, if Ken was doing this, too, he was doing it more allusively and more gracefully. Gradually, it became accepted within the Milne family that Ken's letters, if not quite 'good enough for *Punch*', were good enough for a boy very much older and, in JV's estimation, 'he might make something of it one day.'

He didn't, of course. Alan did, and at *Punch*, too. In Victorian England – indeed, throughout the British empire – *Punch* was the magazine you would find in every civilized drawing room, common room and club library. You would find it in doctors' and dentists' waiting rooms, too. Queen Victoria read *Punch*, so did the Brontës and the Brownings – and the Milnes. Founded in 1841 as a humorous and satirical weekly magazine, it took its name (and logo) from the anarchic puppet Mr Punch. The magazine's celebrated illustrators included John Tenniel (1820–1914), who, from 1850 for more than fifty years, was the chief cartoon artist at the magazine, and who, of course, famously, illustrated the children's books of Lewis Carroll; and, later, E. H. Shepard (1879–1976), who contributed more than 1,500 cartoons and drawings to *Punch* across six decades, and who, quite as famously, illustrated the children's books of A. A. Milne. In its Victorian heyday, *Punch*'s noted literary contributors ranged from William Makepeace Thackeray, author of *Vanity Fair*, to the Grossmith brothers, George and Weedon, whose comic masterpiece, *The Diary of a Nobody*, began life as an occasional serial featured in *Punch* in the late 1880s.

By the mid-1890s, when Ken and Alan were together at

Westminster, the magazine's sales were approaching 100,000 copies a week. 1895 was the year *Punch* published probably its most famous cartoon – the work of George du Maurier (1834–1896), writer and illustrator, whose actor son, Gerald, would one day appear in one of A. A. Milne's plays. George du Maurier was also the author of the celebrated novel *Trilby*, and the father of Sylvia Llewelyn Davies, and so the grandfather of the five boys who inspired J. M. Barrie's *Peter Pan*.

Du Maurier's 1895 *Punch* cartoon carried the title 'True Humility'. It would later be known by the phrase it introduced to the English language: 'The curate's egg'. The drawing depicted the breakfast table at a bishop's palace, with a new curate seated nervously at the bishop's right hand working on a boiled egg:

BISHOP: I'm afraid you've got a bad egg, Mr Jones.
CURATE: Oh, no, my Lord, I assure you! Parts of it are excellent!

As well as 'good in parts', via another, earlier, cartoon, this time satirizing medical care, du Maurier introduced another phrase to the language that has stood the test of time: 'bedside manner'. Du Maurier's novel *Trilby* (1894) told the story of an impoverished artist's model, Trilby O'Ferrall, who is transformed into a great star under the spell of an evil musical genius, Svengali. Songs, dances, soap, toothpaste, and even the city of Trilby in Florida were named after her, as was the soft felt hat with an indented crown worn in the London stage version of the novel. Du Maurier quickly came to dislike the persistent attention the novel was given – exactly as, a generation later, A. A. Milne came to despair at the universal obsession with his children's books.

Within a few years, A. A. Milne would be part of this theatrical, literary and bohemian world. He wouldn't simply be writing for *Punch* as one of its most popular and prolific contributors: his most successful books would be illustrated by E. H. Shepard; J. M. Barrie would become a mentor and friend; he would be having dramatic rows with Gerald du Maurier and cosy correspondence with Margaret Baird, whose sister Dorothea created the title role when *Trilby* opened at the Theatre Royal, Haymarket, in October 1895. Margaret Baird became a friend of A. A. Milne. Dorothea had been a friend of Lewis Carroll. (Dorothea, incidentally, became the daughter-in-law of Henry Irving, the first actor to be knighted. Lewis Carroll had introduced her to Irving's leading lady, Ellen Terry, in 1894. In 1904 she created the part of Mrs Darling in the original production of *Peter Pan*.)

In the summer of 1898, as Ken approached his eighteenth birthday, he left Westminster School. He was not destined to write for *Punch*. He was not sure what he was destined for. According to Alan, Ken had 'no ideas, no ambitions, and little more than average public-school qualifications'. Barry – the cloud in Alan's life, where Ken was the sunshine – was articled to a solicitor and would qualify quite soon. 'It took four long years to become a solicitor; four long years in which you need not wonder what you were going to be, four long years before you had need to prove yourself.'

> 'Where are we going?' said Pooh, hurrying after him, and wondering whether it was to be an Explore or a What-shall-I-do-about-you-know-what.
> 'Nowhere,' said Christopher Robin.
>
> *The House at Pooh Corner*

According to Alan, neither he nor Ken were go-getters – 'but I had a sort of jealous obstinacy, heritage of that childish "I can do it" spirit, which he lacked.' To Ken, the prospect of four years' respite was attractive. 'Since he didn't mind what he was,' said Alan, 'he would be – what was it? – a solicitor.'

So, Ken left Westminster and followed in Barry's footsteps. He was articled to William Bowles Barrett, solicitor, of Weymouth, and embarked on a life that was steady and unspectacular. He continued writing – charming letters, engaging verses (as we shall soon see), even a play – but he was not in competition with anyone, least of all himself. In due course, thinking a solicitors' office might be overly confining, he took the Civil Service exams and passed and found himself starting out on a career in the Home Civil Service in the Estate Duty Office. He did well: in time he moved to the Ministry of Pensions and was awarded a modest honour for his public service. In 1902, aged twenty, in Weymouth, he fell in love with Maud Innes, the sixth of the eight daughters of a successful local builder and developer. They were married in London in 1905, quite quietly at St Paul's Church in Portman Square, and lived, contentedly, first in a flat in Hammersmith and then in a house in Ealing and another in Croydon. They had four children: two girls (Marjorie and Angela) and two boys (Ian, known as Tim, and Antony). Alan visited them often and loved them all dearly. Maud was like a sister to Alan: he had no sisters. Alan was like a brother to her: she had no brothers. Later, in the 1920s, when Alan had found success and Ken was forced to take early retirement and move to the country, to Shropshire, because of his tuberculosis, Alan provided the family with financial as well as moral support. He cared for them, in every sense, always.

When Ken died, on 21 May 1929, at his home, Chanters House, at Pilton near Shepton Mallet, Alan's son, the real Christopher Robin, was eight. Christopher told me he could not remember ever meeting his uncle Ken, though he supposed he must have done. 'I didn't know Ken,' Christopher told me, 'but I know I would have liked him. I think he would have been easier to like than my father.'

Christopher was aware of Ken throughout his childhood. Long before Christopher was born, when Alan and Ken were in their twenties and both working in London, they would regularly take lunch together at one of the capital's many ABC tea shops. When I was a boy, growing up in London in the 1950s, my Saturday morning treat was to go with my father to the ABC in South Kensington for an iced bun and a hot chocolate. It was our special time together – while my mother went to have her hair done. A. A. Milne loved the Aerated Bread Company's tea rooms (established in the 1860s, the last closed in 1982) – they were one of his enchanted places, too, where he and Ken would treat themselves to scrambled eggs on toast or fried fish, coffee and a Bath bun, or tea and 'half a toasted scone and two portions of honey'. For A. A. Milne, as for Pooh, happiness equates with honey. In one of his pieces for *Punch*, celebrating the art of journal writing, Alan conjured up a properly exciting diary entry – and it included a visit to an ABC:

TUESDAY.— Letter from solicitor informing me that I have come into £1,000,000 through the will of an Australian gold-digger named Tomkins. On referring to my diary I find that I saved his life two years ago by plunging into the Serpentine. This is very gratifying. Was late at the office as I had to look in at the Palace on the way, in order to get knighted, but managed to get a good deal of work done before I was interrupted by a madman with a razor, who demanded £100. Shot him after a desperate struggle. Tea at an ABC, where I met the Duke of —. Fell into the Thames on my way home, but swam ashore without difficulty.

Many years later, when Alan was in his early fifties and Christopher Robin was still a boy, the father would take the son to an ABC tea room for an occasional treat. Christopher clearly remembered having scrambled eggs on toast at the ABC. According to Christopher, there were three of them there: himself, his father, 'and the ghost of Ken'.

Although Christopher did not recall meeting his uncle Ken, he did remember happy holidays with Ken's widow, Maud, and her family. In the mid-1930s, across four summers, Alan and Christopher holidayed with Maud and her children in Dorset. Maud organized the holiday. Alan paid the bills. Alan's wife came once, but not again. These summer breaks were important to Alan. Maud and her children, and the memory of Ken, were important to Alan. Christopher, now a teenager, was conscious that his father was conscious that he was now in his fifties – and no longer twelve, the age at which the door to childhood closes. Christopher said that he suspected that his father saw him then 'as a sort of twin brother, perhaps a sort of reincarnation of Ken'.

Christopher believed that during those holidays Alan needed his young son – and Maud's children, Ken's children – to help him escape from being fifty. 'It was a private dream of his,' said Christopher, 'but he did once share it.' It was on one of those Dorset holidays:

Quite naturally, quite unselfconsciously, we skipped, back through the years to our schooldays. I would put our age at around twelve. Five twelve-year-olds playing happily together. I don't for a moment think this was done deliberately in order to level out our assorted ages. Nor do I think it was my father who led us back. I think it just happened because we were all Milnes and this is a thing Milnes can do. We do it without effort and we do it for our own private delight.

Aunt Maud, of course, was not a Milne. She had married into the family, so she understood the Milne magic, but she did not possess it. As Christopher explained, she was not one of the twelve-year-olds: 'Maud, aged about fifty, remained fifty. The rest of us became children.'

Chapter Seven

in which Alan discovers love – and poetry

Was I in love for the first time?

This is a book about childhood, but the problem with childhood is that it comes to an end. Adulthood arrives. Sex rears its ugly head.

In A. A. Milne's 1946 novel, *Chloe Marr*, an elderly vicar says to the twenty-eight-year-old heroine, 'You had a happy childhood?' and Chloe replies, with feeling: 'Until I was thirteen. Then I grew up rather quickly.' A. A. Milne's favourite play was J. M. Barrie's *Peter Pan; or, The Boy Who Wouldn't Grow Up*.

There are no grown-ups in the Hundred Acre Wood. Eeyore can be gloomy in an adult sort of way. Christopher Robin is 'sensible' at times, as a parent might be. Without resolving them, Rabbit and Owl occasionally ponder complicated issues, much as a middle-aged couple might – much in the manner of Vladimir and Estragon in Samuel Beckett's play *Waiting for Godot*:

> 'Well?'
>
> 'Exactly,' said Owl. 'Precisely.' And he added, after a little thought, 'If you had not come to me, I should have come to you.'
>
> 'Why?' asked Rabbit.

'For that very reason,' said Owl, hoping that something helpful would happen soon.

There is an adult world beyond the world of Pooh – we know that. There will be Big Questions that need to be answered one day – but not yet.

Essie, the vicar's wife in *Chloe Marr*, cannot believe that the beautiful and glamorous Chloe was ever happy. She sees the young woman's apparently carefree and frivolous way of life as 'an attempt to hide from herself how unhappy she was'. 'She was happy as a child,' insists the vicar. '"Until I was thirteen," he quoted, "and then I grew up rather quickly." What did she mean by that, Essie?'

Essie has the answer: 'It's the dangerous age, when you accept your nature or are at odds with it, perhaps for the rest of your life.'

Until we are twelve (thirteen at the most), we can be children. According to Christopher Robin (the real Christopher Robin), the Milnes had a key that could take them back to childhood. It is the key that Alan used when he opened the gates to the Hundred Acre Wood and wrote *Winnie-the-Pooh* and *The House at Pooh Corner*. Childhood is the place, the only place, where you find pure happiness. It is Paradise, before the Fall.

In the summer of 1898, when Ken left Westminster School for a solicitor's office in Weymouth, Alan, without his brothers or his mother, went on holiday with his father. The pair of them went on a pleasure-cruise to Norway. 'I was sixteen . . . just beginning to grow up,' said Alan – adding, 'I was, in fact, unbearable.'

This was the summer when A. A. Milne discovered girls. From then on, for the next fifty years, females of all ages both delighted and troubled him. He was not sure he ever understood them, but outside of his four children's books (in which they barely feature), he wrote about women time and time again. They fascinated him and perplexed him. Let's face it (I know this is a book in which our hero is Winnie-the-Pooh, but let's face it all the same), they excited him. In the late 1920s, when D. H. Lawrence's sex-suffused novel *Lady Chatterley's Lover* was first published in Italy and France, in England, in his novel *Two People*, A. A. Milne was writing about sex, too – less graphically than Lawrence, for sure, but with, at moments, as we shall see, a comparable erotic charge.

Back in the summer of 1898, on his teenage Norwegian cruise, Alan noticed 'a very attractive young woman on board who had all the men round her'. Alan was on the outskirts of the crowd, hoping for, and sometimes getting, a smile. He was aware of his own schoolboy charm. 'In my pink-and-white tie (second XI) and green and blue cap (College colours),' he boasted, 'I could probably have got a smile from anybody.' Years later, in his mind's eye, he could still picture her 'swinging her legs on the deck rail' and catching his eye with 'that warm, sudden smile which meant that we two had some secret which the others did not share . . .' He wondered to himself, 'Was I in love for the first time?'

Briefly, he dreamed the impossible dream, but, quite quickly, he woke up and, 'without any embarrassment, I transferred my affection to the charms of deck-cricket and a girl called Ellen.' Ellen was exactly his own age. He never forgot her, but in later life he chose not to reveal her surname 'in case she is no longer my own age'.

He did not forget the older girl, either – the one who had all the men round her when she was swinging her legs on the deck rail. After the publication of his four children's books, when he was in his forties and his fame and fortune were at their zenith, he began writing *Two People*, for adults, and it was all about love – young love, married love, extra-curricular love . . . The central character is an author who dotes on his wife completely and then, by chance, in his early forties, at a supper party, is introduced to a beautiful actress, Coral Bell. She is forty-seven: 'She doesn't look forty-seven.' She was twenty-two when he had first seen her – and last seen her – at a distance, on stage. He had been instantly enchanted by her performance, by her look, by her laughter: 'bubbling happiness coming out of this absurdly attractive face – large eyes, large mouth and very little else'. It all came flooding back to him:

> Coral Bell! Twenty-five years ago none had been so Coral-mad as he. She was in all his day-dreams. When he was batting, she was watching; when he was in his form-room, she was waiting in the Yard outside, and as he crossed it, would ask him the way to the Headmaster's house. It would appear that she didn't want to see the Headmaster very much, for when he suggested an afternoon on the river, and tea at the Rose and Crown, she agreed at once. It meant cutting cricket, and perhaps trouble afterwards, but how gladly one would suffer for her sake.
>
> He was sixteen. Legally you could be married at fourteen, but they might have to wait until he was twenty-one. Five years, and everybody else in the house wanting to marry her too. But if they were wrecked on a desert island together . . . If only.

And then, a few weeks later, in London, he meets her again – again by chance, at the corner of Piccadilly and

Sackville Street. 'Oh, it's *you!*' he exclaims. 'Yes, it's me,' she replies – and she remembers him.

'You were the darling who fell in love with me when you were sixteen. That was – are you any good at arithmetic?'

'Pretty fair as it happens. I was in a bank once.'

'A bank! Oh dear! Then if you happened to know how old I was when you fell in love with me, you'd *easily* be able to work out how old I am now?'

'No . . . Mine was one of those banks where time grew very wild. You couldn't depend on it at all. One might have been eighteen twenty-five years ago, and just about thirty now.'

'And if one had been twenty-two then?'

'Then one could easily be looking twenty-nine in Sackville Street.'

And what happens next you will discover when you read the novel – and you must. *Two People* is one of the best books A. A. Milne ever wrote. P. G. Wodehouse, his contemporary and sometime friend, considered it 'colossal', the work of 'a genius'. Years later, after the Second World War, when Milne and Wodehouse had fallen out, Wodehouse still rated it: 'I can re-read a thing like *Two People* over and over again and never get tired of it.'

What happened to the love life and marriage of A. A. Milne, we will discover in due course. As Coral Bell says in *Two People*, 'It's terribly difficult marriage, isn't it?' – before adding, 'The really difficult thing is knowing when and how to fall *out* of love.'

All that is for later. For now, I am wanting to show you the teenage Alan Milne, in his pink-and-white tie (second XI) and green-and-blue cap (College colours) falling in love for the first time – and how it felt to him.

After the Norwegian cruise, at the end of the holidays, Alan returned to Westminster School – alone. 'I discovered now what delightful letters Ken wrote, but they did not make up for his absence. Without him there seemed to be nothing to do but work and play games.' He did both, and to some effect. He loved his cricket and played on, even when he dislocated a thumb while fielding. Batting as near one-handed as might be, he still managed to hit his personal record of thirty-nine runs. And the following day, he recalled with pride, 'left hand picturesquely in a sling, I collected with the other hand all the mathematical prizes which were available, and was installed as head monitor (under the Captain) for the coming year.'

> It was going to be one of Rabbit's busy days. As soon as he woke up he felt important, as if everything depended upon him. It was just the day for Organizing Something, or for Writing a Notice Signed Rabbit, or for Seeing What Everybody Else Thought About It. It was a perfect morning for hurrying round to Pooh, and saying, 'Very well, then, I'll tell Piglet,' and then going to Piglet, and saying, 'Pooh thinks – but perhaps I'd better see Owl first.' It was a Captainish sort of day, when everybody said, 'Yes, Rabbit' and 'No, Rabbit' and waited until he had told them.
>
> *The House at Pooh Corner*

At sixteen, A. A. Milne was a cricketing mathematician and head monitor (under the Captain) at Westminster School. He was destined, he felt (and his parents felt, too), not for a solicitors' office, but for either Oxford or Cambridge university. Which? He wasn't sure yet. In the autumn of 1898, he tried for a scholarship to Trinity College, Cambridge – and failed to get it. 'Not that it mattered very much,' he reflected. He was still young. Besides, 'Westminster gave three scholarships to Christ Church, Oxford, every year, and I could be certain of one of these.' Anyway, he had his own priorities: 'The important thing now was to get my colours at football.'

Cambridge or Oxford: he would go to one or the other. In England, at the end of the nineteenth century, there was not much choice – and had not been for nearly seven hundred years. Durham and London universities were founded in the 1830s, but Oxford (founded from 1200) and Cambridge (founded from 1209) were 'the universities', the institutions to which every English gentleman would automatically aspire to send his son for higher education. (Women's halls began to be established in Oxford in the late 1870s, but the first matriculation ceremony for women did not take place in Oxford until 1920, the year in which Christopher Robin was born and Oxford women were first awarded degrees. Female students could attend Cambridge University from 1869, confined to women-only colleges such as Girton or Newnham, but they could not receive degrees until 1948, almost eighty years later.) There were ancient universities in Scotland and Ireland, but the assumption in the middle-class homes of the professional classes in England was that your boy, should he prove bright enough, and should you be able to afford it, would go to either Oxford or Cambridge, and probably to a college at one of those universities with which there was already a family or school connection.

The matter of where A. A. Milne would go – indeed, the matter of what his future might hold – was settled, unexpectedly, by something that happened a few weeks before his eighteenth birthday, during the Christmas holidays of 1899. That's when Alan discovered 'the itch for writing', especially the itch for writing light verse. The discovery, he said, was 'odd and accidental'. And it involved girls. Two girls, in fact.

In September 1899, an Anglo-Indian family came to Westgate-on-Sea. The two boys of the family (aged twelve and eight) were enrolled at JV's school, Streete Court. The two daughters (aged fourteen and ten) were sent to a neighbouring girls' school. In the Christmas holidays, while their parents returned to India, the four children stayed with the Milnes, as paying guests. A happy time was had by all, and Ken (back from his solicitors' office in Weymouth for the festivities) and Alan took a particular shine to the older girl, Ghita. One day, after Ken had returned to Weymouth, Alan caught Ghita in the throes of composition. He supposed she was engaged in some sort of holiday homework ('probably in German'), but it turned out she was writing a letter to Ken.

'What can't you spell?' asked Alan, rather patronizingly. Ghita, according to Alan, 'wiped some of the ink off her fingers, put her tongue back, and said that it was poetry,' adding, 'Oh, *do* help me, Alan, I *can't* get it right, it just *won't* rhyme when I want it to.'

Alan did his best to help. The result was copied out by Ghita and sent to Ken. A few days later, Ken replied to Ghita with, according to Alan, 'a set of verses which surprised me: verses in the real Calverley tradition'.

The name Calverley may not mean much to us now, but at the end of the nineteenth century it was a name to reckon with. Charles Stuart Calverley (1831–84) was a Victorian poet, wit and scholar. Notorious for his undergraduate

JV Milne with his three sons, Barry, Ken and Alan, 1886.

JV with Alan as a Westminster schoolboy.

1908. Back Row (left to right): Maria and JV Milne, Maud and Ken with Marjorie. Front Row (left to right): Connie (Barry's wife) with John, Barry and Alan.

Henley House school photo, circa 1889. JV Milne can be seen centrally in the second row from the front (with pince-nez, hands folded), H. G. Wells two places to his right, and Alan can be found behind Wells (his hand on another boy's shoulder) with Ken five places along.

(Left) A. A. Milne serving in World War I as a signalling officer.

(Above) A 1921 photograph of A. A. Milne.

At Easton Glebe, 1921. Back row, centre is Charlie Chaplin between Daphne Milne and H. G. Wells. A. A. Milne is front row, far right.

Irene Vanbrugh and her husband Dion Boucicault Jr on stage in Milne's play *The Truth About Blayds* at the Globe Theatre in 1922.

P. G. Wodehouse   J. M. Barrie   E. H. Shepard

WHEN WE WERE VERY YOUNG.

IX.—TEDDY BEAR.

A BEAR, however hard he tries,
Grows tubby without exercise.
Our Teddy Bear is short and fat,
Which is not to be wondered at;
He gets what exercise he can
By falling off the ottoman,
But generally seems to lack
The energy to clamber back.

Now tubbiness is just the thing
Which gets a fellow wondering;
And Teddy worried lots about
The fact that he was rather stout.
He thought: "If only I were thin!
But how does anyone begin?"
He thought: "It really isn't fair
To grudge me exercise and air."

For many weeks he pressed in vain
His nose against the window-pane,
And envied those who walked
  about
Reducing their unwanted stout.
None of the people he could see
"Is quite" (he said) "as fat as me!"
Then, with a still more moving
  sigh,
"I mean" (he said), "as fat as I!"

Now Teddy, as was only right,
Slept in the ottoman at night,
And with him crowded in as well
More animals than I can tell;

Not only these, but books and things,
Such as a kind relation brings,
Old tales of "Once upon a time,"
And history re-told in rhyme.

One night it happened that he
  took
A peep at an old picture-book,
Wherein he came across by chance
The picture of a King of France
(A stoutish man), and, down below,
These words: "King Louis So-and-
  So,
Nicknamed 'The Handsome.'"
    There he sat,
And (think of it!) the man was fat!

Our bear rejoiced like anything
To read about this famous King,
Nicknamed "The Handsome." There
  he sat,
And certainly the man was fat.
Nicknamed "The Handsome." Not
  a doubt
The man was definitely stout.
Why then a bear (for all his tub)
Might yet be named "The Hand-
  some Cub!"

"Might yet be named." Or did he
  mean
That years ago he "might have
  been"?

For now he felt a slight misgiving:
"Is Louis So-and-So still living?
Fashions in beauty have a way
Of altering from day to day;
Is 'Handsome Louis' with us yet?
Unfortunately I forget."

Next morning (nose to window-pane)
The doubt occurred to him again.
One question hammered in his head:
"Is he alive or is he dead?"
Thus nose to pane he pondered; but
The lattice-window, loosely shut,
Swung open. With one started "Oh!"
Our Teddy disappeared below.

There happened to be passing by
A plump man with a twinkling eye,
Who, seeing Teddy in the street,
Raised him politely to his feet,
And murmured kindly in his ear
Soft words of comfort and of cheer:
"Well, well!" "Allow me!" "Not
  at all."
"Tut-tut! A very nasty fall."

Our Teddy answered not a word;
It's doubtful if he even heard.
Our bear could only look and look:
The stout man in the picture-book!
That "handsome" King—could this
  be he,
This man of adiposity?

"Impossible," he thought; "but
  still,
No harm in asking. Yes, I will!"

"Are you," he said, "by any chance
His Majesty the King of France?"
The other answered, "I am that,"
Bowed stiffly and removed his hat;
Then said, "Excuse me," with an air,
"But is it Mr. Edward Bear?"
And Teddy, bending very low,
Replied politely, "Even so."

They stood beneath the window
  there,
The King and Mr. Edward Bear,
And, handsome, if a trifle fat,
Talked carelessly of this and that...
Then said His Majesty, "Well, well,
I must get on," and rang the bell.
"Your bear, I think," he smiled.
  "Good-day!"
And turned and went upon his way.

A bear, however hard he tries,
Grows tubby without exercise;
Our Teddy Bear is short and fat,
Which is not to be wondered at.
But do you think it worries him
To know that he is far from slim?
No, just the other way about—
He's proud of being short and stout.

A. A. M.

Punch, 13 February 1924, featuring the first Shepard drawings of the bear who would become Winnie-the-Pooh.

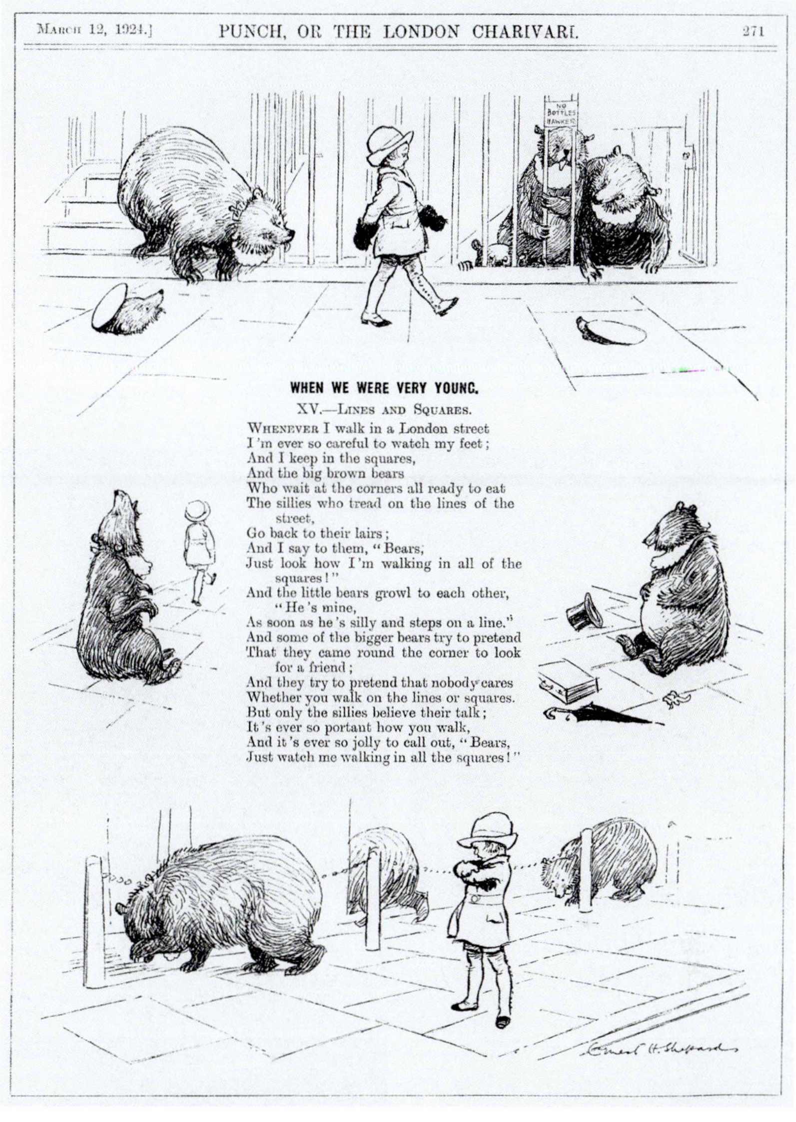

MARCH 12, 1924.] PUNCH, OR THE LONDON CHARIVARI. 271

WHEN WE WERE VERY YOUNG.

XV.—LINES AND SQUARES.

WHENEVER I walk in a London street
I'm ever so careful to watch my feet;
And I keep in the squares,
And the big brown bears
Who wait at the corners all ready to eat
The sillies who tread on the lines of the
street,
Go back to their lairs;
And I say to them, "Bears,
Just look how I'm walking in all of the
squares!"
And the little bears growl to each other,
"He's mine,
As soon as he's silly and steps on a line."
And some of the bigger bears try to pretend
That they came round the corner to look
for a friend;
And they try to pretend that nobody cares
Whether you walk on the lines or squares.
But only the sillies believe their talk;
It's ever so portant how you walk,
And it's ever so jolly to call out, "Bears,
Just watch me walking in all the squares!"

THE EVENING NEWS, Thursday, Dec. 24, 1925.

The Evening News

HOME ED.

London's Predominant Evening Journal. Largest Evening NET SALE in the World.

NO. 13,745. FORTY-FIFTH YEAR. LONDON: THURSDAY, DECEMBER 24, 1925. ONE PENNY.

A CHILDREN'S STORY BY A. A. MILNE.

CHRISTMAS WITHOUT SNOW IN LONDON.

GREAT STORM SWEEPS OVER DERBYSHIRE TO-DAY.

LORD COBHAM'S MANSION ON FIRE.

PRICELESS ART TREASURES INVOLVED.

HISTORIC PAINTINGS.

Christopher Robin.

Page 7 To-night—To-morrow Night's Broadcast.

A new story for children, "Winnie-the-Pooh," about Christopher Robin and his Teddy Bear, written by Mr. A. A. Milne specially for "The Evening News," appears to-night on Page Seven.

It will be broadcast from all sta-

WHITES' DANGER IN TIENTSIN.

LOOTING OUTBREAK BY BEATEN CHINESE.

BARRICADED QUARTER.

MISSING LOAN CLUB SECRETARY FOUND.

FULHAM MAN'S SURRENDER TO SOUTHEND POLICE.

TWICE IN SEA

FROM OUR OWN CORRESPONDENT.
SOUTHEND, Thursday.

At 1.50 a.m. to-day a man, whose clothes were soaked in sea water, went to P.C. Chinnery on

HARRY LAUDER LOSES HIS TRAIN.

BUT SAVES A SHILLING.

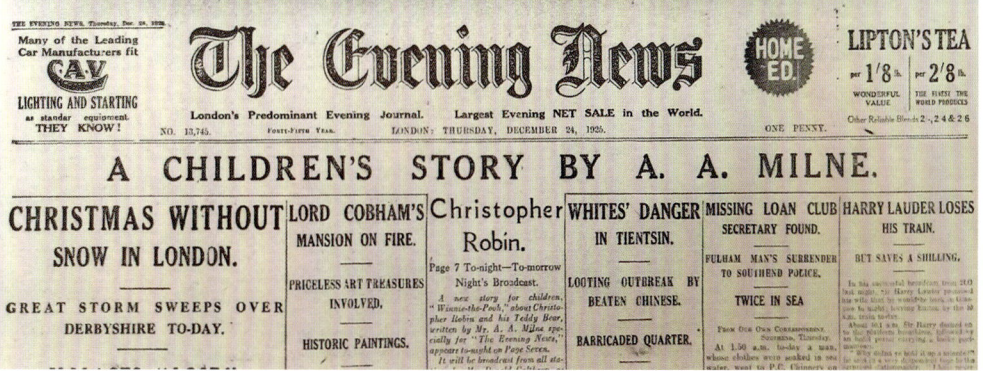

(Top) *Punch*, 12 March 1924, featuring 'Lines and Squares' from *When We Were Very Young*, published later that year. (Above) The *Evening News*, 24 December, 1925.

A. A. Milne and Christopher Robin playing together, 1922.

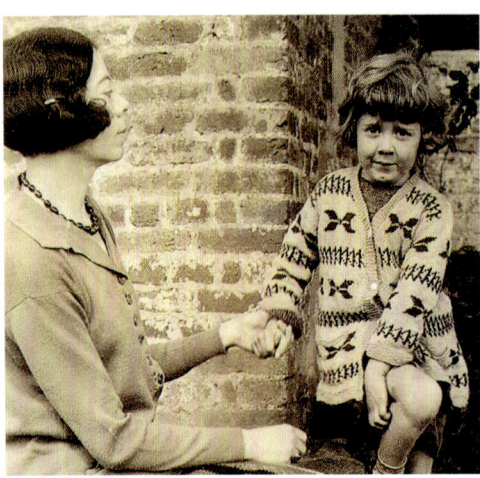

Christopher Robin and Daphne at Cotchford Farm, circa 1926.

Christopher Robin and Winnipeg at London Zoo.

Christopher Robin and Winnie-the-Pooh in Pooh's House, an old walnut tree in the garden at Cotchford Farm, circa 1926.

Christopher Robin with his childhood friend, Anne Darlington, circa 1928.

Mother and son, Daphne and Christopher Robin Milne, circa 1928.

Christopher Robin and his beloved Nanny, Olive Rand. Winnie-the-Pooh and Piglet also on parade.

Christopher Robin and his 'silly old bear', photographed by Marcus Adams, circa 1928.

pranks when he was at Oxford, he moved on to Cambridge, and at both universities won the Chancellor's prize for Latin verse – the only person ever to do so. He became celebrated for his humorous verse, published in *Punch* and elsewhere, and noted for his deft wordplay and skill as a rhymester:

> Should ever anything be missed – milk, coals, umbrellas,
>   brandy –
> The cat's pitched into with a boot or anything that's handy.

Everything about Calverley makes him sound agreeable. He was good company, generous-hearted, reckoned one of the most brilliant classicists of his time, and a master of light verse that was both delightfully memorable and engagingly unpredictable:

> I cannot sing the old songs now!
> It is not that I deem them low,
> 'Tis that I can't remember how
> They go.

A. A. Milne loved Calverley's work, and he loved his brother Ken all the more when he discovered Ken could create verses almost as witty and clever as those of the master. 'I had no idea that he could do it,' said Alan. Ken had added at the foot of the verses he sent to Ghita: 'All my unaided work – and I bet yours wasn't.'

Alan responded to Ken direct, confessing that he had been Ghita's collaborator and – to show what he could do on his own – sending his brother a set of amusingly disparaging odes about Ghita and her three siblings. The first was his 'Ode to Irma', aged ten, and, according to Alan, 'a placidly grubby child whom we all loved'. This, claimed Alan, was his first-ever attempt at light verse:

They say the Dutch prefer their ladies short
    And fat as fat can be, but not as clean as
Is usual here. Out there, dear, you'd be thought
    A Venus.

I am not sure the verse has stood the test of time, but Alan was quite pleased with it and Ken responded immediately, evidently surprised at his brother's facility: 'Good heavens, you can do it too.'

> Written down like this, it doesn't seem a very good song, but coming through pale fawn fluff at about half-past eleven on a very sunny morning, it seemed to Pooh to be one of the best songs he had ever sung. So he went on singing it.
>
> *The House at Pooh Corner*

To the end of his professional life, A. A. Milne was particularly proud of his poetic endeavours. He regarded the art of light-verse writing as 'one of the loveliest of arts'. His verses appeared regularly in the pages of *Punch* and subsequently in three popular anthologies; they became international bestsellers in *When We Were Very Young* and *Now We Are Six*; they featured prominently in the Pooh books, described as 'Hums' and 'Poetry'.

> 'But it isn't Easy,' said Pooh to himself . . . 'Because Poetry and Hums aren't things which you can get, they're things which get you. And all you can do is to go where they can find you.'
>
> *The House at Pooh Corner*

A. A. Milne never took the writing of light verse lightly.
For him, from the outset, it was a serious business. 'Light
verse,' he asserted, 'obeys Coleridge's definition of poetry,
the best words in the best order; it demands Carlyle's definition of genius, transcendent capacity for taking pains; and it
is the supreme exhibition of somebody's definition of art, the
concealment of art. In the result it observes the most exact
laws of rhyme and metre as if by a happy accident, and in a
sort of nonchalant spirit of mockery at the real poets who do
it on purpose.'

'Oh Kanga,' said Pooh . . . 'I don't know if you are inter-
ested in poetry at all?'
   'Hardly at all,' said Kanga.
   'Oh!' said Pooh.

Winnie-the-Pooh

For two years after their first exchange of verses, Ken and
Alan collaborated as poets – sometimes, during the holidays,
working together, drafting lines, searching for rhymes, performing their poems and their parodies out loud; more often,
with Ken in Weymouth and Alan at Westminster, by letter,
building their joint verses by correspondence. (In London
and Weymouth in the late 1890s there were still six postal
deliveries a day six days a week, every two hours, from 7.30
a.m. to 7.30 p.m.; the post was taken around the country
by train and in horse-drawn mail carts, and delivered by
postmen on foot and bicycle.) Alan relished this collaboration – he devoted pages of his autobiography to describing the detail of it – both because it enabled the brothers to
remain close while they were apart and because they both
rather fancied the quality of their endeavours.

He coughed in an important way, and began again: 'What-nots and Etceteras, before I begin, or perhaps I should say, before I end, I have a piece of Poetry to read to you. Hitherto – hitherto – a long word meaning – well, you'll see what it means directly – hitherto, as I was saying, all the Poetry in the Forest has been written by Pooh, a Bear with a Pleasing Manner but a positively Startling Lack of Brain. The Poem which I am now about to read to you was written by Eeyore, or Myself, in a Quiet Moment. If somebody will take Roo's bull's eye away from him, and wake up Owl, we shall all be able to enjoy it. I call it – POEM.'

The House at Pooh Corner

Alan and Ken, now eighteen and twenty, the one in his last year at school, the other in his second year as an apprentice solicitor, took their work seriously: they sought publication. 'We offered our services to *Punch* first,' Alan said, 'but *Punch* was unappreciative.' So they turned instead to the Westminster School magazine, *The Elizabethan*. The magazine's *ex officio* editor was the Captain of the school and, since Alan was his Number Two, 'head monitor (under the Captain)', there was little difficulty in ensuring that *The Elizabethan* gave the early works of 'A K M' (as they called themselves) the prominence the Milne brothers felt they deserved:

Shall I write you a parody, smart and satirical,
After the manner of *Punch* and the rest –
Or something in dialect pretty and lyrical,
Safe to remind you of Burns at his best?

Perhaps you would fancy an 'Ode to an Eider-duck'
Telling his praises with never a pause:
How he was born a duck, lived – yes, and died a duck,
Hampered by Nature's inscrutable laws.

At this stage in his life, according to Alan, he had no thoughts of making a career as a writer. He assumed he would be leaving school to go to university to study mathematics – and it would probably be Oxford, he was told, because Oxford would better suit his particular mathematical talent, which, apparently, was for 'pure', not 'applied', mathematics.

And then – as Milne put it in a poem years later – 'something Oo occurred'. Alan, at school, came across a copy of a magazine called *The Granta*. He saw it by chance – by accident. (As Eeyore observed, 'They're funny things. Accidents.') It was a happy accident that changed his life, set him on the path that would eventually lead him to fame and fortune – and to me writing this book, and to you reading it. They're funny things. Accidents.

The Granta was a student magazine founded by Cambridge undergraduates in 1889. The magazine was named after the river Granta, the medieval name for the Cam, the river that runs through the city of Cambridge. The founding editor was R. C. Lehmann (1856–1929), the son of a Sheffield steel manufacturer and a Scottish authoress and naturalist whose family circle had known the likes of Charles Dickens, George Eliot and the Brownings. Young Lehmann was one of the Cambridge stars of his generation: President of the Cambridge Union, captain of the Trinity College Boat Club, and founder of a student magazine that gained a reputation that extended far beyond the university. It was read by gentlemen in London clubs, and some of the quips and banter of its youthful contributors were repeated in the columns of national newspapers. As Alan Milne explained, '*The Granta* used to call itself The Cambridge *Punch*, until it got the idea of calling *Punch* The London *Granta*.' When he graduated, Lehmann went on to become a mainstay of *Punch*, as well as an MP, a lawyer, and, later, the father of four gifted children, including the novelist Rosamund Lehmann and the actress Beatrice Lehmann. *The Granta* continued as an undergraduate publication for eighty years and published the early writings of assorted authors of note, among them Ted Hughes, Sylvia Plath, Stevie Smith, Michael Frayn – and A. A. Milne.

Back in 1899, Alan Milne 'stood looking at this copy of *The Granta*' with his friend, Arthur Gaye, the Westminster School Captain and editor of *The Elizabethan*, who suddenly said to him, unexpectedly and out of the blue, 'You ought to go to Cambridge and edit that.'

And Alan replied, quite firmly, 'I will.' And he did.

Chapter Eight

in which Alan arrives at Cambridge

I did all the usual things

Alan Milne secured his place at Cambridge University, at the second attempt. He won a minor scholarship, open only to Westminster boys, worth £40 a year, and an open exhibition worth £23. He arrived at Trinity College in the autumn of 1900, aged eighteen and three-quarters.

The city of Cambridge was as beautiful then as it is today, though, of course, quieter and less crowded. There were very few motor cars: the students moved around town on foot, on bicycles and by horse-drawn tram. Today the University of Cambridge boasts around 13,000 undergraduates. In 1850, when Queen Victoria's husband was the University Chancellor, there were just 1,300. By the time Milne arrived (when the 8th Duke of Devonshire had become Chancellor), numbers had doubled. The members of the university, graduates and undergraduates, were all men. The only young women a student at Cambridge could expect to encounter would be the daughters of dons or the sisters of fellow students. Or shop girls. Or prostitutes.

Famously, Henry Labouchère, who was at Trinity some years before A. A. Milne, was seen one evening walking down Silver Street with what would have been described as 'a woman of easy virtue' (or even 'a lady of the night') on his arm. The proctors, the university police who patrolled the streets after dark to maintain both discipline and decorum (ensuring that every student was respectably dressed and wearing his academic gown), stopped Labouchère and challenged him to identify his female companion.

'This is my sister,' said Labouchère, genially, by way of explanation.

'That, sir, is one of the most notorious whores in Cambridge,' countered the proctor sternly.

'I know,' responded Labouchère. 'And Mother and I are so terribly worried about her.'

Labouchère was the antithesis of A. A. Milne. By his own account, Labouchère spent his time at Cambridge 'diligently attending the racecourse at Newmarket', where he lost £6,000 in gambling in two years. He was accused of cheating in an examination, and his degree was withheld. He left Cambridge and was sent to South America to look after family business interests there. Failing at that, he then joined a circus in Mexico, before returning to England and eventually becoming the moralistic member of parliament who introduced the notorious legislation outlawing 'gross indecency' between men under which Oscar Wilde was prosecuted in 1895.

Milne was acquainted with undergraduates of Labouchère's stamp (there were a good number of them at Trinity in his day), but he did not mix with them. He knew, because everybody knew, that the University Chancellor, the Duke of Devonshire, had a mistress (a celebrated courtesan, Catherine Walters, known to her many distinguished friends as 'Skittles'), but he did not approve. Alan Milne held to the middle-of-the-road, middle-class values that he had learned from his parents. Later he espoused radical causes, as we shall see, and was not frightened of controversy, but throughout his life he tended to steer clear of people who did not share his moral code. He did not approve of coarse humour, bad language or loose behaviour. Some of his friends regarded him as a touch prim, even priggish, but I think he simply believed in what he regarded as 'decency'. He was brought up to respect women – and did, even if he sometimes struggled to understand them.

In *Two People*, the novel he wrote at the end of the 1920s, immediately after the triumphs of his children's books, he explores every aspect of love – and lust. At one point, the hero of the book (an author like Milne) thinks his young wife may have run off with another man. If she has, she must actually *love* this other man – 'horrible!': 'Love is much more personal to a woman, he thought, than to a man; physical love. Any decent man could contemplate spending the night with any decent woman, even a stranger, without alarm or disgust. But most women would have to have some strong feeling for the man first. A man could leave his wife and take a mistress, any mistress, just because he was bored with his home. A woman couldn't. Wouldn't.'

In 1900, public men (especially those with the means to do so) took private mistresses. The Prince of Wales, soon to become Edward VII, was notorious for his. The year 1900 was also the end of the century, the *fin de siècle*, the culmination of an era sometimes referred to as 'The Decadence', an era, according to cultural historian Thérèse Taylor, with a peculiar, immediately recognizable style: 'It was mannered, sophisticated, polished and amoral . . . The decadents stopped to rethink the arts, and to bring forward the powerful symbols of the unconscious mind. Their arts glorified their morbid tastes. They liked witty repartee, and disliked moralising. They appreciated costumes and artifice. They preferred the paradoxical to the obvious, moonlight to sunlight, and imagination to fact.'

A. A. Milne's formative years were the 1890s, but he was not drawn to the decadents. He always preferred sunlight to moonlight. He read *Dr Jekyll and Mr Hyde*, but he enjoyed *Treasure Island* more. He could appreciate the paradoxical wit of Oscar Wilde, but he was more at home with the easy-going good humour of *Punch*. Wilde's *The Picture of Dorian Gray* and Jerome K. Jerome's *Three Men in a Boat* appeared within a year of one another (1889–90). Milne was happier reading the latter than the former. Whatever were the powerful symbols in his unconscious mind, they led eventually to the creation of Tigger, Eeyore, Piglet and Pooh.

At Cambridge, A. A. Milne did not mix with any of the latter-day decadents who were there, nor with the fast set. Alan Milne played a straight bat. Occasionally, he met respectable girls who charmed him and with whom he flirted (by doing his best to be amusing), but for his three years as a student his principal companions were middle-class public school boys like him. 'I did all the usual things in my first term,' he recalled. 'I bought two pipes, silver bound, in a Morocco case. I started a banking account, and established my cheque-signature as "Alan A Milne".'

He particularly relished the food on offer at Trinity, the largest and the wealthiest of all the Cambridge colleges. 'I need not be hungry again,' he realized. 'After seven years of starvation at Westminster it was delightful to be ordering one's own breakfast and lunch.' On each staircase within the college there was a servant, known as 'a bedder', whose job was not only to make the students' beds each morning, and to look after their laundry, but to lay and clean out the coal fires in the students' rooms, bring up hot water for them to shave and wash, and bring in their morning and midday meals.

According to Alan, even in the evening in Hall, 'one was safe' – so long as you understood what was on the menu. On his very first evening dining in Hall, a shy freshman sitting opposite Milne was totally confused when a college waiter offered him capercailzie or beef. Capercailzie is a Scottish Gaelic word for a kind of grouse – delicious but not easily pronounced. Milne recalled the scene:

WAITER: Capercailzie or beef, sir?
FRESHMAN *(startled)*: What?
WAITER: Capperkelly or beef, sir?
FRESHMAN *(very pink)*: Er – I didn't – er –
WAITER: Kepper—
FRESHMAN: Beef, please.

Milne settled in easily, comfortably. He liked Trinity College. He felt at ease with the very fabric of the place. He first had rooms (all undergraduates had sitting rooms as well as bedrooms) on P staircase in the Victorian buildings in Whewell's Court, named after the former Master of Trinity who paid for them. Alan's sitting room was enhanced by elegant blue velvet curtains made for him by his doting mother. She also supplied him with cushions bearing the arms of both Westminster School and Trinity College. Both his parents were immensely proud of their son's academic achievements. In his final year, the curtains and cushions came with him when his seniority allowed him to move into Great Court, reckoned the largest enclosed courtyard in Europe and dating from the early seventeenth century. Alan relished the heritage of the college (founded by Henry VIII in 1546) and enjoyed his encounters with the college's

celebrated and long-serving Master, Dr Henry Montagu
Butler (1833–1918), clergyman and Latinist, recognized as
the foremost classical versifier of his time.

Anecdotes about Dr Butler abound. My favourite is the
one in which he falls fast asleep during a college meeting
and wakes up with a start and a timely and forthright declaration: 'A strong case, tellingly put.' Alan's favourite was
the one in which Dr Butler comes into the college breakfast room one wintry morning to find half-a-dozen nervous
freshmen awaiting him. The Master looks out of the window
and remarks genially: 'Well, well, we have a little sun this
morning' – to which the most nervous of the freshmen
responds: 'I hope Mrs Butler is all right.'

Milne survived his first breakfast with Dr Butler. In fact,
he seems to have survived all the hurdles of undergraduate
life with relative ease. He saw himself as a 'typical freshman':
'I kept lectures, cut chapels, got up as late as I could, was
called on by strangers and, shyly, returned calls. I also played
outside-left in the Freshman's match and a silent Greek
maiden in *Agamemnon*.'

Milne's friends at Cambridge were mostly mainstream
men, like him, and included a number of Westminster
School contemporaries, like Arthur Gaye, the School
Captain who had suggested he go to Cambridge and edit
The Granta. While the aesthetic decadents passed him by
entirely, he did get to know three or four future members of
what would become known as the 'Bloomsbury Group', the
set of writers and intellectuals who made their mark in the
first third of the twentieth century, remembered for 'loving
in triangles and living in squares'. All the male members of
the Bloomsbury Group, except for the artist Duncan Grant,
were educated at Cambridge, either at King's College or

Trinity. At Trinity in 1899–90, Saxon Sydney-Turner, Lytton Strachey, Leonard Woolf and Clive Bell became friends with Thoby Stephen, and it was through Thoby and his brother Adrian that Woolf and Bell, when they came down to London from Cambridge and began to live in and around Bloomsbury, met their future wives, the Stephen sisters, Virginia and Vanessa.

A. A. Milne got to know them because he and Saxon Sydney-Turner had been near contemporaries at Westminster. Sydney-Turner was an odd cove. Lytton Strachey remembered him 'as a wild and unrestrained freshman who wrote poems, never went to bed, and declaimed Swinburne and Sir Thomas Browne till four o'clock in the morning in the Great Court at Trinity'. Alan Milne was grateful to know him because, when he arrived at Trinity, it was good to see a familiar face among so many strange ones, and he was intrigued to meet Sydney-Turner's friendship group, while accepting that he wasn't much like them and thinking to himself that he was glad he wasn't much like them. They were intellectually brilliant (Sydney-Turner secured a Double First) and conscious of it. They were 'serious' and, already, A. A. Milne was beginning to protest against 'seriousness', either as a self-protective mechanism because he felt uncomfortable or even inadequate among self-styled intellectuals, or because he was beginning to believe – as a lifetime credo – that when you get up in the morning you can probably do without a sense of tragic awareness, but you will definitely need your sense of humour.

Looking back, Leonard Woolf acknowledged, 'We were very serious young men,' while Milne regarded public displays of seriousness as 'bad form'. That said, Alan was happy to be invited by Woolf and his friends to attend meetings of the Trinity College Shakespeare Society (and in due course to be elected a member), reading out loud from the plays of Shakespeare. Alan was content to be given the more minor roles, though when they read *The Merchant of Venice* and Woolf played Shylock and Lytton Strachey was Portia, Milne read both Antonio and Nerissa. The group also invited him to join the X Society, at which plays not by Shakespeare were given moved readings. One of them was Webster's bloody revenge tragedy, *The White Devil* – a work of literature probably as far removed from *The House at Pooh Corner* as it is possible to get.

Alan was probably more in sympathy with Leonard Woolf than the rest of the Sydney-Turner/Lytton Strachey circle. Woolf and Milne were quite traditional (they shared a love of cricket) and pretty strait-laced: they eschewed ribald gossip and vulgar jokes. They both loved the novels of Jane Austen, while regarding the great Thomas Hardy (1840–1928) as the living writer most to be reckoned with. In 1903, when Samuel Butler's *The Way of All Flesh* was posthumously published and regarded as a tract against Victorian hypocrisy, both Woolf and Milne felt it spoke for them. Years later in a collection of his essays entitled (in typical 'unserious' Milne vein) *Not That It Matters*, A. A. Milne wrote: 'Once upon a time I discovered Samuel Butler; not the other two, but the one who wrote *The Way of All Flesh*, the second-best novel in the English language. I say the second-best, so that, if you remind me of *Tom Jones*, or *The Mayor of Caster-bridge*, or any other that you fancy, I can say, of course, that one is the best.'

Milne was reading serious books at Cambridge, but doing his best not to say serious things about them. He was pursuing his mathematical studies, but not too seriously. His one serious passion was still 'the serious business' of writing light verse, and his collaborator was still his brother – although they were now living and working almost two hundred miles apart. Alan was in Cambridge, Ken was in Weymouth, but they corresponded every week, and every week, according to Alan, 'A K M' was sending in a set of verses to *The Granta* – and receiving them back again. 'It was not until the beginning of my second term,' Alan remembered with pride, 'that we had our first contribution accepted.'

The editor of *The Granta* who accepted the Milne verses was Edwin Montagu, another Trinity man, though three years older than Alan. Montagu went on to become President of the Cambridge Union and, later, as only the third practising Jew to become a member of the British cabinet, he served in the governments of H. H. Asquith and David Lloyd George. Famously, in 1912, Montagu went on holiday to Sicily with his friend Asquith, then prime minister. Asquith's daughter Violet came on the holiday, too, bringing her friend, Venetia Stanley, with her. Venetia turned twenty-five that summer and, on the holiday, both Montagu, then thirty-three, and Asquith, then almost sixty, fell in love with her. Montagu eventually married her, and Asquith's obsession with her is now the stuff of legend. In the same year, 1912, Milne published a book called *The Holiday Round*, a collection of sunny essays whose simple, innocent, carefree tone was a world away from the complicated angst developing between Montagu, Asquith and Stanley on holiday in Sicily.

In time, A. A. Milne got to know Asquith's eldest son, Raymond, and described him as 'the most brilliant man I have ever met'. A barrister and a remarkable intellect, Raymond became a war hero. His death in September 1916 affected Milne deeply. At the Battle of Flers-Courcelette, he

was shot in the chest but lit a cigarette to hide the seriousness of his injuries so that his men would continue the attack.
Edwin Montagu (whose marriage to Venetia survived, despite
the unhappiness of it and her several affairs) remained very
proud of having given Alan his first break in *The Granta*.
Indeed, he regarded it as his 'proudest' achievement as
editor. 'I remember,' he said, looking back, 'how I rejected –
how arrogant we were! – his first contributions, telling him to
persevere and that he might one day learn to write.'

The material that Montagu accepted in Alan's second
term was a type of nonsense verse, invented by Ken, 'a little
in the limerick vein', that the brothers fondly hoped might
become known as a Milnick – 'it was not to be.'

Montagu published half-a-dozen of these verses.
Here's one:

> He was a violincello
> > And she was a wedding-bell
> He loved 'not wisely' (Othello)
> > But she didn't love 'too well'.
> One day she addressed him as 'Fellow!' . . .
> > And they buried him there where he fell.

Here's another – the one Alan was most proud of:

> He was an ardent philosopher
> > And she was a girl of physique.
> He said he was dying because of her,
> > But she told him she couldn't stand cheek.
> Then he recklessly said it was cross of her . . .
> > And he hopes to be well in a week.

A day or so after these verses appeared in *The Granta*,
Trinity, Cambridge, was playing football against Trinity,

Oxford. Alan was in the Cambridge team and, by his own account, on the way back from Oxford after the match, 'inevitably' they stopped in Bletchley and went for a drink. 'And while I was shyly drinking my ginger-beer,' he recalled, 'and wishing that I liked beer and whisky more than I liked rice-pudding, which was not at all, I heard no less a person than the Captain of the Side say to no less a person than one of the "blues" in the side: "Did you see those awfully good verses in *The Granta* this week – a new sort of limerick by somebody called A K M?"'

Alan plunged 'a glowing face' into his ginger beer and reflected: 'If only Ken had been next to me, so that we could have nudged, so that we could have nudged each other and grinned, and talked it over happily together afterwards.' But, of course, Ken wasn't there: he was almost two hundred miles away, in Weymouth. Alan wrote to him to report how well their joint published efforts were being received, and together they continued making combined contributions to *The Granta* over the next five terms, until Alan was at the end of his second Cambridge year in the summer of 1902. If anyone asked (but few did), Alan always made it clear that A K M was two people, not just one, but, understandably, the assumption in Cambridge was that A K M was A A M choosing to write under alien initials, 'presumably from modesty'.

Eventually, Ken decided to withdraw from the partnership, telling Alan he could do 'this sort of thing' just as well without him. It was true. Ken acknowledged the loving rivalry that there had always been between them, but when Alan became the darling of *The Granta* and then became editor of *The Granta*, he accepted defeat. 'Whatever I did,' Ken wrote to his brother, 'you did a little better or a little sooner . . .' It was ever thus: 'And so it went on.' But Ken had believed there was one area of endeavour that was his special territory. 'I should always be the writer of the family,' he had told himself. 'And now,' he conceded, 'you have taken that too. Well, damn you, I suppose I must forgive you. My head is bloodied but unbowed. I have got a new frock coat and you can go to the devil. Yours stiffly, Ken.'

In his autobiography, having told the story of Ken's acceptance that his brother was now 'the writer of the family', Alan quoted the famous 1838 poem by Leigh Hunt that was a mid-Victorian and Milne family favourite:

> Jenny kiss'd me when we met,
>   Jumping from the chair she sat in;
> Time, you thief, who love to get
>   Sweets into your list, put that in!
> Say I'm weary, say I'm sad,
>   Say that health and wealth have miss'd me,
> Say I'm growing old, but add
>   Jenny kiss'd me.

Alan included the poem simply so that he could follow it with this: 'Throughout his life I never lost Ken, nor he me. Time, you thief, who love to get sweets into your list, put that in.'

Chapter Nine

*in which Alan discovers people in
London are talking about him*

The Thing to Do

'Well,' said Owl, 'the customary procedure in such cases
is as follows.'

'What does Crustimoney Proseedcake mean?' said
Pooh. 'For I am a Bear of Very Little Brain, and long
words Bother me.'

'It means the Thing to Do.'

'As long as it means that, I don't mind,' said Pooh
humbly.

Winnie-the-Pooh

So far as Alan Milne was concerned, the Thing to Do when
he got to Cambridge was to become editor of *The Granta*.
Generalized ambition is all very well, but clarity of ambition
is everything. Alan knew what he wanted and, in only his
fifth term, he got it. Then, and later in his working life,
A. A. Milne mostly set himself clear goals and usually
achieved them, doing what he wanted, what he preferred,
what he felt best, even when others close to him were urging
him to follow a different course.

What is odd is that when he was offered the post, he claimed it came as a complete surprise – 'almost the biggest surprise of my life'. Each editor of *The Granta* had in his gift the power to choose his successor. Edwin Montagu was succeeded by Clement Jones (another Trinity man), who knew Milne, liked his stuff, and in the autumn of 1901 wrote to him to persuade him to take on the job. What also surprised Alan was that Jones took twenty pages to expatiate on what a marvellous job it was and how well suited Milne would be for it, 'when four words "Will you be editor?" would have been enough'.

R. C. Lehmann, the founding editor of the magazine, had been a Trinity man and in its early years most of *The Granta*'s editors were Trinity men, too. On reflection, after the initial surprise, Alan concluded that perhaps, after all, he had been 'the only possible person in sight' when Clement Jones decided he needed to get 'the paper off his hands somehow'. Suddenly, it seemed a little disappointingly easy: 'There is no fun in saying "I will" grandly, and then being as good as told that, willy-nilly, you've got to.'

There was to be one stumbling block, however, and in overcoming it Alan showed a stubborn determination that would give a foretaste of his approach to authority figures (agents, producers, publishers, the public) who, in the years to come, might have ideas that did not chime with his own. Milne was offered the *Granta* editorship at the end of the Cambridge Michaelmas Term 1901 and expected to take it up at the beginning of the Lent Term in January 1902. But on the first day of that term, his tutor asked to have a word with him. Alan recalled the conversation in detail:

'I hear you are editing *The Granta* this term?'

'Yes.'

'Well, you can't.'

'Why not?'

'You had no business whatever to commit yourself to anything like that without consulting me.'

'Oh!' I decided to consult him. 'Well – may I?'

'If you had consulted me, as you ought to have done, I should have forbidden it.'

'But why?'

'You're a mathematician—'

'Well—'

'And the College pays you for being a mathematician—'

'Not very much.'

'And from what I hear you will have to work a great deal harder, even as it is, in order to get the degree that is expected of you. And this is the moment you choose to take on other responsibilities—'

'I always meant to edit *The Granta*. I simply must.'

'I warn you that the College may decide to withdraw the money it pays you—'

'I simply must. I always meant to.'

There is a long pause. I am not looking heroic. I am looking sulky and stubborn and uncomfortable.

'I'd rather do it,' I mumble, 'than have the money.'

'And you think you can edit *The Granta* and do your legitimate work properly?'

'How many hours a day do you call properly?'

'I should expect at least six from anyone with any pretensions to be a scholar.'

'All right. Six.'

'Very well then. You will keep a record of your working hours, and show it to me every week.'

So there it was. Alan Milne had achieved his first major ambition. For two terms he edited *The Granta* – writing much of the magazine himself. The regular features included 'Motley Notes' (random musings on issues of the day), 'Union Notes' (reporting on the speeches and antics of the aspiring student politicians as they strutted their stuff in the university's debating society), 'Theatrical Notes' (which, in time, Alan dropped when it became clear that complimentary seats for the editor would only be forthcoming if the local theatre's management was satisfied that every review would be a favourable one: Alan was not to be bought), 'Sporting Notes', and a feature called 'Those in Authority', a weekly portrait of a notable figure with Cambridge connections.

Boldly, for this feature, in June 1902, for the special May Week* issue of *The Granta*, Alan wrote about the soon-to-be-crowned new king, Edward VII, who had succeeded his mother, Queen Victoria, on her death in January 1901. The King had definite Cambridge connections; better still, he was another Trinity man. As a young Prince of Wales, he had spent a term at the University of Edinburgh and had matriculated at Oxford University, but it was not until he got to Cambridge, and to Trinity College, in 1861, that the future sovereign acknowledged enjoying his time at university. In 1902, he was the patron of the ADC, the Amateur Dramatic Club, founded in 1855 and the oldest university

---

* At Cambridge University, May Week takes place in June, after the end-of-year examinations, and at the end of the summer term, known at Cambridge as the Easter Term.

dramatic society in the country, and that gave Alan the excuse he needed for his playful piece about His Majesty.

'Little or nothing is known of his early life,' wrote Alan, 'but it is believed that even in this stage of his career he evinced that love for the drama which was destined to make him President, and afterwards Patron, of the ADC. Anyhow there is evidence to show that he frequently came on at Her Majesty's and the Court about this time, while the Princess of Wales first saw him in 1861 with the part of Leading Gentleman, a part to which he has always lived up.'

Alan was quite pleased with this right royal play on London theatre names and later claimed that he had intended to send 'a specially printed copy' to the King, 'but finance or laziness intervened.'

Alan certainly wasn't lazy as editor of *The Granta*. Apart from the Union, Sporting and other Notes, 'The rest of the paper,' according to Alan, 'was filled with "humorous" articles and verses' – and most of these he was supplying himself. Other undergraduates were offering contributions, of course, but the editor felt he had a duty to provide his readers with the best stuff – and he rather felt that what he was writing was the best stuff. 'No doubt it was only better in my own opinion,' he admitted, 'but, as editor, whose opinion could I consult but my own?'

In his very first issue, he published the first of a series of 'dialogues' which ran through the term and were precursors to the kind of pieces he would soon be writing for *Punch*, as well as the dialogue for his plays and eventually for the conversations that help make the Pooh books the masterpieces that they are. These first dialogues, written when he was twenty, led directly to what would become one of the

most popular of the AAM features in *Punch*: a series about a
group of young people known as 'The Rabbits'.

The Rabbits, as they called themselves, were the very
antithesis of Milne's serious-minded real-life friends like
Saxon Sydney-Turner, Leonard Woolf and Clive Bell. The
Rabbits were neither the Bloomsbury Group in the making
nor the Decadents on the slide. The Rabbits were sunny,
fresh-faced, unashamedly frivolous and fun-loving, gay
(very much in the traditional sense of the word) and playful.
Indeed, they were almost always playing games: tennis,
cricket and golf, mostly, with a bit of weekend shooting and
the odd game of billiards and, once, when they all went on
a spree to Monte Carlo, a few spins at the roulette table.
The group comprised six friends, six carefree companions,
six of the best: Archie Mannering and his sister Myra, their
chums Samuel Simpson and Thomas of the Admiralty, plus
Dahlia Blair and the narrator, with occasional guest appear-
ances from like-minded pals and assorted parents, uncles and
aunts.

The older characters were of a type:

'My father, Major Mannering,' said Archie, 'will now
relate an anecdote of Waterloo.'

The very first story is all about cricket and opens
over breakfast with a passing reference to the great Cam-
bridge-born cricketer Jack Hobbs:

'By Hobbs,' cried Archie, as he began to put away the
porridge. 'I feel as fit as anything this morning. I'm absolutely safe for a century.'

'You shouldn't boast with your mouth full,' Myra told
her brother.

'It wasn't quite full,' pleaded Archie, 'and I really am good for runs today.'

'You will make,' I said, 'exactly fourteen.'

'Hallo, good morning. Didn't see you were there.'

'I have been here all the time. Fourteen.'

'It seems a lot,' said Myra, doubtfully.

Archie laughed in scorn.

The world Milne depicted in his early dialogues in *The Granta* and in the forty-five outings he gave to The Rabbits in the pages of *Punch* echoed the world of Jerome K. Jerome's *Three Men in a Boat* and anticipated the world created by P. G. Wodehouse in his Jeeves and Wooster stories.

The first full-length Jeeves novel, *Thank You, Jeeves*, was not published until 1934, but Jeeves and Bertie made their first appearance in print together in a 1915 Wodehouse short story called 'Extricating Young Gussie', in which Jeeves has quite a minor role and, intriguingly, Bertie's surname is not Wooster but Mannering-Phipps.

The world of The Rabbits, conceived at Cambridge in 1902 and brought to full flower in the pages of *Punch* between 1909 and 1914, is a pre-war middle- and upper-middle-class world of house parties, amateur theatricals, sailing weekends, summer games and winter sports, in which people regularly use phrases like 'By Jove', 'Right O', 'Good man' and 'You silly ass' and almost every story could be called 'A Happy Ending', although only one of them is.

H. G. Wells loved The Rabbits. 'If I could do any one thing as perfectly as you do that,' he told his former pupil, 'I should be perfectly happy.' The Rabbits were the pieces that first made Milne a name to reckon with. People loved them. Some people even learned chunks of the dialogues by heart and performed them as party pieces. When Alan first met the young woman he was destined to marry, he was delighted to discover that she could quote episodes from The Rabbits line by line. Perhaps that's why he married her. Seriously. He liked that. He liked it very much.

Indeed, looking back, Alan acknowledged that he was drawn to his future wife because she reminded him of Myra, Archie's sister in The Rabbits. Myra was fun: jolly, genial, carefree, confident, competent, and she always got on well with the boys. Milne was clear that The Rabbits were not based on particular individuals. He had to accept that he was probably most like the narrator, but the other five, he insisted, were conjured up from his imagination. Having invented Myra and put her into The Rabbits, he admitted in a letter to Dorothea Baird in 1914, 'As for Myra, she is my wife now; though she too (as Joseph Conrad once said) "came out of my ink-pot" at the beginning. But when I write of her now, I think of my wife, and I like other people to think of her too.'

What Milne (and others) came to think of her as time went by, we shall be exploring in due course. The nature and challenges of matrimony became a major Milne pre-occupation over time, but, pre-war, Alan and The Rabbits lived beneath a blissfully cloudless sky.

'Why. What's the matter?'

'Nothing, Pooh Bear, nothing. We can't all, and some of us don't. That's all there is to it.'

'Can't all *what?*' said Pooh, rubbing his nose.

'Gaiety. Song-and-dance. Here we go round the mulberry bush.'

'Oh!' said Pooh. He thought for a long time, and then asked, 'What mulberry bush is that?'

'Bon-hommy,' went on Eeyore gloomily. 'French word meaning bonhommy,' he explained. 'I'm not complaining, but There It Is.'

Winnie-the-Pooh

Critically acclaimed in their day (with Milne likened to Lewis Carroll, among others), hugely enjoyed by readers, and remembered with real affection over the next two to three generations, The Rabbits have not stood the test of time in the way the Pooh books (or Jeeves and Wooster) have, but they are still fun to dip into and they reflect perfectly the middle-class mores and the carefree way of life of the well-to-do young in the early years of the twentieth century, before the horrors of the Great War changed everything.

'So here they all are,' said Milne of The Rabbits. 'Whatever their crimes, they assure you that they won't do it again.'

On the brink of the Second World War, thirty years after he had first brought them to life, Milne reflected, 'I don't want to read "The Rabbits" now, but I can do it without feeling uncomfortable.' He was less sanguine about their precursors, the sketches in the same vein that he had published in *The Granta* in 1902. 'These earlier dialogues,' he said in 1939, 'fill me not only with unease, but with a profound surprise that they led me anywhere.' Yet they did – undeniably. They settled his destiny. They led him, he acknowledged, 'away from the Civil Service, schoolmastering, chartered accountancy, all the professions which I might have followed, into the profession of writing.'

At the beginning of Milne's second term at the helm of *The Granta*, a letter addressed to The Editor arrived from London. It was from R. C. Lehmann (Rudolph Chambers Lehmann, known to family and friends as 'Rudie'), founder-editor of the Cambridge magazine, and now one of the mainstays of the national institution that was *Punch*. In the letter, Lehmann asked for the name of the author of a series of dialogues 'of which I and many others in London have a very high opinion', in the hope that, if it interested him, 'work of a similar nature might be put in his way'.

Lehmann's was a name to reckon with. Former President of the Cambridge Union, future politician (a Liberal MP from 1906 to 1910), author of *The Complete Oarsman* (he coached both Cambridge and Oxford crews, despite at the Henley Royal Regatta, when on the water himself, finishing last in every heat he entered, from 1877 to 1888), versifier (nicknamed 'The Poet Laureate of Rowing'), lyricist (contributing to operettas in the Gilbert and Sullivan tradition), barrister and humourist, he wrote the first-ever series of Sherlock Holmes parodies in *Punch*, collected in 1901 as a book entitled *The Adventures of Picklock Holes*. Lehmann had first been invited to contribute to *Punch* while he was still an undergraduate and editing *The Granta* in 1889. Now he was extending the same invitation to A. A. Milne. Alan was overwhelmed. *Punch* wanted him as a contributor.

It was overwhelming. *Punch* was everything then. It was a bit like being an aspiring model today and being invited to feature on the cover of *Vogue* magazine. As a personal aside, I remember, in 1969, when I was an Oxford undergraduate, President of the Oxford Union and an editor of *Isis*, the Oxford equivalent of *The Granta*, I was invited by the then editor of *Punch*, William Davis, to contribute to the magazine. As Milne said in 1939, 'The undergraduate of today will find it difficult to appreciate the thrill which I received from this letter.' It was such a thrill. I was even invited up to London to the *Punch* offices, to lunch at the magazine's celebrated dining table – onto which, from the 1850s to the 1970s, the magazine's owners and editors and leading contributors carved their initials. Distinguished visitors, from James Thurber to John Betjeman, were invited to make their mark, too. King Charles III, when a young Prince of Wales, carved a C onto the table – though his personal protection officer, when inspecting the dining room before the lunch, was unimpressed. 'My God,' he said to the staff member showing him round, 'you've certainly had trouble with vandals, haven't you?'

In time, Alan Milne carved 'A A M' into the *Punch* table. In the summer of 1902, young Alan ('I was twenty and very young for that') simply revelled in the news that 'people in London' were talking about him. 'I was thrilled,' he said. 'There was only one person to whom I could communicate, and with whom share, that thrill. I wrote at once to Ken.'

He wrote to Ken, and then he wrote back to Rudie Lehmann, thanking him for his kind and flattering interest, and humbly offering to pen a series of sketches for *Punch* (for *Punch*!), promising to deliver them as soon as term was over. He did exactly that. The series of six articles then went forwards and backwards between Milne and *Punch*'s Assistant Editor, Owen Seaman, for some weeks, until, as Alan remembered it, 'they were all to his liking.'

Owen Seaman would soon become a pivotal figure in the life of A. A. Milne. Alan would one day become Seaman's assistant and marry Seaman's god-daughter. Seaman had been a schoolmaster and university lecturer before he joined

Punch. His own first successful submission to the magazine had been a parody of Rudyard Kipling: 'Rhyme of the Kipperling'. Once he knew him well, Milne had mixed feelings about Seaman, describing him as a 'strange, unlucky man'. 'All the Good Fairies came to his christening, but the Uninvited Fairy had the last word,' according to Milne. 'Humour was drowned in Scholarship and Tact went down before Truth.' Some have suggested that Seaman's difficult and dour disposition was the model for the gloomy character of Eeyore.

But back in 1902, Seaman, aged forty-one, did his best to help Milne, age twenty, get his first *Punch* offerings into shape. When Seaman deemed them worthy, they were submitted to the editor of *Punch* himself: the great Sir Francis Burnand (1836–1917), the panjandrum of literary humour in Victorian and Edwardian England, knighted for his service to the nation that very year. In his heyday there was none so great as he. As an undergraduate at Cambridge (he was another Trinity man, of course), Burnand founded the Amateur Dramatic Club. In 1866 he wrote the libretto for Arthur Sullivan's first comic opera, *Cox and Box*. He was the author of numerous popular plays, burlesques and pantomimes, some so successful they ran in the West End (and in New York) for a year and more. From 1880 to 1906, he was the editor of *Punch*, the third to fill the role, and the one, in A. A. Milne's estimation, to give the magazine its special standing. According to Milne, under Burnand, *Punch* 'became more catholic in its appeal; it began to discard its air of a Family Joke and aspired to be the National Institution which it has since been proclaimed. Yet he always kept for it a note of irresponsibility.'

If Seaman (knighted himself as editor of *Punch* in 1914: such was the standing of this now-almost-forgotten magazine only a century ago) was clean-shaven, bald, gloomy and morose, Burnand, by contrast, was burly, bearded and genially outgoing. Burnand lived in Ramsgate, on the Kent coast, but held court in London at the Garrick Club. 'I think Frank Burnand is the most amusing man to meet,' said George Grossmith, the leading baritone in nine of Gilbert and Sullivan's most famous operettas and co-author, with his brother Weedon, of *The Diary of a Nobody*, first published by Burnand in *Punch*. 'He is brimful of good humour. He will fire off joke after joke, and chaff you out of your life if he gets a chance. His chaff is always good-tempered. No one minds being chaffed by Burnand. I will not sing a song when he is in the room if I can possibly help it. He will sit in front of me at the piano, and either stare with a pained and puzzled look during my comic song, or he will laugh in the wrong places, or, what is worse still, take out his pocket-handkerchief and weep.'

Unfortunately, by 1902, as *Punch* editor, Burnand was reckoned past his prime. By all accounts, he had become rather grand and a bit lazy. Milne's tyro offerings reached Sir Francis at the beginning of October 1902, but nothing more was heard of them until May 1903 when Alan made tentative 'apologetic enquiries' of Rudie Lehmann, who then wrote to Burnand, 'who replied that he had been very busy with his autobiography lately, and hadn't had time to give them the anxious consideration which they deserved, but he would be going down to Ramsgate for the weekend and hoped to be able to read them in the train'. According to Alan, 'Rudie waited another month or two (Burnand having met a friend in the train) and then got them away from him, and sent them to a paper called *John Bull* which had just been started as "a rival to *Punch*". This editorship seemed to be in more lively hands, for the series was accepted at once; but the financial arrangements were equally volatile, and the paper went bankrupt at once. Whether before or after the first of my articles appeared I never discovered.'

Milne's first professional appearance in print was on hold, but Cambridge life went on. By the end of his second year, 'The Thing to Do' had been done. He had edited *The Granta* for two terms and with some success. People in London were talking about him. He was now in touch (or at least in correspondence) with the people from *Punch*. What next? Inevitably, the next Thing to Do was face the harsh reality of what university is ultimately about: passing your final examinations and securing your degree. As he put it, 'My last year at Cambridge was sacrificed to the Mathematical Tripos.' In the event, the sacrifice was in vain. At school, he had been destined for a First – indeed, in the eyes of his father (and of H. G. Wells) for the best of Firsts. 'I had hoped,' he admitted, 'that I might just get a Second,' but it was not to be. 'It sounds well to say that one has got an Honours Degree; it looks well to write BA (Maths. Honours) after one's name; to a maiden aunt one can explain how well her nephew has done. But one cannot explain a Third Class to one's father.'

J. V. Milne was so bitterly disappointed that for a week he did not talk to his son. When someone joked to Alan that he rather wished he could be sure *his* father wouldn't talk to him for a week, Alan smiled wanly but reflected that in the Milne family, 'we dreaded Father's unhappy silences much more than we dreaded his anger.'

When JV did come to talk to his son about life after a Third, he resolved to make the best of it. He had once hoped to see his brilliant boy rising through the ranks of the Civil Service, becoming a Permanent Secretary in the fullness of time, securing a knighthood or even a baronetcy for services to the nation, but that did not seem a likely prospect now. JV had an alternative plan. A more realistic plan, which he hoped might be achievable. He had thought it through carefully, and a little later that summer – it was an August evening: Alan remembered it vividly for the rest of his days – he shared it with his boy. Father and son sat side by side on a garden seat, at the end of the croquet lawn in the garden at Streete Court: 'Father had his notebook out, and was checking figures: adding this up, subtracting that, and telling me the result. Twiddling the end of a croquet-mallet between my feet, my eyes on the ground, I said "Oh, yes", and "Yes", and "I see" in a reserved, rather obstinate voice. We were settling my future.'

JV had been a schoolmaster all his working life: he had built up a successful, respected and now quite profitable independent preparatory school. He was ready to give his son the opportunity of succeeding him. He outlined his plan for his boy: 'A year in Germany studying the latest educational systems, a year or two at a public-school, then to Streete Court, first as assistant master, then as junior partner, finally in full control.' JV had worked out all the details in his notebook: 'the salary I should get at first, my share of income as partner, the allowance to be paid to him when he retired, the compensation to be made to my brothers for inheriting the whole patrimony, the value of the inheritance in fifteen years' time when I should be my own master, all obligations discharged.' Alan pictured his father's precise writing in the notebook: 'Blue-black ink, red ink, little ticks in pencils, as he checked each item: a labour of love and pride and hope that morning in his study, while I fooled about on the fashionable beach with the prettiest of the many pretty visitors to Westgate.'

'Well, dear, what do you think of it?' asked the loving father.

'It's all right,' said the ungrateful son. He corrected himself. 'It's very generous,' he said – but he said it reluctantly. He was thinking: 'The prettiest of the pretty visitors lived in London.' He was still only twenty and he was to be sent to Germany. 'It seemed wrong.'

'Well, you must think it over,' said JV. 'I don't want to hurry you.'

But Alan didn't need time to think it over.

'Father?' he said.

'Yes, dear?'

'I think I – I think I – I'd like to try to be a writer.'

'It's for you to decide.'

'Yes . . . I think I have decided.'

JV closed his notebook and put it back in his pocket. Years later, in his autobiography, Alan relived the moment, pictured the scene in his mind's eye, and wondered how much heartache was hidden in that notebook now put away for ever. In retrospect Alan was painfully aware of the hurt he had caused his father that day. Alan's son, Christopher Robin, would one day – and at about the same age – disappoint and hurt his father, too. The rift – the misunderstanding – the failure to connect – between Alan and his son would run deeper and last longer than the hurt Alan inflicted on his father in rejecting JV's plans for his future, but, in time, both Alan and Christopher Robin lived with a sense of anguish and regret about the ways they had responded to their loving fathers at particular moments in their lives.

At that moment, in the garden at Streete Court in August

1903, Alan Milne rejected what his father was offering him. At the time, he did so perfectly reasonably, without rancour, because, quite simply, it was not what he wanted. Later, of course, he realized that he had rejected what amounted to his father's life's work: 'this dream of the little Kilburn schoolmaster, B.A. (Lond.) with his old-fashioned clothes and his old-fashioned beard' – a school, a successful school, 'that could hold its own with all the fashionable schools of Thanet'. J. V. Milne was fifty-eight in 1903. A. A. Milne was fifty-seven in 1939 when he published his memoir and pictured his father sitting at the edge of the croquet lawn looking up at Streete Court, his great achievement, remembering 'all the ugly schools through which he had struggled on his way to this loved place'. Alan knew that his father, as he surveyed the school that was the achievement of his life, 'was on his knees to God, as he had been every night of his life, in gratitude for the fulfilment to which he had been led'.

In due course, Christopher Robin came to reject what millions regarded as the great achievement of his father's life because, as he bluntly put it, 'It seemed to me almost that my father had got to where he was by climbing upon my infant shoulders, that he had filched from me my good name and had left me with the empty fame of being his son.' Alan simply rejected his father's generous proposal because it held no appeal for him. He was twenty and had no desire to be a schoolmaster. 'I'd like to try to be a writer,' he said.

'How do you mean to set about it?' asked his father, reasonably enough.

'I thought I'd just go up to London and – and write.'

'Write what?'

'Well – anything. Everything.'

'Just think a moment, darling, of all the people who want to write, and who think they *can* write, and how very few of them—'

'Naturally I'm thinking of the very few of them.'

'We can't all be Dickenses, you know.'

'Dickens isn't the only man who has made a living by writing.'

'Even Mr Wells had to do other work for a long time before he could support himself by writing.'

Whenever JV mentioned H. G. Wells to Alan he referred to him as 'Mr Wells', even though, by now, Wells was a family friend.

'Wells hadn't got any money,' countered Alan. 'I've got £300 or so. Haven't I? I mean you said – I mean I know it's your money, and it's awfully good of you, but you did say – I mean the others had a thousand pounds.'

'I think it's £320,' said JV, who knew exactly how much it was. 'Of course, that would help.'

'But, Father dear, three-twenty, just think, I could live for three years on that if I had to, and do you mean to say that in three *years* I couldn't – why I nearly had a whole series in *Punch* when I was still at Cambridge, I mean everyone thought I was going to, and it isn't as if – I mean I did edit *The Granta*, and people do read *The Granta* in London. Besides, there's—'

Alan stopped suddenly. 'What, dear?' asked his father.

'Nothing. Anyhow I *know* I can do it. Three years!'

In his head, he thought (though he did not say it out loud), 'In three years I could be editor of *Punch,* of *The Times*, of – should I? Yes, for Ken's sake of *The Cornhill*' – the great literary magazine of the age, once edited by the scholar and celebrated mountaineer Leslie Stephen, father of Virginia Woolf and Vanessa Bell. There was no summit Alan could not conquer.

> 'Pooh's found the North Pole,' said Christopher Robin. 'Isn't that lovely?'
>
> Pooh looked modestly down.
>
> 'Is that it?' said Eeyore.
>
> 'Yes,' said Christopher Robin.
>
> 'Is that what we were looking for?'
>
> 'Yes,' said Pooh.
>
> 'Oh!' said Eeyore. 'Well, anyhow – it didn't rain,' he said.
>
> *Winnie-the-Pooh*

'Look at me,' thought Alan, looking intently at his father. 'There is nothing I can't do.'

'Then you want to go to London and take some rooms there,' said JV, not having heard his son's thoughts, of course. 'Would you live with Barry?' Barry, now twenty-three, was in London finishing his articles as a solicitor.

'Good Heavens, no,' said Alan out loud. 'Sorry. Ken will be in London this year, but I wouldn't even live with *him*. I *must* be alone.'

'You do understand, don't you,' said his father, Eeyore-like, 'that you have no more money to come after this three hundred? And it will be too late then to be a schoolmaster. You'll just have to be a bank clerk.'

According to Alan, it had always been held over JV's sons, this threat of servitude in a bank. 'Other sons,' he recalled, 'might be told that they had to enlist, or emigrate, if they failed in their chosen profession; even to sweep a crossing; but from childhood we had been taught that it was in banks

that human driftwood ultimately grounded. What qualifications were necessary for a bank-clerk other than that of being
a disappointment to his father we never discovered.'

'Of course,' Alan said to his father. 'Of course. But I can
do it. I know.'

Chapter Ten

in which Alan confronts his money worries

Application

And he did.

Christopher Milne told me that when his father, aged twenty-one, came to live in London in September 1903, he chose to live alone. 'But he wasn't lonely,' said Christopher, 'as I might have been, as most young people of that sort of age probably would be. All his life, he was self-sufficient, self-contained. Except when it came to Ken, my father did not seem to need other people. He did not reveal himself to other people. How much he revealed of himself to himself within himself, I don't know. All I know is that he was content with his own company, even at a young age, and I suspect that most of what was happening in his head, then and later, was to do with his work rather than his personal relationships.'

Work – or the hope of work – was certainly what made him decide to find his first digs as an independent adult in the area around Fleet Street. Fleet Street, in the City of London, a short road, a third of a mile long, just east of the Strand and Royal Courts of Justice and close by St Paul's Cathedral, was then the thoroughfare synonymous with newspaper and magazine publishing. It still is, though nothing at all is published there now. The capital's first daily newspaper, the

Daily Courant, was published in Fleet Street in 1702. By the beginning of the twentieth century, every British newspaper and journal of note had its offices in Fleet Street or nearby. As an aspiring writer, Alan knew where he wanted – where he needed – to live. He rented two rooms in Temple Chambers at the bottom of Bouverie Street – the street just off Fleet Street, where *Punch* was based for almost all of its history.

Alan's ambition was clear. He set it out in a letter that September to the Milne family's notable friend, H. G. Wells: 'I thought I would write and tell you that I am going to try my luck at journalism. Thanks to an arrangement with my father made some years ago, I have enough money to keep me somehow in London for two years – even if I earn nothing. But I'm going to earn something. You see!' He was not interested in compromise: 'I believe it is better to go the whole hog – rather than to pretend to be a school-master during term, and play at journalism in the holidays.'

Wells was a mentor and lifelong family friend. Mark Twain (1835–1910) was a hero and role model, whom Alan never met but whose writing he admired and whose advice he took. Mark Twain, the great humorous writer of the age (reckoned by William Faulkner 'the father of American literature'), told every aspiring author that success simply required 'application': 'You need to apply the seat of the pants to the seat of the chair.'

Every day, young Alan did exactly that, committing himself to producing a minimum of one thousand words a day – seven days a week. He wrote articles, verses, dialogues – some topical, some satirical, on sport, on travel, on 'life', mostly on everyday domestic themes – and sent them off in assorted directions. In the pre-broadcasting era, the printed press was everything: it provided you with your news and your entertainment. Scores of newspapers and magazines were published from Fleet Street. At the time, there were eight evening newspapers in London alone, published six days a week. The one Milne most hoped to appear in was the *St James' Gazette*, before it was merged into the *Evening Standard* in 1905. Oscar Wilde and Thomas Hardy had been published in the *St James'* in the 1890s. Kenneth Grahame and P. G. Wodehouse were getting their pieces accepted by the *St James'* now. Alan was determined to be of their number.

He read the paper every evening and one evening was struck by an article on 'the miserable existence of the usher in a preparatory school'. Given his experience as a headmaster's son, Alan felt he had something to contribute on the subject. He sent in his piece. The *St James' Gazette* published it and, as a consequence, 'always every week, sometimes every day, I sent up an article to *The St James'*.' The next day, he would dash out to buy the first edition to see if the editor had deemed his offering worthy of publication. 'Looking for it in vain,' he recalled, 'and feeling that if one is looking for a thing one may as well look thoroughly, I read every word of *The St James'* every evening, leading article and all.' Reading the paper so assiduously was, Milne claimed, what made him both a Free Trader and a Liberal – though he was in no sense a political writer until he was confronted by the horror of the First World War. As a writer, A. A. Milne, from first to last, was foremost an entertainer. He made a virtue of not dealing with the overtly political, the apocalyptic and the existential. He liked to keep it simple and close to home. He was interested in the complexities of the everyday.

> Pooh looked at his two paws. He knew that one of them was the right, and he knew that when you had decided which one of them was the right, then the other one was the left, but he never could remember how to begin.
>
> *The House at Pooh Corner*

He was also interested, right from the start, in being properly paid. He had been introduced by Rudie Lehmann to someone at the *Daily Telegraph* who advised him never to accept less than 'two guineas a thousand'. 'Never accept advice like this,' was Milne's advice to aspiring freelancers in later years: 'The important thing at first is to be printed.' The going rate when he started was 'a guinea a thousand' and the *St James' Gazette* was the first publication to pay him a full guinea. His very first fee was fifteen shillings and that came, not from the *St James'*, nor from *Punch*, as he might have hoped, but from *Vanity Fair*. The magazine, which took its name from Thackeray's great novel, was founded in 1868 and subtitled 'A Weekly Show of Political, Social and Literary Wares'. Especially famous for its caricatures of the leading personalities of the day (drawn by Max Beerbohm, 'Spy' and others), its noted contributors included Lewis Carroll (who contributed word puzzles), Willie Wilde (Oscar's older brother) and the young P. G. Wodehouse.

In 1903, with much fanfare, the *Strand* magazine published 'The Adventure of the Empty House' by Arthur Conan Doyle. It was the story that marked the return of Sherlock Holmes a decade after his duel with his arch-enemy Moriarty and supposed death at the Reichenbach Falls. (Conan Doyle could never escape from his most famous creation, just as A. A. Milne in time would never be able to escape from his. Doyle reluctantly but repeatedly bowed to popular demand, writing thirty-two Holmes short stories – out of a total of fifty-six – and two full-length Holmes novels after he had first hoped to get shot of his great detective by killing him off in 1893. Milne was made of sterner stuff. Resisting all offers, he resolutely refused to return to the Hundred Acre Wood after the publication of *The House at Pooh Corner* in 1928.)

The 'return of Sherlock Holmes' was a huge event, nationally and internationally. Young A. A. Milne wrote a burlesque of the new Doyle story and sent it to *Punch*. *Punch* refused it so, undaunted, he sent it to *Vanity Fair*.

Alan was particularly happy with the way his spoof ended, with this unexpected exchange between Dr Watson and Sherlock Holmes:

> 'And Moriarty?' I said. 'What of him?'
> 'There was no such man,' said Holmes. 'It was merely the name of a soup.'

Not long after submitting the piece, Alan was due to have dinner with Ken and was waiting for his brother 'at a nondescript club which he had joined'. In the smoking-room, Alan picked up the latest issue of *Vanity Fair* and was leafing through it, wondering on which page one day his parody might appear. And then, to his utter dismay and disappointment, he found he had been forestalled: somebody else had written a Holmes parody. 'Jealously,' he recalled, 'I read the opening paragraph. Dash the man, he had even got my joke about the Persian slipper! I read on . . . and then suddenly with beating heart glanced at the end:

'There was no such man,' said Holmes. 'It was merely the name of a soup.' A A M

He saw his own initials. He was in print at last. His work was there for all to see. A A M had his very own page in *Vanity Fair*. He read the piece through again – 'lingeringly: line by matchless line, loving every beautiful word of it'.

He had time to read it through twice more before Ken arrived. On seeing Alan's masterpiece in print, Ken, now a qualified solicitor with his first job in London (which he was not much enjoying), was, of course, at least according to Alan, 'as excited and happy as I'. The brothers – aged just twenty-one and twenty-three – decided to celebrate the momentous moment in style. After the best dinner the club could provide, and a bottle of something to 'wash it down', they decided to take in a show and made their way to the St James' Theatre to see the great actor-manager George Alexander in a happy play called *Saturday to Monday*. By happy chance, King Edward VII and Queen Alexandra were in the Royal Box that night, alongside George and Mary, the Prince and Princess of Wales. Alan allowed himself to think that the royal party had also all just read *Vanity Fair* and also felt A A M's professional debut called for a celebration.

Alan was overjoyed with this success, if a tad disappointed when he discovered that the fee for the Holmes parody was to be fifteen shillings rather the guinea he had been hoping for. He rejoiced, too, when, at last, in May 1904, eight months after he had first set up shop in Temple Chambers, *Punch* finally accepted an A A M contribution, a satirical verse that earned him a modest eight shillings and threepence, not much more than a third of a guinea. 'The paying power of *Punch* was rather a blow,' he told H. G. Wells in a letter in

July 1904. He sent his mentor an account of his earnings to date:

TOTAL EARNINGS £ 17.8.0

made up of (I am doing the details in my head, so it may not add up right)

	£ s d
St James Gazette (6 articles)	6.16.6
Black & White (2 articles)	2.18.0
Bystander (2 contributions)	2.2.0
Express (1 contribution)	1.15.0
Manchester Guardian (odd jobs)	1.17.6
Vanity Fair (1 contribution)	15.0
Punch (2 contributions)	16.6
Daily Chronicle (one roundel)	7.6

He kept going. A regular place in the pages of *Punch* remained his goal, and he remained hopeful, but it was not easy: 'Every week I sent something in, and every week it came back again. It was difficult to know what to do with the rejected contributions. If *The St James'* didn't like 'Spring in the Black Forest' (1,200 words), there was a chance that *The Westminster* might love it; and if *The Westminster* hated it, then it might be just the thing for *The Globe*. One could go on hoping, and hope was what, of all things, I wanted. But it was difficult to feel any hope about a six-hundred-word sketch which *Punch* had rejected. There seemed to be no place for it but the waste-paper basket, a place, no doubt, entirely suitable.'

He persisted (he would always persist), but it wasn't easy. He was making progress, slowly; he was beginning to make a name for himself, of sorts; but he was not earning enough money. He loved his life in his two rooms in Temple Chambers (comfortably done up for him by his caring mother): he had breakfast brought in daily; he usually lunched at the nearby ABC tea room; he often dined in Ye Olde Cock Tavern at 22 Fleet Street, which he loved because of its heritage (the wood carving in the bar said to be the work of Grinling Gibbons) and because he was eating and drinking where Samuel Pepys and Charles Dickens had eaten and drunk before him.

He was extravagant – in small ways. He spent, he admitted, 'a good deal on tobacco', but, he claimed, 'hardly any on drink'. He enjoyed life's little luxuries. He would take a hansom cab to Lord's to watch the cricket ('for only by hansom should one approach Lord's'), but the rest of the time be happy on the 'bus – especially the open-topped buses of the Edwardian era. He would book the best seats when he and Ken went together to the theatre; when he played golf, he didn't fuss over the cost of the lost golf balls. He said that he had 'a gift for extravagance' inherited from his father. JV liked to say that Nature had made him for a millionaire. But, according to Alan, 'the extravagance was combined with a Scottish common-sense and a Presbyterian horror of getting "wrong" about money'.

As his reserves began to dwindle, Alan accepted that he needed to find cheaper accommodation. He advertised for 'two unfurnished rooms with use of bath, central', rejected invitations to rent either a bed-sitting room in Ponders End or a maisonette in Park Lane, and settled for two rooms on the top floor of a police sergeant's house at Number 8 Wellington Square, Chelsea. In a letter to H. G. Wells, he described the rooms as 'cheap and dirty'. They cost him ten

shillings a week. Breakfast was provided by the police sergeant's motherly wife ('a big, friendly soul') for an additional
sevenpence. There was a smell of gas in the sitting-room,
a music-hall singer of some description renting the room
below his, and a variety of children belonging to the police
sergeant habitually on the stairs. He was on the stairs quite
often because the bathroom had been, until lately, a sort of
conservatory linking up the backyard with the ground-floor
passage.

To buy a house in Wellington Square in 2025 would cost
you up to £8 million. In the late autumn of 1904, when Alan
arrived, it was not such a fashionable address. 'I found 3
beetles in my sugar the other day,' he told H. G. Wells. 'Now
I ask you – is this luxury? (You will probably say it was lux-
urious of me to have had 3 beetles when 2 would have done.)'

Of course, as many authors have found across the years,
the quality of the work – or at least its success and saleability
– is often in inverse proportion to the size of the study. The
pieces he sent to *Punch* from his garret in Wellington Square
found more favour than the ones he had been submitting
from his more comfortable rooms in Temple Chambers. As
1904 gave way to 1905, *Punch* began to use A A M more
regularly – and to pay him a little better. Everyone was paying
him a little better. 'Once,' he recalled, thinking back to the
Wellington Square days, 'I got three guineas for a story in
The Westminster Gazette, my top price so far and therefore to
be celebrated with Ken in some way, and reduced, in effect,
to two guineas.'

The financial crisis of his early years came to a head on
17 January 1905, the day before his twenty-third birthday.
It was a Tuesday; he had lunched with Ken; and together,
after lunch, they went to Alan's bank in Fleet Street. Alan

was planning to withdraw £2 in cash – the amount he needed each week to cover his regular expenses: fourteen shillings for rooms and breakfast, another fourteen shillings for lunches and dinners, and two shillings for coal – 'leaving ten shillings a week for teas, 'buses, stamps, stationery, doctors, dentists, games, clothes, holidays and club-subscriptions'. As they arrived at the bank, Alan told his brother proudly that he had a balance of nearly six pounds. Alan handed over his cheque for £2 made payable to 'Cash'. The cashier took the cheque, went away and returned – but not alone. The bank manager was with him and the bank manager explained to Alan that, alas, he was already overdrawn. Alan protested. The bank manager reminded him that he had signed a Banker's Order for the National Liberal Club subscription of six guineas, which had just been paid. 'Oh!' said Alan. There didn't seem to be anything else to say.

It was at that moment that the young A. A. Milne realized that he had finally run through the entirety of the £320 his father had given him. He confronted the reality of the free-lancer's lot: you live by what you earn. It is as simple, and as harsh, as that. In the event, his immediate embarrassment was overcome – by JV. Alan remembered that this was the very eve of his birthday: 'Father had sent me a fiver last year. Would he do it again? Probably.' He announced, with dignity, that he would be paying £5 into the bank the next day. His cheque for £2 was cashed.

Club-subscriptions were important to A. A. Milne, then and all his life. He valued the safe haven of a London gentleman's club, where no women were allowed (except as cleaners, maids or waitresses) and where like-minded chaps could meet and dine and drink together on friendly terms, within unspoken rules and without unnecessary intimacy. In the heyday of his fame and fortune, Alan was a member of the Athenaeum (established 1824), the Garrick (est. 1831), and the Beefsteak (est. 1876). The first club he joined was the National Liberal Club, established in 1882 by William Gladstone as a place where Liberal Party supporters could meet in comfortable surroundings. Gladstone himself laid the foundation stone of the impressive Italianate club building at 1 Whitehall Place (where the club still lives), remarking, 'I should say there could not be a less interesting occasion than the laying of the foundation-stone of a Club in London. For, after all, what are the Clubs of London? I am afraid little else than temples of luxury and ease. This, however, is a club of a very different character . . .'

It was London's largest club (with some 6,500 members) and, so long as you were happy to call yourself a Liberal, and you were a man, more open and accessible than most. That Alan Milne was able to join aged twenty-three was thanks to H. G. Wells, who told him he had to join a club, both for what we would now call 'networking' and, chiefly, so that he could read for free all the London and provincial newspapers and magazines and understand what sort of contributions editors were looking for. Wells kindly suggested that he would propose Alan for membership . . . 'And we'll get Archer to second you.'

'William Archer?' asked Alan in awe. He was still two months off his twenty-third birthday.

'Yes,' said Wells, then thirty-nine. 'You'll have to meet him, of course. I'll arrange it.'

He did.

William Archer, then forty-eight, was the great theatre critic of the age, famous as the man who first promoted the works of Henrik Ibsen in Britain (and translated several of his plays, including *A Doll's House*, *Peer Gynt* and *The Master Builder*), a champion and friend of George Bernard Shaw, a committed advocate of spelling reform ('nue spelling', he called it), a formidable intellect and, according to A. A. Milne, an individual with 'more gravity than any man I have met'.

'At some horribly early hour on a cold November morning,' Milne recalled, 'I breakfasted with Wells and William Archer.' The meal was a serious affair. Archer was the dourest of Scotsmen: 'One felt that humour in his presence would have as little chance of establishing itself as would some practical joke on a Bishop during the final blessing.' Young Alan struggled to contribute to the conversation. Archer and Wells talked, wisely, profoundly, unceasingly: 'together they seemed as old and wise as God.' However, when breakfast was over, Archer filled in the required form, saying, according to Alan, 'he had known me intimately for several years, in the course of which I had proved a most entertaining companion. I was elected.'

For many years afterwards, Archer and Milne would bump into each other at the club. They would greet one other cheerily – and then not know what to say. 'After a period of intense thought,' Milne recalled, 'a smile would light up our faces and we would say simultaneously: "Have you seen Wells lately?"' They hadn't. They said so – simultaneously. Then Archer would say, 'Well – er—' and give a little nod, and Milne would nod back and say, 'Well,' and they would hurry away from each other and that would be that. Until the next time.

By the time he joined the National Liberal Club, Alan was already thinking of writing a play, but he did not turn to the great drama critic William Archer for advice. H. G. Wells remained Milne's literary mentor and Wells suggested that, before he try his hand at playwriting, he might make a bit of the money he so needed by producing a novel – and why not a novel based on the amusing stories he had been writing for the *St James' Gazette*, stories revolving around the happy-go-lucky adventures of Amelia?

Amelia is no Nora Helmer or Hedda Gabler. Amelia is fun. And flirtatious. Breezy, bright and beautiful, ever on the brink of being proposed to, never lost for words, ever on the move, looking for a party or a game of tennis, she's very much in the mould of the angst-free, intelligent, interesting, free-wheeling young women who featured prominently in Milne's writing throughout his twenties and thirties. Perhaps they featured in his daydreams, too? 'Clarissa' and 'Lilian' were two others he liked to write about; 'Myra' and 'Dahlia' two more, who turned up a little later in his hugely popular series of stories about the group of friends called 'The Rabbits'. The girls were all charming and much of a muchness. Except that Amelia was American. She wasn't very American. It was simply convenient to make her American to explain 'why she wants to go to places like the Tower', as Milne explained to Wells.

Alan came up with a strong title for his first book – *Lovers in London* – and to his delighted astonishment, J. B. Pinker, Wells's literary agent, agreed to represent him. Pinker (1863–1922) was one of the first 'agents' in the modern sense of the term: he looked after the interests of authors, negotiating with publishers on their behalf in return for a percentage of their earnings. Pinker boasted an extraordinary roster of literary luminaries at the time, including Henry James, Joseph Conrad, Rudyard Kipling and Arnold Bennett, as well as H. G. Wells. (Later, James Joyce and D. H. Lawrence joined his list. Later still, less happily, Pinker's two sons drove the Pinker agency into the ground and ended up facing imprisonment, accused of embezzling their own authors' funds.) Back at the beginning of 1905, Pinker secured Milne an impressive £15 advance for his novel. That is the equivalent of about £1,500 today.

Milne was ever grateful for the money, but never proud of the book. In later years, he deleted it from the list of his works and bought back the copyright (for £5) to stop the possibility of a reprint. When admirers got in touch to enquire about it, he advised them to avoid it altogether. He dismissed it as 'Humorous Juvenilia . . . You're much better away from it.'

The book had a strong title, but no plot, sparkling dialogue and mixed reviews. On publication, Wells wrote to young Milne to congratulate him on having his first book in print. Alan replied:

8 Wellington Square

Chelsea

6.iv.05

My dear H G

I've only this evening found your letter here. Many thanks for what you say about the book. I've had very nice reviews from *Punch*, *Evening Standard*, and *Scotsman* (Hoots) but may I quote the *Sheffield Independent* in full to you?

The only readable portion of this book is its title which might stand for something good. It is a series of jerky dialogues with the author's comments and the readers' suppositious reflections interjected so that it is difficult to distinguish one from the other or guess what the author desires to convey. The book is devoid of style, lucidity, and is unintelligible to the reader. We sympathise with those who had to see it through the press.

Almost as soon as *Lovers in London* appeared, its author was ready to disparage it. Later in the same letter to Wells, Alan gave an indication of where his future as an author might lie: 'I'm all for playwriting,' he declared. He had recently been to see *Peter Pan*, which had opened to great acclaim at the Duke of York's Theatre on 27 December 1904, and told Wells he was soon to see Barrie's next play, *Alice Sit-by-the-fire*. He ended his letter:

Have you seen *Peter Pan*? It's too wonderful to live. My heroes in real life are J M Barrie and the editor of the *Sheffield Independent*.

Good bye

Ever Alan

Barrie remained a lifelong hero for A. A. Milne. In due course, they would meet and become friends. And the spirit of *Peter Pan; or, the Boy Who Wouldn't Grow Up*, to give the play its proper title, entered Alan's soul and never left it.

Chapter Eleven

in which the Teddy Bear is born
and Alan finds happiness

Those Were the Days

There must have been something in the air in 1904. *Peter Pan* opened in London. Chekhov's *The Cherry Orchard* opened in Moscow. Puccini's *Madam Butterfly* had its premiere at La Scala in Milan and the first Rolls-Royce motor car was shown at the Paris Salon. In Spain, Picasso painted *The Two Sisters*. In France, Rodin sculpted *Le Penseur*. In Austria, Freud published *The Psychopathology of Everyday Life*. And in the United States of America, Theodore 'Teddy' Roosevelt was elected President.

Formerly the Governor of New York, Roosevelt had been elected as William McKinley's Vice-President in 1900 and assumed office as President when McKinley was assassinated by an anarchist in 1901. At forty-two, Roosevelt became the youngest president in US history and went on to become one of the most remarkable. His personal story is extraordinary: a sickly, asthmatic child, he deliberately set out to become a great outdoorsman and succeeded. While adversity dogged him (his first wife and his mother died on the same night when he was twenty-three), he rose to every challenge. An historian, a war hero, a conservationist, a reformer, the first American to win a Nobel prize, his achievements were so many, from establishing America's national parks to founding the Panama Canal, but his legacy is to be remembered by most as the man who gave his name to the teddy bear – annoying for 'T R', as he preferred to be called: he loathed the diminutive 'Teddy'.

In November 1902, Roosevelt was on a bear-hunting expedition in Smedes County, Mississippi. He had not caught a bear, but after a long chase with hounds some of his followers had. They tied the animal to a willow tree and invited the President to shoot it. Roosevelt declined to make an 'unsportsmanlike' shot and the incident inspired a political cartoon by Clifford Berryman that appeared in the *Washington Post* on 16 November 1902. In its turn, the cartoon inspired Morris Michtom, a shopkeeper in Brooklyn, New York, to create a small soft toy bear and put it in the window of his candy store, calling it 'Teddy's Bear'. The Brooklyn bear was an immediate success and Michtom went on to found the Ideal Novelty and Toy Company and make his fortune.

Coincidentally, that same winter of 1902/3, in Europe, the German plush-toy company founded by Margarete Steiff, having been manufacturing animal toys for children since the 1880s – including monkeys, donkeys, horses, camels, pigs, mice, dogs, cats, rabbits, giraffes and elephants – decided to broaden its range by introducing bears. The rest is history: in Europe and America and beyond, from the middle of the first decade of the twentieth century to the present day, year in, year out, bears of every kind have been the bestselling soft toys in the world.

The American name 'Teddy's Bear' quickly morphed into 'teddy bear' and became universal. The first British teddy bear arrived in 1906, manufactured by a London company, J. K. Farnell, established by a silk merchant, John Kirby Farnell, in 1840, making pin cushions and tea cosies, and later expanded into a soft-toy-making business by his children, Henry and Agnes. The bear bought at Harrods for Christopher Robin's first birthday in 1921 was a Farnell bear and, initially, Christopher, his parents and nanny all called him Edward Bear. Teddy bears in Britain often were called Edward because Teddy is a diminutive of Edward as well as Theodore and many in Britain in the Edwardian era assumed, wrongly, that the teddy bear had been named after King Edward VII rather than President Roosevelt. His Majesty (or 'TumTum', as he was nicknamed by some of his bolder friends) also looked more like a teddy bear than did the twenty-sixth President of the United States.

> Edward Bear, known to his friends as Winnie-the-Pooh, or Pooh for short, was walking through the forest one day, humming proudly to himself.
>
> *Winnie-the-Pooh*

We will come to how Edward Bear came to be called Winnie-the-Pooh in due course. In 1904 Milne had no thought of writing children's books. He was piecing together his first novel, *Lovers of London*, thinking about the possibility of writing a play, and placing one-off humorous pieces wherever he could, increasingly in the pages of *Punch* – which was gratifying, but not hugely remunerative.

Writing for *Punch* was an honour. It was an honour he had long aspired to. He was conscious of the honour, but, as he reflected, 'I couldn't afford to sustain it.' He thought he might apply for a regular job. *Country Life*, founded in 1897, wanted an assistant editor. So did the *Hibbert Journal*, launched in 1902 as a 'Quarterly Review of Religion, Theology and Philosophy'. Alan applied simultaneously to both: 'To *Country Life* I quoted my games record, my editorship of *The Granta*, and my early collections of birds' eggs and butterflies. To *The Hibbert Journal* I quoted my profound interest in philosophy and theosophy, my early collections of birds' eggs and butterflies, my games record and my editorship of *The Granta*.' Neither application was successful.

The world around him was changing. As J. V. Milne turned sixty, he retired from schoolmastering. He had to accept that none of his sons wanted to succeed him at Streete Court. Sons can disappoint and hurt their fathers, even when they love them very much. The Milnes sold their school and moved to the lovely (and charmingly named) village of Steeple Bumpstead on the Suffolk/Essex borders. It was an idyllic Edwardian English village, with two churches, two pubs and cricket throughout the summer on the village green. This is where the Milnes lived until the outbreak of the Great War in 1914. Their sons came to visit often. Barry, the oldest, the solicitor, his mother's favourite, arrived on his motor bike, sometimes bringing Ken in the sidecar. Ken, now a civil servant, maintained good relations with both his brothers. Alan loved Ken and ignored Barry. The older brothers were getting married – Barry to Connie and Ken to Maud – and starting families of their own. Alan was fond of both his sisters-in-law and, when they arrived, of his young nephews and nieces, too. His affection for both Connie and Maud was real and lifelong. Barry he never liked and, as we know, came to despise.

I asked Christopher Milne about his uncles and his father. 'I can't tell you anything,' he said. 'I don't know. He loved

Ken, of course. Barry he never mentioned.' He shrugged and smiled: 'Families.'

In 1905, the average age of marriage in Britain was just under twenty-two years for women and just under twenty-six years for men. Ken and Barry were twenty-five and twenty-six, settling down, starting families, establishing careers. Alan was twenty-three, rising twenty-four, not yet looking for a wife, but in want of money and not entirely satisfied with the freelance life. *Punch* was taking more of his stuff. He was happy about that. In the first half of the year, they had accepted a dozen of his contributions. In the second half, they asked him to write a series for them. He did it. 'It wasn't very good,' he recalled, 'and it wasn't very bad.' He made about £120 that year: Ken was earning £200. 'Where should I be in five years' time?' he asked himself. 'At twenty-four,' he reflected at the beginning of 1906, not long after his birthday, 'one must be certain of fame at thirty.' He asked himself: 'How could I achieve fame at thirty?' Sitting in Battersea Park, 'in a pair of tight boots, on a mild February day which seemed to make them tighter', he came up with the answer: 'Only, it seemed, by writing a novel' – a real novel 'which would be the talk of every dinner table'.

These were the years when H. G. Wells, G. K. Chesterton, Arnold Bennett and John Galsworthy were producing novels of note. Joseph Conrad's *Nostromo* was published in 1904. E. M. Forster published his first novel in 1905: *Where Angels Fear to Tread*. A. A. Milne decided he would follow their example. Back in his room in Wellington Square, he took off his tight boots and, 'sitting in my slippers before the fire I resolved to begin my novel on Monday.' Years later, all he could remember of the novel was the proposed title, rather a good one: *Philip's Wife*. To prove to himself that this was no empty resolution, he wrote to *Punch* to tell them that they shouldn't expect any further contributions from him in the coming months. He was retiring to the country to write a novel.

What happened next changed and redefined his life. *Punch* wrote back saying, 'Don't rush to the country, there might be something for you here.' Two days later, 'on another mild February day, in another pair of boots', Alan made his way to the *Punch* office. After twenty-six years as editor, the great Sir Francis Burnand had been persuaded to retire. He was sixty-nine and reluctant to go. He believed he still had much to offer. (He continued contributing to the scripts of the pantomimes at Drury Lane, continued coming up to London from Ramsgate to hold court at the Garrick Club, became editor of *The Catholic Who's Who*, and published one more book, in 1917, the year he died: *The Fox's Frolic: or, a day with the topsy turvy hunt*.) Burnand was succeeded by his Assistant Editor, Owen Seaman, forty-four, and Seaman, of course, now needed his own Assistant Editor. Seaman thought young Milne might be ideal for the job. When he heard the proposed terms, Alan very much agreed. 'The pro-prietors thought,' said Seaman, 'seeing that they wouldn't require your full time, that £250 a year would – er – meet the case.' That was a quarter more than Ken was earning at his desk in the Estate Duty Office. 'As regards your own contri-butions,' Owen Seaman went on, 'they would be paid for at double rates, and naturally we should expect you to contrib-ute every week.'

On the bus going back to Wellington Square, Alan worked out that his new income would amount to around £500 a year. Enough to live on (and live on well), enough to afford the subscription to another club (or two), enough to move from dank Chelsea back into the heart of town. He exchanged his room in Wellington Square (with shared outdoor facilities) for an apartment in St James's Park Chambers, Queen Anne's Gate, Westminster (with a personal bathroom so large he turned it into a bedroom-with-bath and made the bedroom his library). He was overjoyed. His boyhood dreams were coming true. He wanted to tell his father. He wanted to share the news with Ken. Looking back, he remembered, 'I could not think for happiness.'

On Tuesday 13 February 1906, just four weeks after his twenty-fourth birthday, A. A. Milne started work as Assistant Editor of *Punch* and embarked on the happiest years of his adult life. The *Punch* week started on a Tuesday and, for Alan, involved doing what he described as the editor's 'donkey work' – chasing contributors, correcting proofs, having bright ideas for cartoons. Alan was not yet to be invited to sit with the magazine's grandees around the famed *Punch* table at the Wednesday dinner, when, over champagne and brandy, smoking their pipes and cigars, the senior men would consider and choose the look and theme of the week's principal cartoon, but he could come up with suggestions and Owen Seaman took those suggestions to the dinner and shared what he considered the best of them – with or without acknowledgement, Alan was never sure.

Friday was his busy day, the day 'I sat down after breakfast to make my own personal contribution to *Punch*: a gay (I hoped) article of twelve hundred words, with a smile in every paragraph, and a laugh in every inch. (I was paid by the inch.)' He could, of course, have begun his article on any day of the week, but, of course, like almost every columnist before and since, he needed a deadline to concentrate the mind. His article had to be with the printer by four o'clock on Friday afternoon. On Friday morning at 9.30 he sat down to search for 'the idea': 'At 10.30, my brain in ruins, I was still searching. At 11.30 I was telling myself that even if I did find it, I had to find fifty-one more before the year was over; and that if I stayed on *Punch* until I was seventy, as everybody seemed to do, then I should have to find about 2,500 ideas before I died. Yet now, in my prime at twenty-four, I couldn't even find one. Why hadn't I become a schoolmaster?'

At twelve he was saying: 'Well, it's not very good, but I may as well begin, and see what happens.' At 12.30 he was saying: 'It's not so bad.' At 1.30 some variation of the idea came to him and he started again. It was now definitely going to be good. At 3.30 it was finished. He sent it down to the printers and went out in search of something to eat.

Soon after four he was back in the office – writing a review of the play he had seen the night before, writing a book review, writing 'the paragraphs'. The paragraphs were cuttings taken from other newspapers, given an added twist, a touch of *Punch* – for example, 'Peacock and Peahen for sale: unrelated: 1906 chicks,' to which might be appended the quip: 'Then it's quite time they *were* related.' At seven o'clock, the proof of his own contribution came up from the printer and required close attention, and tweaking towards perfection, before dinner at eight. At ten o'clock, he was back in the editor's office as the set pages were beginning to arrive. Painstakingly, Owen Seaman pored over them line by line, Alan Milne standing at his side ready to make any necessary emendations – 'interesting to cut ten lines out of somebody else's article, and annoying to have to cut two out of my own.' Owen Seaman was punctilious as an editor, with, according to Alan, a heart of gold concealed beneath a rugged exterior. Could Alan kindly explain 'the point' of one of the paragraphs: 'Not more than twenty people will see it. Can't you make it clearer?'

'Easily. But it will spoil it for the twenty.'

'We can't edit a paper for twenty readers.'

'Wouldn't it be heavenly if we could? . . . Is that better?'

'H'm. It isn't too clear now.'

'One must keep it funny somehow.'

'Oh, well, all right. You may find a better one tomorrow.'

This editorial fine-tuning went on until one in the morning, when Seaman called it a day and the Editor and his Assistant went home. At 10 a.m. on Saturday, Alan was back (an hour before Seaman) to go through the pages for final correction before sending them off to press by lunchtime – when he could set off to play cricket at Steeple Bumpstead or watch cricket at Lord's or have lunch (and then dinner) with Ken and Maud at their home in Ealing.

Alan loved his life at *Punch* – and the readers of *Punch* loved his contributions. Over the next few years, these *Punch* pieces made him a household name. This was two and three decades before the advent of radio and television, when a regular column in a popular publication could make a writer properly famous – if the writer had the right touch. And A. A. Milne did. In the early days, when Alan sent a piece to the *Evening News*, the Literary Editor, C. E. Burton, asked to see him. 'I liked your article,' said Burton, 'it's going in tomorrow.'

'Good,' said Alan.

'It was funny without really trying,' said Burton.

'That's what it tried to be,' said Alan.

As the years went by, A. A. Milne became increasingly frustrated that people thought because what he wrote was easy to read it must also be easy to write. He took the business of being 'effortlessly amusing' seriously. He did not like it when his lightness of touch made people take him for a lightweight.

His pieces for *Punch* took a variety of forms: sometimes they were straightforward essays, or an imagined correspondence, or a burlesque of something in the news. Often they were duologues or playlets: dialogue was always his forte. They were, in modern terms, accessible and relatable. He gave you portraits of people you might know (and he did know) – a solicitor, a painter, a civil servant, an actor, 'the younger son' – and wrote about everyday life – being in the train going to work, playing croquet at the weekend, going to a dance, washing up – with a keen observer's eye and a wry smile. He wasn't arch or arcane – which might be said of some of the established *Punch* contributors: he was modern and amusing. His readers looked forward to his pieces because they entertained, they lifted your spirits, and they rang true.

> Eeyore was saying to himself. 'This writing business. Pencils and what-not. Over-rated, if you ask me. Silly stuff. Nothing in it.'
>
> *Winnie-the-Pooh*

So popular did A. A. Milne become – and so quickly – that his *Punch* pieces were republished in book form and became bestsellers. The titles he chose for each volume tell their own story:

The Day's Play (1910)
The Holiday Round (1912)
Once a Week (1914)
The Sunny Side (1921)

In 1929, when all four books were brought together and published in one volume, he called the collection *Those Were the Days*. Looking at my copy of the first edition (kindly inscribed to me by Christopher Milne on 15 December 1981), I see that A. A. Milne gives the origin of the title he has chosen with an epigraph on the title page:

> Life's morning radiance hath not left the hills,
> Her dew is on the flowers. Those were the days . . .

The Prelude

The author of *The Prelude* is not mentioned. Probably in 1929 Milne and his publisher assumed that every educated reader would know that *The Prelude* is by William Wordsworth and is the poem in which Wordsworth takes us with him on his life's journey to becoming a poet, beginning with his childhood memories – ice-skating, flying kites, climbing hills and mountains, feeling the breeze on his skin, revelling in nature.

What Wordsworth had known, Milne had known, too. Alan's childhood was his enchanted place. But it was not just his childhood that was special to him. His twenties and early thirties were magical to him, too – the time he spent in the happy, innocent, everyday world he depicted week in, week out, for more than a decade in the pages of *Punch*.

Until the cataclysm of the First World War changed everything, Alan loved his life. He loved his work. It was rewarding; it was satisfying; it was making him famous. He loved his time away from work: going to the theatre, going to Twickenham to watch the rugby, playing golf, playing cricket, going to the Lake District to climb the Napes Needle. He made time to visit his parents at weekends. Always once, and often two or three times a week, he would go over to Ealing to have dinner with Ken and Maud. The brothers in their twenties would enjoy the kinds of treats they had enjoyed when they had been at school ten years before. 'While Maud stayed at home and boiled the potatoes,' Alan recalled, 'Ken and I would go out and buy all the things at the grocer's which we would have bought so gladly at Westminster: sardines, tongues, tinned fruit, soft drinks and, more adulty, cherry brandy.' Then, after dinner, 'while Maud washed up, we men sat in front of the fire, replete, and smoked and chattered.' *Those* were the days!

Ken and Maud's children added to Alan's happiness. Their first daughter, Marjorie, arrived in 1906, followed by Angela in 1909. In time, as she became a talkative little girl, Alan featured Marjorie in some of his *Punch* pieces, disguising her lightly as Margery. 'You are Margery to me,' he explained to his niece. 'I hope I have a mind above your common-place Marjories.' He gave her a catchphrase which became a Milne family favourite: 'Well, that's a *silly* thing to say.'

In September 1910, when *The Day's Play* was published, he denied the existence of *Lovers in London* and described the new book as his first book, inscribing it to Ken and Maud:

To the dear authors of Marjorie
from the author of Margery
('Well, 'at's a silly fing to say.')

His domestic life with Ken and Maud and the girls was comfortable and cosy. His working life was exciting. Through *Punch* he got to know most of the leading journalistic and literary figures of the day. Some, usually a little older than Alan, became friends and mentors. Charles Turley Smith

(1868–1940) was a regular book reviewer for *Punch*. Known to his friends simply as Turley, he had started out as a tutor, then became the author of a number of popular school-boy yarns, before poor health took him to live in Mullion in Cornwall, where he played a lot of golf – and introduced Alan to the game. A A M was not sure about golf to begin with. 'Why do I hit the ball with a ridiculous club like this?' he asked his readers. 'I could send it farther with a cricket bat. I could push it straighter with a billiard cue.' Quite quickly, he became a golf-obsessive, enjoying 'many holidays at Mullion' and enjoying Turley (incidentally the name of one of the Lost Boys in *Peter Pan*), because Turley combined 'an innocent goodness with a keen sense of humour, and intelligence with a boyish devotion to games'.

Not so innocent was E. V. Lucas, humorist, essayist, play-wright, biographer, editor, publisher, poet, novelist, short-story writer and possibly (after Frank Richards, the creator of Billy Bunter) the most prolific author of his time. Edward Verrall Lucas wrote well over one hundred and fifty books. Max Beerbohm reckoned 'he spoke fewer words than he wrote' – and he talked a good deal. Brought up as a Quaker, he was apprenticed to a bookseller aged sixteen, moved into journalism, joined *Punch* in 1904, and worked for the publisher Methuen & Co. from 1908. He read everything (spending days as a young man in the Reading Room of the British Museum) and made it his business to know every-body. By dint of charm and endeavour he managed to become 'thick with royalty'. It was through his friendship with Princess Marie Louise that he became involved in the creation of Queen Mary's Dolls' House, helping to select the authors invited to contribute miniature volumes and publish-ing *The Book of the Queen's Dolls' House Library* in 1924. In time he received honorary degrees from St Andrew's and Oxford universities and became a Companion of Honour. In 1897 he married the daughter of an American colonel and collaborated with his wife in writing children's books and having a daughter of his own.

Towards the end of his life, in the 1930s, Lucas left his family and lived alone in Marylebone, dining out most days at one of his several clubs – which included two of A. A. Milne's favourites: the Garrick and the Athenaeum. He was a good friend to young Alan and became his publisher. Alan was ever grateful to E V for his constant encouragement. 'I thrive on your praise,' he wrote to him, 'for there is none that I value more.' When writing something, Alan would think, 'E V will like that,' and keep going. Lucas understood that 'you can't be light and gay and off-hand and casual and charming in print, unless you are continually reassured that you are being some of those things.' Alan enjoyed E V's company (almost everyone did), and felt that they were proper friends, but probably did not know that Lucas's wide range of literary and artistic interests included building a substantial personal collection of pornography.

Or perhaps he did. When Owen Seaman, as editor of *Punch*, was away, E. V. Lucas stood in as acting editor. E V, according to Alan, 'had as many concerns outside *Punch* as Owen had few'. After the magazine was put to bed on a Friday night, 'Owen had nowhere to go but home, and a lonely home at that. E V had a hundred mysterious activities waiting for him.' It was E. V. Lucas who took A. A. Milne through the stage door of a West End theatre for the first time. It was E V who suggested to Alan, when *The Day's Play* was published, that he send a copy to Rudyard Kipling. Alan was going to do so, and drafted a letter to Kipling, but then lost his nerve and sent the letter and the book instead to the contemporary writer he most admired: J. M. Barrie, the author of *Peter Pan*.

Barrie was charmed and invited Milne to lunch. Better still, Barrie asked Alan to become the 'last member' of his celebrated cricket team. In 1887, Barrie had founded an amateur cricket team for cricketing friends of mixed ability and named it the Allahakbarries, under the misapprehension that 'Allah akbar' meant 'Heaven help us' in Arabic, rather than 'God is great.' Most of the best-known (male) British authors of the day played on the team at various times, including Kipling, H. G. Wells, Arthur Conan Doyle, P. G. Wodehouse, G. K. Chesterton and Jerome K. Jerome. A. A. Milne got to know them all. E. V. Lucas and Owen Seaman played for the team, too, as did young George Llewellyn Davies, the eldest of the five young brothers who inspired the characters of the Lost Boys in *Peter Pan* and whom Barrie unofficially adopted after their parents' death. In 1915, serving as a second lieutenant in the King's Royal Rifle Corps in Flanders, George (impossibly handsome and universally liked) died of a gunshot wound to the head aged twenty-one, killed by a German sniper.

Until the advent of the Great War – the 1914–18 war, 'the war to end all wars' – A. A. Milne was happy. Looking back in 1939, he reflected: 'The world was not then the damnable world which it is today; it was a world in which imaginative youth could be happy without feeling ashamed of its happiness.' Alan remembered how young he had once been, how light-hearted, how confident of himself, how confident of the future: 'I loved my work; I loved not working; I loved the long weekends with the delightful people of other people's delightful houses. I loved being in love, and being out of love and free again to fall in love. I loved feeling rich again, and having no responsibilities but only the privileges of a benevolent uncle. I loved hearing suddenly that some Great Man, full of serious purpose, had loved my last article. And if anybody says that all this is a misuse of the much misused word "love", well, it is, but I like misusing it, for it conveys my simple happiness.'

A. A. Milne played cricket and crossed paths with an extraordinary generation of writers. J. M. Barrie created Peter Pan. Rudyard Kipling wrote 'If', often voted the best-loved poem in the English language. Arthur Conan Doyle invented Sherlock Holmes. G. K. Chesterton invented Father Brown. P. G. Wodehouse conjured up Jeeves and Wooster; Jerome K. Jerome wrote *Three Men in a Boat*. And A. A. Milne? In *Winnie-the-Pooh* he brought us 'simple happiness'. Who could ask for anything more?

Chapter Twelve

in which Alan finds a wife and writes a play

She laughed at my jokes

Marriage is an honourable estate, but one that is fraught with challenges. I know. I have been married for more than fifty years. A. A. Milne was married for forty-three years. I am not sure how much I understand my own marriage – which I would say (and I hope my wife and our children would agree) has been a happy one (so far). Overall, I suspect A. A. Milne's marriage was less happy than mine has been, but I am less certain of how much of what it was really like I can reveal to you. I will do my best. Like most marriages, of course, it had its ups and downs: sometimes the tide was in, sometimes out. In the early years, it was very happy. In the middle years, less so. I think I understand the nature of the relatively safe harbour where it came to rest.

I can tell you exactly what Alan Milne felt about his brother, Ken, and his brother, Barry, about his sisters-in-law, about his parents and his own son. I can tell you how he viewed his professional achievements and his disappointments – and how much he loved his special friends and mentors, like E. V. Knox, Owen Seaman, Turley and H. G. Wells. About his marriage I will give you what I have gleaned from those letters in the Milne archive in Texas, from my conversations with Milne's son, Christopher, and his wife, Lesley, and from the sketchy and mostly guarded recollections (sometimes contradictory) of those who knew the Milnes. I cannot give you much on his marriage from Milne himself, because he does not appear to have shared his personal feelings with either family or friends, and in his 1939 memoir he states plainly: 'This is the autobiography of a writer, not of a married man.'

However, he also said: 'Whatever subject an author chooses or has chosen for him, he reveals no secret but the secret of himself.' Helpfully, his pieces for *Punch*, his plays and his novels also give us some of the story.

It all began happily, of course. Most marriages do. 1910 was a significant year for the British empire (Edward VII died and George V became King), and for A. A. Milne. His first collection of pieces for *Punch* was published. He was invited to join the senior *Punch* men at the fabled Wednesday-evening editorial dinner and to carve his initials into the *Punch* dining table. And in December 1910, *Punch*'s editor, Owen Seaman, took his Assistant Editor, Alan Milne, with him to his goddaughter Dorothy de Sélincourt's twenty-first-birthday dance.

Born in London, in Albert Road, Battersea, on 2 November 1889, Dorothy, who preferred from an early age to be known as either Daphne or Daff, belonged to an interesting, achieving family. Her grandfather, Charles Alexandre de Sélincourt, had escaped from France at the time of the 1848 February Revolution. Her father, Martin de Sélincourt, described himself as a 'mantle manufacturer' on her birth certificate, when the family was living south of the river Thames in a household with (according to the census of the time) just two servants. On his daughter's marriage certificate, Martin is described as a 'merchant'. By then the family

is living in Kensington, with four servants. Martin did well
for himself. Eventually, he became chairman of the Deben-
hams Trust and the Piccadilly department store Swan and
Edgar.

Martin de Sélincourt made money, while his siblings –
Daphne's aunt and uncles – also made their mark in their
time. Agnes de Sélincourt was a Christian missionary in
India, founding missions and becoming the first principal
of Lady Muir Memorial College in Allahabad. Later she
became the principal of Westfield College in London. Ernest
de Sélincourt was the leading Wordsworth scholar of his day
and Professor of Poetry at Oxford between 1928 and 1933.
Basil de Sélincourt was a musicologist, essayist and authority on Walt Whitman and William Blake. Hugh de Sélincourt
was a prolific author, drama critic of the *Star*, literary critic
of the *Observer*, best remembered for his novel *The Cricket
Match*, published in 1924, the same year as *When We Were
Very Young*, and still regarded as one of the classic accounts
of English village cricket.

I am mentioning the de Sélincourt family's considerable intellectual credentials chiefly because most accounts of
Daphne – including those of her own son – seem to suggest
she had none. I am not sure that is quite right. Or fair.
Daphne was not a writer, but she was witty, sparky and (so far
as I can tell) far from lacking in intelligence. I think Christopher had reservations about his mother because she was often
absent during his childhood (and he loved his nanny 'Nou'
like a mother) and, I suspect, because he was encouraged to
disparage her by his wife, Lesley, who was the daughter of
Daphne's younger brother, Aubrey. How that came to be we
shall come to in a page or two.

> 'Owl,' said Rabbit shortly, 'you and I have brains. The others have fluff. If there is easy thinking to be done in this Forest – and when I say thinking I mean thinking – you and I must do it.'
>
> *The House at Pooh Corner*

When I talked to Christopher about Daphne he was at best non-committal, at worst dismissive. He had come to see his mother as a lightweight – both intellectually and emotionally. He told me he felt she connected more with her garden than she did with people and that she was much more interested in clothes than in books. 'She wasn't brainy,' he said. 'Others in the family were. She wasn't. Her famous Uncle Ernest, the Wordsworth man, he had a colossal brain. So did her brother, Aubrey. She didn't. She had fluff. And a family can find itself divided by that – with the unbrainy ones finding the brainy ones quite unbearable.' He illustrated the divide in his memoir of his childhood: 'One can imagine Uncle Ernest sweeping Aubrey off to the Tate Gallery or the Queen's Hall, leaving Dorothy [Daphne], to whom *chiaroscuro* and *allegro* meant absolutely nothing at all, upstairs in her bedroom, contemplating her wardrobe and humming her own private homemade hums.'

By every account, Daphne was always well dressed and nicely groomed. Judging from the photographs she was not noticeably 'pretty', but at twenty-one she was attractive (someone said, not meaning it unkindly, that, with her pug-like nose and beady dark eyes, she had the look of a Pekinese) – and she was fun. Her aunt Agnes had secured a first at Girton College, Cambridge, and was proficient in fourteen languages. Whether Daphne had been taught at home by a governess or had gone away to school no one seems to know. Christopher told me he had 'no idea' where or how she had been educated, but she spoke some French, he said, because she had been to France in her late teens 'to be finished'. Time at a finishing school on the Continent (to acquire some domestic skills, good deportment and a touch of sheen), followed by 'the London season' and 'a coming-out dance': that was the way it was for most, if not all, upper-middle-class girls of her time.

When Alan met her, she was just twenty-one, he was soon to be twenty-nine, and he was taken with her at once. Not surprisingly. She knew exactly who he was and, better still, 'she had my contributions to *Punch* by heart before she met me.' Alan said, with satisfaction: 'She laughed at my jokes.'

Daphne and Alan became immediate friends, good companions who began doing everyday things together in an everyday way. 'When I wanted a present for a sister-in-law or a new suit for myself,' he recalled, 'I would summon her to help me; when she wanted a man to take her to a dance she would ring me up.' Each had something to offer the other: 'she had (it is now clear) the most perfect sense of humour in the world; and I, in my turn, had a pianola to which she was devoted, and from which I could not keep her away.'

Their easy friendship bubbled along happily for a couple of years – 'We might have gone along like this for ever' – until one day, at the beginning of 1913, they found themselves in a boot-shop. He remembered it well – as though it were a scene from Noël Coward's *Private Lives* or one of his own yet-to-be-written plays:

'Any sort of boots,' she asked, 'or just boots?'

'Skiing boots,' said Alan.

'I bought mine yesterday,' she said.

'What for?'

'Skiing.'

'Where? Hampstead Heath?'

'Switzerland.'

'But that's where *I'm* going!'

'Well, there's plenty of room for both of us. I'm going to a place called Diablerêts.'

'Dash it, so am I.'

'What a very small—'

'Don't say it. Are you at the Grand?'

'Yes. What fun. I've got a pair of orange trousers.'

'I shall be wearing a red carnation in my button-hole. We're bound to recognise each other. What are you like with a lot of other people about?'

'Heavenly.'

'So am I. I do hope we shall like one another.'

They did – but Alan found the 'other people' got in the way. He proposed to her in Switzerland at eleven o'clock one morning in a snowstorm. He said he had to, 'because she was going back to London that afternoon, where also there were other people, and it was clear to me now that it was my mission to save her from them.'

Alan was happy with 'other people', now and then, when they were playing silly games at a weekend house party or sharing sandwiches and squash in the pavilion after a cricket match, but as time went by – at parties, at dances, in crowded rooms – he found 'other people' increasingly tiresome. He was more of a one-to-one man. He preferred good conversation over a quiet supper, or a country walk with three or four friends, to the brittle laughter and 'fun company' of a roomful of bright young things. Daphne was eight years his junior and always enjoyed a party.

Alan Alexander Milne, aged thirty-one, bachelor, journalist, of 32 The Broadway, Westminster, married Dorothy de Sélincourt, twenty-three, spinster, of 13 Palace Court, W, on 4 June 1913, at St Margaret's, Westminster. It was a fashionable church and a big wedding. A. A. Milne was a well-known journalist and Martin de Sélincourt was a wealthy merchant. 'We go to Dartmoor for the honeymoon,' Alan wrote to a friend, 'Jokes about convicts are not being made this year.' There would be walks across the moor, perhaps some golf, but no fishing. Said Alan: 'I should hate to catch a fish who was perhaps on his honeymoon, too.'

There was sex, presumably. That's likely, isn't it? Or is it? My parents got married in 1937 and went to the West Country for their honeymoon, too. They had rented a caravan to stay in, and found, when they got there, that all it had to offer were narrow bunk beds. The well-off Milnes were staying in a comfortable hotel, but there is no account of their wedding night. For newly-weds sex could be a fraught business in the years before premarital sex became acceptable to many (in the West, from the 1960s, coinciding with the advent of oral contraception) and, from the 1970s, the norm for most.

Back in the day, even men of the world expected to marry a virgin bride, and a virgin bride might be woefully ignorant of the facts of life.

Nobody seemed to know where they came from, but there they were in the Forest: Kanga and Baby Roo. When Pooh asked Christopher Robin, 'How did they come here?' Christopher Robin said, 'In the Usual Way,

> if you know what I mean, Pooh,' and Pooh, who didn't,
> said 'Oh!' Then he nodded his head twice and said, 'In
> the Usual Way. Ah!'
>
> *Winnie-the-Pooh*

Not everyone was equally innocent, of course. Daphne's
uncle, Hugh de Sélincourt, only four years Alan's senior,
became notorious for his 'open marriage'. He and his wife,
Janet, did what they pleased with whom they pleased. Hugh
was a friend of Havelock Ellis (1859–1939), who, famously,
researched and wrote about every aspect of human sexual-
ity – even before his own marriage, aged thirty-two, when
he was still a virgin. Havelock Ellis's wife, the writer and
women's rights campaigner Edith Lees was openly lesbian.
She and Havelock Ellis led sexually separate lives. Havelock
Ellis went on to have a relationship with Margaret Sanger,
the American sex educator and birth-control pioneer, who
reportedly also had an affair with Havelock Ellis's friend
Hugh de Sélincourt. Later, when Havelock Ellis was in a
relationship with a young French woman, Françoise Delisle,
Hugh had an affair with her, too. (That's when the friendship between Havelock Ellis and Hugh de Sélincourt cooled.)
Whether or not Daphne de Sélincourt knew anything
of her uncle's interesting sex life, or had read any of the
works of Havelock Ellis, we do not know. It is doubtful. We
do know that when Christopher Robin, her only child, was
born, in 1920, seven years after her wedding, she was bewil-
dered – and distressed – by the physical aspects of giving
birth. In one of the boxes in the Milne archive in Austin
in Texas I came across the notes from a conversation that
Ann Thwaite had had in the 1980s with an elderly friend of

Daphne's who remembered Daphne telling her that, at least in later life, she was 'anti-sex'.

Mrs Patrick Campbell, one of the leading actresses of the day, who was about to star in Bernard Shaw's *Pygmalion* in 1914 and was a good friend of Milne's friend J. M. Barrie, yearned, she said, for 'The deep, deep peace of the double-bed after the hurly-burly of the *chaise-longue*.' Never mind the double bed: Alan and Daphne preferred separate bedrooms. That was not unusual for people of their class and time. Indeed, it was what was recommended in the pioneering marital guides of the period, such as *Facts about Marriage Every Young Man and Woman Should Know* by S. Dana Hubbard MD (Dermatologist) and *Married Love or Love in Marriage* by Dr Marie Stopes, the controversial advocate of birth control.

Celia and Ronald, one of the couples A. A. Milne writes about in his *Punch* pieces, have separate bedrooms in their first flat. Celia is a girl very much like Daphne. Myra, the girl from his stories about The Rabbits, *was* Daphne, according to Alan in 1914 – though, as you will remember, he had conjured her up from his ink-pot well before he met the real thing. These were the kinds of girls he liked – and went on liking all his life. They were central to his pieces in *Punch* and turned up in each of his novels, from the disowned *Lovers in London* in 1905 to *Chloe Marr* in 1946. As time went by, he tended to idealize her, but she is essentially the same young woman. In his 1921 novel, *Mr Pim*, she is called Olivia:

> She had a sense of humour. You could tell her your most subtle joke and she would laugh at it, but her sense of humour was more to her than that. It had been her shield since first she was married, from over the top of which she

smiled at the world when it was being bad, and rejoiced with it when it was good again . . . Whatever came, Olivia was ready for it, funny old world. The guards who sit in the stalls and laugh at the human comedy could never laugh at her; she was so much more at ease than they.

The year after Alan married Daphne, he published his next book, *Once A Week*, another collection of his *Punch* pieces. He dedicated it to his young wife, now twenty-four:

To

MY COLLABORATOR

who buys the ink and paper

laughs

and, in fact, does all the really difficult

part of the business

this book is gratefully dedicated

in memory of a winter's morning

in Switzerland

For the first twenty years of their marriage, Daphne was very much Alan's collaborator. She took his dictation, she dealt with his correspondence, she looked after the domestic side of life – all of it, and ably, too. They found their first flat together (15 Embankment Gardens, Chelsea), but Alan left Daphne to look after the furnishing and decorations. She brought her taste – good taste – with her, as well as an income and her personal maid, Gertrude. Daphne was a wealthy man's daughter. She was used to the best. Alan was happy with that. Alan was happy with Daphne: 'She laughed at my jokes.'

Inevitably, with marriage, Alan's life changed. The Milne family dynamic changed. Alan spent fewer cosy evenings with Ken and Maud and their children in Ealing. Alan and Daphne went to see Alan's parents, who had now moved to a Victorian house at Burgess Hill in Sussex, but they visited less frequently than Ken and Maud or Barry and Connie did, and, as the years went by, increasingly Alan made these family visits on his own, without Daphne. JV and Maria were easier and more relaxed with Maud and Connie than they ever would be with Daphne – who they referred to as 'Dorothy' until the end of their days.

When Alan and Daphne went away for the weekend it was more often to stay at Brooklands, Daphne's father's country house at Sarisbury Green in Hampshire, or to stay with one of Alan's successful and interesting older friends – such as Alderson Hall, a solicitor who moved from the law into the theatre and had a large house, Ditton Place, near Balcombe, just nine miles from Alan's parents in Burgess Hill. Ditton Place, built in 1904 (and now a school), had a fine formal garden created by the noted architect and garden designer Sir Reginald Blomfield. Throughout their married life Alan and Daphne shared a love of gardens.

They soon found they had something else, and perhaps something more unusual, in common. Each of them had a serious antipathy to one of their own siblings. Alan, as we know, had never really liked his brother, Barry. Barry was their mother's favourite, so possibly he was jealous of him. Certainly, he mistrusted him from an early age. He was fond of Barry's wife, Maud, but avoided Barry when possible, and once he had formed the view that Barry had 'not been straight' in the matter of their father's money, he had no further dealings with him. They did not speak for many years, and when Barry died, in 1942, aged sixty-three, there was no death-bed reconciliation.

Daphne was never fond of her younger brother, Aubrey. He was talented: a sailor, an artist, a classical scholar (his translations of Herodotus and Livy are still in print), a popular schoolmaster at the Dragon School and, later, at Bryanston. But Daphne did not like him. And when he tried to set up his own school and came to Alan for financial help, the rot set in. Alan gave Aubrey loans that were not repaid on time or at all – according to Daphne. Aubrey's children remembered it differently. All we know of Alan's view on the matter we can glean from a line in one of his novels: 'Cousins, brothers-in-law, aunts – God what a crowd. All trying to borrow money or asking him to use his influence.' Daphne did not speak to her brother for many years and, again, when Aubrey died, in 1962, aged sixty-eight, there was no death-bed reconciliation.

The one difference between Alan and Daphne regarding their despised siblings is that Alan was truly fond of Barry's wife, Maud, and was fond of their children, too, while Daphne positively loathed Aubrey's wife, Irene, and felt nothing towards their offspring. Irene Rutherford McLeod was a playwright, poet, novelist, sometime actress and active suffragist. She was not Daphne's sort of woman. Irene and Aubrey had two daughters: Lesley and Anne. When Daphne and Alan's son, Christopher Robin, married Irene and Aubrey's daughter Lesley in 1948, it was the first time Daphne and her brother Aubrey had spoken to one another in many years.

Irene McLeod appeared in two notable plays of the Edwardian era: *The Voysey Inheritance* by Harley Granville-Barker and *The Eldest Son* by John Galsworthy. From 1910 she began writing plays in support of the suffragist cause. Alan's marriage to Daphne coincided with him taking his first serious steps towards becoming a playwright – though his plays would always be fantastical or domestic rather than overtly political. J. M. Barrie was his role model, rather than Ibsen or Bernard Shaw, let alone Irene McLeod. Alan had been toying with the idea of playwriting for several years: his *Punch* pieces were often written as playlets. *Peter Pan* was constantly revolving in his head. When his friend Alderson Hall, who had started out as a solicitor but, under the name Anmer Hall, became a theatre producer, director and actor, suggested Milne might write him a one-act play as a curtain-raiser, Alan rose to the challenge.

The play was called *Make-Believe*. 'My collaborator,' Alan recalled, 'sent it off to Alderson and bought a new dress for the first night.' Unfortunately, 'after a few exciting days' the play came back.

Curtain-raisers were played at the start of the evening, before the main attraction, and designed, as Alan put it, to entertain 'the cheaper seats while the stalls were finishing their dinners'. The curtain-raiser was often performed by the understudies from the main play and Alderson Hall's reason for rejecting *Make-Believe* was that the characterization was 'too subtle for understudies to put over the footlights'.

Undaunted, Milne shared the play with J. M. Barrie, who liked it, too, and shared it with Harley Granville-Barker, playwright-and-actor-turned-director, who was putting on Shakespeare at the Savoy Theatre at the time. Granville-Barker loved it, accepted it, and told Milne he would put it on – 'on condition you should immediately write me a full-length play'.

Make-Believe was never produced. The script has not survived. Later, Milne used the title for another play. The original *Make-Believe* never saw the light of day. But for

Alan, it did not matter. He had written a play and a manager of note had accepted it: 'The thing had happened . . . I was going to be a dramatist.'

But not immediately. This was the summer of 1914 and, on 4 August 1914, war was declared.

Chapter Thirteen

in which the world goes to war

A cushy billet

Aubrey de Sélincourt, Daphne's despised younger brother, had just turned twenty at the outbreak of the 1914–18 war – the Great War as it became known, the 'war that will end war', as H. G. Wells optimistically called it, a war that involved more than sixty million fighting men, more than nine million of whom were killed: an average of six thousand dead per day.

A year earlier, Aubrey had won an open scholarship to University College, Oxford. The moment war was declared, he abandoned his studies and signed up for military service. On 29 August he was gazetted to the 7th Battalion of the North Staffordshire Regiment. A year later he was one of the survivors in the three-week long Battle of Sari Bair, the final failed attempt by the British to seize control of the Gallipoli peninsula from the Ottoman empire. In 1916 he requested a transfer to the fledgling Royal Flying Corps, the air arm of the British army, and was awarded his 'wings' early in 1917. On 28 May 1917, he was shot down flying over Douai in German-occupied northern France, close to La Brayelle airfield, the base of Manfred von Richthofen, the notorious 'Red Baron', ace of air aces among German fighter pilots.

Aubrey was shot down by Werner Voss, a pilot von Richthofen described as his 'dear friend' and 'most redoubtable competitor'. Aubrey was Voss's thirty-first victory. Aubrey was twenty-two, Voss was twenty. Voss's last stand came four months later, on 23 September 1917, just hours after his forty-eighth victory, when in single airborne combat he fought eight British pilots, putting bullets into every one of them, before he was killed. One of the eight, James McCudden VC, described Voss as 'the bravest German airman'. On 9 July 1918, McCudden was killed in France when his aircraft crashed on take-off due to engine failure. He was twenty-three. When Voss brought down Aubrey's FE2d biplane, Aubrey survived and spent the rest of the war in a German prisoner-of-war camp.

If Aubrey de Sélincourt was a young hero, his brother-in-law, A. A. Milne, thirty-two at the outbreak of war, could fairly be described as 'an old pacifist'. Conservative in appearance and manner, Alan was a radical at heart. He had campaigned on behalf of Herbert Asquith's Liberal Party in the 1910 general election. Not that he discussed it with Daphne or her family (Daphne was never much interested in politics), but he claimed to have been a pacifist since at least 1910. In his autobiography, written in the run-up to the Second World War, he admitted he would have preferred not to mention the First World War at all. 'I would like to put asterisks here,' he said, to avoid the subject altogether, 'for it makes me almost physically sick to think of that nightmare of mental and moral degradation, the war.'

In 1934, he published a personal pacifist tract, *Peace with Honour*. It became a bestseller. Later he wrote to his American publisher: 'You have always told me that personally you have always thought more of *Winnie-the-Pooh* than any book I have ever written. Please let me tell you that I think more of *Peace with Honour* than any book I have ever written.'

Was *Winnie-the-Pooh* written as an anti-war book, as some people believe? I don't think so. Certainly, in his Pooh stories Milne conjures up a world without war, a world that includes elements of drama and danger certainly, but essentially a world of innocence, joy and kindness. There is no evidence – or reason – to believe that Milne was setting out deliberately to write an anti-war children's book, let alone a book designed (as some claim for it) as a primer on how to cope with the challenges of post-traumatic stress disorder.

BANG!!!???***!!!

Piglet lay there, wondering what had happened. At first he thought that the whole world had blown up; and then he thought that perhaps only the Forest part of it had; and then he thought that perhaps only *he* had, and he was now alone in the moon or somewhere, and would never see Christopher Robin or Pooh or Eeyore again. And then he thought, 'Well, even if I'm in the moon, I needn't be face downwards all the time,' so he got cautiously up and looked about him.

He was still in the Forest!

'Well, that's funny,' he thought. 'I wonder what that bang was. I couldn't have made such a noise just falling down. And where's my balloon? And what's that small piece of damp rag doing?'

It was the balloon!

'Oh, dear!' said Piglet. 'Oh, dear, oh, dearie, dearie, dear! Well, it's too late now. I can't go back, and I haven't another balloon, and perhaps Eeyore doesn't *like* balloons so *very* much.'

Winnie-the-Pooh

Though the term was not coined and defined until 1980, the symptoms of PTSD have been recognized and reported for centuries. As a result of the First World War and his time at the front, A. A. Milne may have been the victim of some of them. Both bursting balloons and buzzing bees feature in the Pooh stories. Did the bang of a burst balloon or the proximity of buzzing bees trigger in A. A. Milne traumatizing memories of being part of the Battle of the Somme in 1916 – a battle that cost the lives of 300,000 men and that Milne described as 'a lunacy which would shame the madhouse'? Possibly. But to suggest, as the film *Goodbye Christopher Robin* does, that Milne in the 1920s was a full-blown victim of PTSD is to over-egg the pudding.

Over the years, there have been assorted speculations that each of the animals in the two Pooh books represents a different psychological disorder. For example, in 2000, the *Canadian Medical Association Journal* published a learned paper entitled 'Pathology in the Hundred Acre Wood: a neurodevelopmental perspective on A. A. Milne'. The paper argued that Pooh is suffering from ADHD (attention deficit hyperactivity disorder) of the 'inattentive type' and possibly OCD (obsessive-compulsive disorder), too. Tigger, like Pooh, has a form of ADHD, but his belongs to the hyperactive/impulsive subtype. Piglet suffers with generalized anxiety, and Eeyore, inevitably, is a victim of persistent depressive disorder (formerly known as dysthymic disorder). Rabbit was diagnosed with narcissistic personality disorder.

In 2019, clinical psychologist and trauma specialist Dr Valentina Stoycheva published an interesting paper in *Psychology Today* suggesting that each animal in the Pooh stories features characteristics consistent with a trauma response. Piglet, for example, is a representation of anxiety and hypervigilance. Adverse experiences can overwhelm the nervous system, leaving the victim in a perpetual state of anticipating danger. Loud noises may startle more; tight spaces may seem tighter.

Piglet also experiences social anxiety, not uncommon when the trauma experienced is interpersonal in nature. Once hurt or betrayed by others, especially those with caregiving or an intimate role in our lives (e.g. parents, grandparents, siblings, romantic partners), we may react by becoming suspicious or even frightened by emotional closeness. On the one hand, we may become untrusting and guarded, while, on the other hand, constantly seeking reassurance.

Piglet sidled up to Pooh from behind.

'Pooh!' he whispered.

'Yes, Piglet?'

'Nothing,' said Piglet, taking Pooh's paw. 'I just wanted to be sure of you.'

The House at Pooh Corner

Tigger is unsettled and hyperactive, as we know, but rather than simply describing him as having ADHD, Dr Stoycheva argues that Tigger is experiencing some of the arousal and reactivity symptoms of PTSD. Difficulty concentrating and constantly feeling your mind is racing are prominent features of trauma response. Eeyore is depressed and illustrates several cognitive and emotional symptoms of PTSD. Rabbit's rigidity may be a response to the unpredictability of traumatic events. Owl is really demonstrating his own difficulties with intimacy. He is aloof and can only connect through intellectualizing, in stark contrast to his friends. Withdrawal and isolation, physical or emotional, are hallmark symptoms of PTSD. So, according to Dr Stoy-cheva, is the loss of playfulness seen in both Owl and Rabbit.

All this is intriguing and fun, which, of course, the reality of trauma and war are not. Milne was not deliberately creating psychological stereotypes. He was simply creating characters with characteristics which we recognize and with which we empathize. What a writer writes reflects that writer's experience. Whatever A. A. Milne wrote following the First World War inevitably will be touched in part by what happened to him – and to the world – during it.

A. A. Milne was revolted by the horror of war. In the 1930s, in the run-up to the Second World War, he wrote: 'It seems impossible to me now that any sensitive man could live through another war. If not required to die in other ways, he would waste away from soul-sickness.'

In 1914, Milne's view was not the general view. He followed international developments that summer with growing despair, conscious that others around him (his colleagues at *Punch*, his de Sélincourt in-laws) were following them almost with growing excitement. On 28 June 1914, Archduke Franz Ferdinand, heir to the Austro-Hungarian throne, was assassinated in Sarajevo by a Serbian nationalist. That served as the spark for the conflict that had long been brewing. On 28 July, Austria-Hungary, with German encouragement, declared war on Serbia. Russian support for Serbia brought France into the conflict and led to Germany declaring war on Russia and France. Germany's violation of Belgian neutrality and British fears of German domination in Europe brought Britain – and the British empire – into the war on 4 August.

The underlying roots of the war – nationalistic impulses, imperial ambitions, a complex web of international treaties – were neither here nor there for most people. We had to stop the Hun and – by jingo! – we would. And we did. Milne was neither cowardly nor unpatriotic. On paper, and in his heart, he was a pacifist. But if this was – as his mentor H. G. Wells maintained – a war to end war, he would play his part. He would volunteer: he would become a serving soldier.

He hated it, but not because he lacked courage. 'To people like myself,' he said, 'the Great Sacrifice was not the sacrifice of our lives but of our liberties.' Ever since he had left Cambridge a dozen years before, he had been his own master, as perhaps only the freelance journalist can be: 'I fixed my own hours, I was under no discipline; no bell rang for me, no bugle sounded.' Now he was thirty-two, married, 'with a happy home of my own and engaged happily in work which I loved'. The prospect of soldiering was not inviting: 'To be a schoolboy again, to say "Yes, sir" and "No, sir" and "Please, sir" and "May I, sir?" was no hardship to schoolboys, no hardship to a million men in monotonous employment, but it was hell itself to one who had been as spoilt by good-fortune as I.'

That said, when he joined up, he was lucky. He acknowledged it: 'If a special order had gone round the British Army: "For your information and necessary action: Milne is joining us. See that he is given the easiest and best possible time, consistent with ultimate victory," I could not have had more reason to be grateful . . .'

He was commissioned to the 4th Battalion of the Royal Warwickshire Regiment, stationed on the Isle of Wight. It was what was known as 'a cushy billet'.* Officers' wives could

---

* A term used by British soldiers during the First World War to describe any military posting that was agreeable.

   The phrase was made popular during the First World War. The word 'cushy' has roots in the Urdu word *kusi* (pleasure) and the Hindi word *khush* (happy, easy, or pleasant).

come along, too, so 'Daphne joined the married strength, and from then on, whenever it was possible, she shared the war with me.' They rented a cottage in Sandown. Alan became a signalling officer and, after a nine-week course at the Southern Command Signalling School at Wyke Regis near Weymouth, an instructor – and so good an instructor was he (marked out as 'Indispensable to the Training of the Battalion') that he was kept at home, on the tranquil Isle of Wight, far from the front line, until July 1916. He could almost pretend there wasn't a war on, 'and having the whole battalion behind me on route marches could almost imagine that I was taking a brisk country walk in civilian knickerbockers'.

He was even able to carry on writing – and, better still, to develop his writing in new directions. Mrs Williams, the colonel's wife, 'mother of five children and the regiment', became great friends with Daphne. Daphne had a gift for certain types of friendship. Together the two wives decided to organize an 'entertainment' for the troops ('whether the troops liked it or not') featuring a little play in which the colonel's five children would act.

Daphne told Alan he must write the play. Alan reminded Daphne that he was the signalling officer in charge of instruction, 'Indispensable to the Training of the Battalion', and far too tired in the evenings to write anything. Daphne said she would do the writing. All he had to do was 'lie in an armchair' and tell her what to write. He'd dictate, she'd transcribe: 'Easy work.' So together they wrote a 'little play' about a Prince and a Princess and a Wicked Countess (Daphne's role) and a magic ring. It went down rather well and, after the performance, the collaborators agreed that some of the dialogue *was* rather funny, and Daphne said, as according to Alan she often did, 'You mustn't waste this.' But, of course, it was only a scene in a children's play. Never mind that, said Daphne: 'Write a book round the people in it.'

'I've never written a book,' Alan protested, 'not straight off.'

'Well, now's the time to start.'

So, as war raged across Europe, and beyond, in Turkey, Egypt and Africa, on the Isle of Wight at Sandown, in 'the prettiest cottage in the town with lilacs and cherry-trees in the garden', Alan dictated the book. He called it *Once on a Time* and described it as 'a Fairy Story for grown-ups'. It is a very funny book. It begins:

> King Merriwig of Euralia sat at breakfast on his castle walls. He lifted the gold cover from the gold dish in front of him, selected a trout, and conveyed it carefully to his gold plate. He was a man of simple tastes, but when you have an aunt with the newly acquired gift of turning anything she touches into gold, you must let her practise sometimes. In another age it might have been fretwork.

'This is not a children's book,' Alan explained in the introduction to *Once on a Time* when it was published in 1917. 'I do not mean by that . . . "Not for children," which has an implication all its own. Nor do I mean that children will be unable to appreciate it . . . But what I do mean is that I wrote it for grown-ups. More particularly for two grown-ups. My wife and myself.' Alan loved writing the book and loved writing it with Daphne: 'We began every evening at half-past five, I in my chair before the fire, my collaborator, pen in hand, brown head bent over table, writing, waiting, laughing: it made the war seem very far away.'

> She also considered very seriously what she would look
> like in a little cottage in the middle of the forest, dressed
> in a melancholy grey and holding communion only with
> the birds and trees; a life of retirement away from the
> vain world; a life into which no man came. It had its
> attractions, but she decided that grey did not suit her.
>
> *Once on a Time*

On Sundays, Alan managed to excuse himself from
Church Parade so that he and Daphne could go for long
walks over the cliffs near Sandown, with a picnic lunch in
their pockets – 'and the characters in the book came with us,
listening to us as we settled their fate for the next chapter.'
(My favourite character in the book is Roger Scurvilegs.)

Until the 1920s, Alan thought *Once on a Time* his best
book, and he remained fond of it always, accepting that it
never sold well because no one could quite work out what
sort of book it was. Were some of the characters intended
to be satires on the German Kaiser and Herbert Asquith
and David Lloyd George (who succeeded one another as
British prime minister in December 1916)? They weren't.
Did Alan see the book in the tradition of Lewis Carroll's
Alice books? Possibly. 'Read in it,' he said, 'what you like;
read it to whomever you like: it can only fall into one of the
two classes. Either you will enjoy it, or you won't.'

The American critic, poet and fantasy writer Thomas
Burnett Swann (1928–76) reckoned it 'a classic' fit to stand
alongside J. M. Barrie's *Peter Pan* and T. H. White's *The
Sword in the Stone*. It is odd that it is so little known, given
that it does what the Pooh books do: it allows children's

characters to have experiences and responses that readers can relate to whatever their age. *Once on a Time*, like the Pooh books, is simple, but not simplistic. Milne said he wanted his readers to realize 'Life in Fairyland was not so straightforward as the romancers pretend. The dwellers therein had much our difficulties to meet.'

Milne dedicated the book 'To the officers and men of the 4th Royal Warwickshire Regiment (among whom it was written) in affection for their good fellowship.' He was ever grateful to it because it was the first proper, full-length book he had written. 'I had thought that I could never write more than two thousand consecutive words, and I had written sixty thousand. I had written a book. It was finished.'

The book was finished and Alan Milne had begun a new phase in his life – as an author, rather than a journalist. A A M contributed barely a handful of pieces to *Punch* during his time in the army. For *Punch* he could have written humorously about life in uniform; for other publications, he could have shared some of his feelings about the horrors of war. He did neither. Instead, he wrote a play, his first full-length play, a drawing-room comedy, a piece of engaging nonsense called *Wurzel-Flummery*.

The idea sprang from a humorous piece he had written before the war deploring the unimaginative way in which millionaires chose to leave their money. 'How much more amusing,' he had suggested, 'to leave £20,000 to each of fifty acquaintances on condition that they all take the same ridiculous name. Fifty Spiffkinses in the same club, just because you said so.' For the play, Milne chose the name Wurzel-Flummery. To play the part of the solicitor in the piece, he and Daphne thought Dennis Eadie (1875–1928) would be ideal. Eadie was a popular leading man who they had seen and enjoyed in Arnold Bennett's comedy *The Honeymoon*. Eadie was in the news in 1916 because that year he became the first man to portray the former prime minister Benjamin Disraeli on screen. The Milnes did not know Eadie, but J. M. Barrie did, and Barrie effected an introduction. With the colonel's permission, Alan was given a day's leave to go to London for lunch with Eadie at the Carlton Grill.

Eadie liked the play, liked it very much, but there was something about it that wasn't quite right. 'If I knew what it was,' he said to the author, 'I would tell you, but I don't.' But Eadie did not want to let go: 'When you've got it right, send it back to me. I want to do it.'

Alan returned to the Isle of Wight and shared the encouraging news with Daphne. They had a happy dinner, 'chattering excitedly, building the wildest castles in Shaftesbury Avenue'. At half-past ten they went to bed, still chattering. At eleven there was a heavy knocking on the front door. Alan answered. An orderly saluted and said that the colonel would like to see Lieutenant Milne in the Mess immediately. Alan found he was bound for France in forty-eight hours.

This was July 1916 and A. A. Milne, fresh from an exciting lunch at the Carlton Grill and a delightful evening with his young wife on the Isle of Wight, fresh from writing *Once on a Time* and *Wurzel-Flummery*, was transferred to 11th Battalion of the Royal Warwickshire Regiment and sent across the English Channel to northern France to join the Battle of the Somme, one of the deadliest battles in human history. The Somme offensive took place between 1 July and 18 November 1916. On the first day alone, nearly 20,000 British soldiers were killed and 40,000 wounded. As the battle wore on, more than 10,000 men were killed or wounded every day.

Chapter Fourteen

in which Alan goes to the Front

Hell itself

Alan travelled to France with a young subaltern, not long out of school and the younger of two sons. The boy's elder brother had been killed a few months before. Alan remembered his travelling companion when later he wrote his book *Peace with Honour*. The young soldier's parents had bought for him – 'you may laugh or cry as you will' at this, said Milne – 'an under-garment of chain mail, such as had been worn in the Middle Ages to guard against unfriendly daggers, and was now sold to over-loving mothers as likely to turn a bayonet thrust or keep off a stray fragment of shell'. The young man did not know whether or not to wear it. Would putting it on be somehow unsporting or even a little cowardly? Milne told him to wear it, and to tell his mother he was wearing it, and to tell her how safe it made him feel. 'I do not know whether he took my advice,' said Milne. 'Anyway, it didn't matter; for on the evening when we first came within reach of the battle-zone, just as he was settling down to his tea, a crump came over and blew him to pieces.'

Alan had no chain-mail vest to keep him safe, but in his uniform pocket he kept a tiny toy dog, a good-luck mascot, that Daphne had tucked into his bag on the day he left England: 'Just to look after you.'

'I miss Daff dreadfully,' Alan told Ken in one of the first of his letters home. This was on 28 July 1916. His battalion had been 'in the thick of it', but was now resting away from the front line before 'going up again in a few days'. They were camped in an orchard: they could not forget the war (there was always the noise of distant gunfire and, overhead, occasional aerial dogfights between young heroes like Alan's brother-in-law, Aubrey, and his German counterpart, Werner Voss), but they could lie in the grass under the trees eating peaches, bought by one of the men in Amiens nearby, and listening to sentimental songs played on a wind-up gramophone that another of the men had managed to find somewhere. Alan told Ken it was 'a heart-rending business', lying there, listening to the music he had listened to with Daff, 'smoking and listening and thinking of London'.

Heart-rending. And deadly, too. On 31 July, three days after his letter to Ken, the peaceful orchard was shelled by the Germans. The battalion command had wrongly assumed they were out of range of enemy fire. Fifty-one men were killed, including the company chaplain and Alan's young subaltern friend, the boy with the chain-mail underwear.

Years later, in *Peace with Honour*, Alan recalled the young soldier's death, quoting the famous Latin phrase from the Roman poet Horace – '*Dulce et decorum est pro patria mori*': 'It is sweet and fitting to die for one's country' – and adding, 'But just why it was a pleasant death and a fitting death I still do not understand. Nor, it may be, did his father and mother; even though assured by the Colonel that their son had died as gallantly as he had lived, an English gentleman.'

Alan was bitter about the war even in the midst of it. In retrospect he was glad to have been in the midst of it, because that allowed him to be bitter about it, from the standpoint of one who had taken part in it – who had been there, amid the muck and bullets. He despised the jingoism of those back home who had never seen the horror of life on the front line. As he said in a letter to Ken, he had a special contempt for every fat newspaper editor who told his readers, 'However long this war lasts we must clench our teeth and hold on until we gain a complete victory.' Said Alan: 'I want to slap him. It's easy work clenching teeth in London.'

He had no time for those at home who glorified the war. He had all the time in the world for the fighting men he was serving with. He loved them. He had a particular soft spot for his commanding officer, Lieutenant-Colonel C. S. Collison. 'I seem to have fallen for him, as they say, at once,' he told Daphne in one of his letters home. Later he wrote to her: 'The C.O. is heavenly; I love him; frightfully funny in a particular way of his own. He was in grand form tonight; in fact, we all were; at least, he made us think we were.'

Christopher Robin and Pooh and Piglet were left on the bridge by themselves.

For a long time they looked at the river beneath them, saying nothing, and the river said nothing too, for it felt very quiet and peaceful on this summer afternoon.

'Tigger is all right, *really*,' said Piglet lazily.

'Of course he is,' said Christopher Robin.

'Everybody is *really*,' said Pooh. 'That's what *I* think,' said Pooh. 'But I don't suppose I'm right,' he said.

'Of course you are,' said Christopher Robin.

The House at Pooh Corner

Charles Collison was a good man by any standard; he was also very much A. A. Milne's kind of good man. 'His humour asked for humour in return,' said Alan, 'but his military façade kept you from taking liberties; he was intimate and aloof, human and astringent; in his manner always on parade, in his mind alert for companionship.' Collison told Alan about Mrs Collison, at home in Chatham, and said, 'I write to her every day because I have dinner every day. If there's time to have dinner there's time to write to your wife.'

When Collison returned to England, before the close of the Somme offensive, he did not forget his men. He sent Alan a box of fifty Corona cigars. He told him it would have been a hundred but he 'couldn't afford 100 owing to the extortions of the mess president'. Alan was the mess president. (Alan was collegiate in the army in a way he was not always at home.) Collison was also kept busy writing letters of condolence to the families of men who lost their lives under his command. This is the letter he wrote to the father of one of Alan's fellow lieutenants, Alec Boucher, who was killed in action, aged twenty-seven:

Dear Mr Boucher,

It is only the fact that I left the 11th Royal Warwickshire Regiment (which I commanded for one and a half years) and had some difficulty getting your address, that prevented me from writing to you before, to tell you how extremely I sympathise with you and your family in the death of your gallant son, who won his Military Cross when under my command last year.

Colonel Rooke who is now commanding that Battalion (11th Royal Warwickshire) has told me of your son's extraordinary gallantry in the recent heavy fighting in which the Battalion was engaged, and I was not at all surprised to hear of it, as I can say I have never met an officer of a more correct bearing, of a greater intelligence, of a more pronounced bravery in my over 20 years experience of the Army.

Up to the moment of his death which I rejoice to know was instantaneous he was engaged in most important work, which required not only great courage but also great intelligence, and he carried out that work in a manner worthy of him.

Again with my most sincere sympathy

Yours truly

C. S. Collison Lt. Col.

Alan Milne returned to England on 8 November, ten days before Alec Boucher was killed. Boucher never returned: he is buried in the Ancre British Cemetery, near the village of Beaumont-Hamel on the Somme, alongside 2,539 other men, of whom 1,335 were unable to be identified.*

Alan survived the Somme. He had several lucky escapes. When he arrived in France he found he had been sent, with (as he put it sarcastically) 'the military efficiency of those days', to a battalion which already had a signalling officer, a new man just appointed, named Harrison. The brigade was about to go into action with the aim of capturing a small village called Bazentin-le-Petit. Milne was ordered to join

---

* There were three British attacks on Beaumont-Hamel during the Battle of the Somme. The first on 1 July 1916 failed, with the British suffering over 20,000 killed and 37,000 wounded in three failed waves. The second attack on 3 September was also unsuccessful. On 13–14 November 1916 the village was finally captured.

Harrison in the signallers' dug-out. 'I liked signallers,' he said, 'and felt at home with them.' There was a camaraderie among signallers because their role was specific, essential and notoriously hazardous. Signallers were responsible for communication, often working near the front lines, sometimes under enemy fire, laying and maintaining telephone lines, and using visual signals like flags or lamps to relay messages.

In the dug-out, Alan got chatting with one of the men, a Lance-Corporal Grainger. 'He was a Welsh miner,' he remembered, 'as well educated as most of them are, quiet, friendly, charming.' Milne and Grainger did not talk about the technical challenge that awaited them: running out a line to the front trench. They talked about books. They found they shared a passion for Jane Austen.

The attack on Bazentin-le-Petit was timed for midnight. On the day before, Harrison and Milne and three men ran out a line to the front trench 'by a devious route' because they were told the existing line would never stand the opening counter-barrage. On the way they fell into 'a burst of whizz-bangs and Harrison was knocked out'. They got him back to the first-aid post; Milne reported to the colonel and found he was now the signalling officer in charge. The following morning, at 4 a.m., they went out again, this time by the ordinary communication trench, 'such as it was', and laid a line 'guaranteed to withstand any bombardment'.

Of course, it didn't. As Alan remembered, 'At eleven that night the Colonel, the Major, the Adjutant and I sat round a table by candle-light smoking and talking, waiting for our barrage to begin.' But the Germans began theirs first. And the line went.

A sergeant-major began to climb out of the dug-out to assess the situation 'and was blown out of existence before he reached the top'. 'We sat there completely isolated,' Alan recalled. 'The depth of the dug-out deadened the noise of the guns, so that a shell-burst was no longer the noise of a giant plumber throwing down his tools, but only a persistent thud, which set the candles dancing and then, as if by an afterthought, blotted them out.'

'Should I try to get a line out?' asked Alan, nervously, feeling that their total isolation was his fault.

'Don't be a bloody fool,' said the colonel.

At about two in the morning a runner got through to them. The attack had been a total failure. Many men had been killed. He couldn't rightly say how many: it had been 'coming over something cruel'.

'All right,' said the colonel.

'Am I to go back, sir?' asked the runner.

'No,' said the colonel, catching the major's eye. The major got up and strapped on his revolver. Alan realized, 'It was all too clearly the moment for me to strap on mine.'

'Use your common-sense,' said the colonel. 'If it's impossible, come back. I simply cannot lose three signalling officers in a month.'

Alan promised, but said afterwards he felt quite unable to distinguish between common-sense and cowardice: 'The whole thing was so damned silly.'

The major went first – he was going, he said, to 're-organise the troops'. Alan went second – 'God knew why,' he said. They were followed by a sergeant and a signaller who, according to Alan, ran out a line 'neatly and skilfully': 'From time to time the Major flung himself down for a breather, and down we flopped and panted, wondering if he would get up again. To our relief each time he was alive, and so were we. We passed one of the signal-stations, no longer a station but a pancake of earth on top of a spread-eagled body; I had left him that evening, saying, "Well, you'll be comfortable here." More rushes, more breathers, more bodies, we were in the front line. The Major hurried off to collect what men he could, while I joined up the telephone. Hopeless, of course, but we could have done no more. I pressed the buzzer, and incredibly heard Daffy's slow, lazy voice: not my Daffy in England, but Corporal Daffy, ex-gardener from Buxton, with the gardener's heavy drooping moustache and heavy stoop, unalterably a civilian. There was only that one other voice in the world which I would have sooner heard.'

Alan asked to speak to the colonel. He told him what he knew and then, boldly, he recalled, 'I ordered – what were telephones for? – a little counter-bombardment.' That done, with a sigh of utter content and thankfulness and the joy of living, he turned away from the telephone – and found Lance-Corporal Grainger behind him.

'What on earth are *you* doing here? You weren't detailed, were you?'

'No, sir.'

'Well, then—'

'I thought I'd just like to come along, sir.'

'But *why*?'

'Well, sir, I thought I'd just like to be sure *you* were all right.'

Alan thought that the greatest tribute to Jane Austen he had ever heard.

For A. A. Milne, his four months in France reinforced his feelings about the stupidity and horror of war. Thousands of lives were lost as valiant men fought over small patches of ground – moving forward, retreating, moving forward again. Bazentin-le-Petit, for example, was in German hands until mid-July, then taken by the British, then recaptured by the Germans in April 1918, before being taken once more by the British in August 1918.*

War, to Milne, was 'hell itself', but he was, in his own way, grateful to have been briefly part of it, both so that he could say that he had seen the horror of it at first hand and because it introduced him to men like Lance-Corporal Grainger and Colonel Collison, men he had not met at home, men he instinctively loved and admired to his dying day. And his time on the front line in France made him realize how much he loved Daphne, how much he missed her.

'Oh Maudie,' he wrote to his sister-in-law, Ken's wife, on 16 October 1916, 'When the war is over Daff and I are going to sit hand in hand for the rest of our lives. We shall never go and see anybody, and if anybody comes to see us they will have to shake Daff's right hand and my left. If you want to know what being in love is like come out here.'

Alan told his sister-in-law that Daff had bet him ten shillings that he'd be home by 20 October – 'nothing but a nice cushy wound can do it now, so I look by being 10/- up. I have already chosen my present – a case for her letters. At present, I carry them in my pocket, and there are enough now to make a bullet think twice.'

Alan arrived in France just after the beginning of the Battle of the Somme and left just before the end – a week before the end. As Milne put it in his autobiography, the 'blood-bath of the Somme' was not quite full. There was to be 'yet one more display of G.H.Q.'s bulldog tenacity', an

---

* The British military cemetery at Bazentin was begun at the end of July 1916 (initially called Singer Circus Cemetery) and used as a front-line cemetery until May 1917. It contains 182 First World War burials, fifteen of them unidentified.

attempt to take the village of Beaumont Hamel. The battalion's objective was called Beauregard Dovecote. According to Alan, 'it was the only attractive thing about it': 'If ever any place looked a death trap on a military map this did.' But it rained and rained – and rained – and the attack was postponed. The battalion marched west, for thirty kilometres, from the edge of German-held Beaumont Hamel to British-held Doullens. 'It went on raining: one never ceased to be wet through.'

They marched through mud, past dead horses, dead mules, dead men. The soldiers sang as they marched. According to Alan, they sang loudly, defying the cold and the rain and the mud. On the battlefields in the heat of August, flies carried pestilence from the bodies of dead animals and men to the encampments. Diarrhoea was rife; the troops were inoculated against typhoid. But this was November, when the cold and the wet alongside the unsanitary conditions meant that trench foot and trench fever were the enemies within. Trench foot causes skin and tissue breakdown, increasing the risk of infection and morbidity. Trench fever is spread by body lice and characterized by fever, chronic weakness, pain behind the eyes, and severe pain in the back and shins. It was not 'a nice cushy wound' but trench fever that took A. A. Milne back to Daphne.

The rain had stopped. November sunshine had appeared. Alan had taken his men out 'on a little hill' one morning, and was walking 'from station to station to see how the messages were coming through'. But he could barely walk, barely drag his legs across the ground. At lunch he went to sleep in the HQ mess. He was seen by the medical officer. Next morning his temperature was 103°F. The MO got an ambulance to take him to the clearing station. His temperature rose to 105°F.

Trench fever is infectious. Milne was ordered home. And the next day the battalion got its order to move: the attack was about to begin. 'My sergeant came to say goodbye to me,' he remembered. 'I handed over my maps, commended the section to his care, wished him luck, and went to sleep again. He only lost a leg.'

Ten days later Alan was at Southampton: 'Some kind woman offered to write a telegram for me. It was to Daphne, saying she would find me in hospital at Oxford. I woke up one afternoon and saw her at the end of the bed, crying.'

The capture of Beaumont Hamel on 18 November 1916 marked the end of the Battle of the Somme.[*]

> . . . When the War is over and we've finished up the show,
> I'm going to plant a lemon-pip and listen to it grow.
>
> Oh, I'm tired of the noise and the turmoil of battle,
> And I'm even upset by the lowing of cattle,
> And the clang of the bluebells is death to my liver,
> And the roar of the dandelion gives me a shiver,
> And a glacier, in movement, is much too exciting,
> And I'm nervous, when standing on one, of alighting—
> Give me Peace; that is all, that is all that I seek . . .
> Say, starting on Saturday week.
>
> *From a Full Heart*

[*] Beaumont Hamel continued to be fought over for the rest of the war. By 1918, the village had been almost totally destroyed. In the Beaumont Hamel British Cemetery there are 180 men buried, 98 identified, 82 unidentified.

Chapter Fifteen

*in which A. A. Milne arrives in the West
End and Christopher Robin is conceived*

Surprised, excited, delighted

The Battle of the Somme was over. It had cost much and
achieved little. The war itself had two more full years to run.
Alan and Daphne did not sit holding hands for the rest of
their lives. But they were close, the closest they would ever
be – as husband and wife, as good companions, as 'collaborators'. That's the word Milne used most often when talking
about their relationship over the years.

Soon they would 'collaborate' in bringing Christopher
Robin into the world. Immediately, they worked together
forging Alan's new career – as a playwright. In April 1917, as
the Russian Revolution took hold in St Petersburg, as President Woodrow Wilson in Washington DC asked the House
of Representatives to declare war on Germany to make the
world safe for democracy, as in the Pas-de-Calais in northern
France four divisions of the Canadian Corps attacked the
German-held Vimy Ridge as part of the Arras offensive, in
London's West End *Wurzel-Flummery* opened for an eight-
week run at the New Theatre on St Martin's Lane, heralded
by *The Times* as 'the first acted play of A. A. M. of *Punch*'.

Alan's first West End success coincided with 'Bloody
April'. The play opened on Saturday 7 April. The Arras

offensive was launched on Monday 9 April. The month came to be known as 'Bloody April' because of the toll taken by the Royal Flying Corps giving air support to the fighting men below. In under four weeks, the British lost 245 aircraft, with 211 aircrew killed or missing and 108 men taken as prisoners of war. The Germans recorded the loss of just 66 aircraft during the same period. Aubrey de Sélincourt, Daphne's younger brother, survived 'Bloody April'. He was shot down and taken prisoner on 28 May 1917, just as *Wurzel-Flummery* was coming to the end of its run.

Alan, still a serving soldier, was given forty-eight hours' special leave to go with Daphne to his play's first night. He remained in the army until his discharge in February 1919, but a medical board declared him unfit for active service at the front. The Somme had taken its toll. On his return from France, after his time in hospital in Oxford, he went back to Sandown on the Isle of Wight. He was happy to be home for Christmas, grateful to be nursed by Daphne, and happier still, on 18 January 1917, his thirty-fifth birthday, to receive an unexpected letter from his hero and mentor, J. M. Barrie.

Generously, Barrie had sent a copy of *Wurzel-Flummery* to Dion Boucicault, actor-manager, good friend of Barrie's and older brother of Nina Boucicault, the first actress to play the title role in *Peter Pan*. Nina (who also starred in the first production of *Charley's Aunt*) and Dion (full name: Dionysus George Boucicault Jr, generally known as 'Dot') were the children of the great Irish actor and playwright Dion Boucicault, famous in his day for his melodramas, and remembered still for his first comedy, *London Assurance*. Dot, who had produced *Peter Pan* in 1904, now wanted to produce two of Barrie's one-act plays in a triple bill and thought Milne's *Wurzel-Flummery* might fit nicely in between them

– if Milne could be persuaded to cut his original three-act play into two. He could, of course, but it was not a comfortable task: 'To cut even a line is painful, but to cut thirty pages of one's first comedy, slaughtering whole characters on the way, has at least a morbid fascination.'

The tightened *Wurzel-Flummery* worked. Dot played the solicitor in the piece; another noted actor-manager of the time, Nigel Playfair, played the pompous MP obliged to change his name to claim his inheritance. The critics thought the conceit delightful and the dialogue witty and the play earned A. A. Milne a handsome £30 a week – roughly £2,500 per week in today's money. On the opening night, Alan and Daphne were introduced to Dot's celebrated wife, the actress Irene Vanbrugh. She had created the part of Gwendolen in Oscar Wilde's *The Importance of Being Earnest* in 1895. Over the years, Barrie, Bernard Shaw, Somerset Maugham and Noël Coward were among those who created roles for her. Dot suggested Alan should set about writing a play for her now.

He did. Leafing through the boxes of Milne's surviving papers in the library in Texas, I found script after script: one-act plays, three-act plays, correspondence about plays, ideas for plays, scenes from plays that were produced and weren't produced. 'The play's the thing' seems to have been A. A. Milne's motto from now on in. He was still in the army, of course: 'My job was soldiering and my spare time was my own affair. Other subalterns played bridge and golf; that was one way of amusing oneself. Another way was – why not? – to write plays.'

Alan now – and for the future – saw himself as a playwright. 'Meanwhile,' he acknowledged, 'the War Office was getting on with the war.' The powers-that-be decided to establish a signalling school at Fort Southwick, one of the forts on Portsdown Hill, overlooking the naval base of Portsmouth on the English south coast. The school was divided into four companies and Milne ('Indispensable to the Training of the Battalion') was chosen to be the head of one of them. Reluctantly, Daphne left Sandown and the Milnes took a cottage in Porchester. Every morning, at 7.30 a.m., Alan had a two-mile walk up the hill to the Fort and every evening a two-mile walk down, getting him home by 5.30 p.m. 'Then, after tea, we could begin Irene's play.'

Irene's play did not come easily. 'Unfortunately,' Alan recalled, 'the play which I had in mind offered no possible part for her.' He tried to forget about the idea he had, but the more he tried to put it out of his mind, the larger the idea loomed. 'It was no good,' he said. 'The only way to forget it was to write it.' So, he wrote – or, 'more accurately' as he put it, 'dictated to my collaborator' – a play called *The Lucky One*. It wasn't a play for Irene. Nor was his next effort: a one-acter called *The Boy Comes Home* about a young soldier coming home from the war and finding himself at odds with the values and attitudes of his parents' generation.

The play for Irene Vanbrugh just wouldn't come. Alan was struggling. Daphne was increasingly concerned about his health. He got tired so easily. 'Well, it was a tiring life, getting up at 6.30, walking two miles up hill, running a company for eight hours (which included teaching ploughboys the theory of induced currents), walking two more miles and then doing my ordinary work of writing for another five hours.' He told Daphne he wanted to go to sleep for a year. Daphne told him to see the MO, which he duly did. He was sent to the Military Hospital at Cosham, kept in overnight, 'thumped all over in the morning' and despatched to the forces' convalescent home at Osborne House, Queen Victoria's former residence, on the Isle of Wight.

Life at Osborne House was Milne's idea of 'the ideal life'. There was a nine-hole golf course running down to the Solent, croquet lawns, an excellent library of 'light novels', and good food – 'incomparably better than anything we had had lately'. Alan ate, slept, read, 'played games gently' and wished it could go on for ever. Settling down with a novel in a deck chair immediately after breakfast, 'safe from the reproaches of conscience', was Alan's idea of heaven on earth. 'And if this were the day when Daphne was coming over to tea, then life had at the moment no more to offer.'

After three weeks at Osborne House, he was given three more weeks of sick leave and then, recovered, reinvigorated, ready for action and reporting for duty, he was ordered, with his battalion, to move from Portsmouth to Dover the following week. In Dover, there were nightly air-raids, which meant Daphne could not join him there, so 'if we were to write Irene's play together, we must write it in the next week'.

He approached the task exactly as he used to approach the challenge of writing his weekly piece for *Punch*. On Thursday afternoon at 5.30, he settled into a deck chair, saying, 'I shall now think of something.' He thought about Irene Vanbrugh, a very stylish leading lady and a natural comedienne. Now in her early forties, she had made her London début, aged sixteen, in December 1888, playing the White Queen and the Knave of Hearts in a West End production of *Alice in Wonderland*. (Lewis Carroll was a university contemporary and friend of Irene's father, a fellow clergyman. Carroll saw Irene as a teenager performing in a seaside show at Margate and was charmed. People were charmed by Irene Vanbrugh.) By dinner-time, Milne reckoned he had found the charming idea he needed for the charming Miss Vanbrugh. He was ready. At 8.30 p.m., he began to dictate *Belinda*, and by Tuesday evening it was finished. 'My collaborator took charge of it while I went off to Dover. A week later I got a telegram from Boucicault: "I like the play, my wife likes the part, I would like to do it."'

Belinda: An April Folly in Three Acts opened at the New Theatre in London on 8 April 1918. Milne called it 'a purely artificial comedy whose only purpose was to amuse'. It achieved its purpose and provided Irene Vanbrugh with one of her favourite roles.

ACT ONE

It is a lovely April afternoon – a foretaste of summer – in Belinda's garden.

Betty, a middle-aged servant, is fastening a hammock – its first appearance this year – to a tree. In front there is a garden-table, with a deck-chair on the right of it and a straight-backed one to the left. There are books, papers, and magazines on the table. Belinda, of whom we shall know more presently, is on the other side of the open windows which look on to the garden . . .

We can't see Belinda as the curtain rises and the play begins. We can hear her voice. She is talking with the servant. We know she is coming. The anticipation is building – and then she appears, through a portico centre stage. She makes a proper entrance, as a West End leading lady should, carrying a parasol and looking quite lovely: the moment we see her, we greet her arrival with a welcoming round of applause.

Belinda is a beautiful woman in her early forties, witty and flirtatious, and currently enjoying the attentions of two very different suitors: one, Claude Devenish, a twenty-two-year-old poet, the other, Harold Baxter, a middle-aged dullard. Do either of these two deserve Belinda? Which one does she fancy? And what is she going to do when her eighteen-year-old daughter, Delia, arrives unexpectedly from Paris? (Pretend she's her niece, of course.) But first, before the plot unfolds, Milne has given his leading lady five minutes' worth of delicious comic business as she attempts to board her hammock and arrange herself decorously in it.

BELINDA: Are you sure you're tying it up tightly enough, Betty?

BETTY (*coming to front of hammock*): Yes, ma'am; I think it's firm.

BELINDA: Because I'm not the fairy I used to be.

BETTY (*testing hammock*): Yes, ma'am; it's quite firm this end too.

BELINDA: It's not the ends I'm frightened of; it's the middle where the weight's coming . . . It looks very nice.

BETTY: Yes, ma'am.

BELINDA (*trying the middle of it with her hand*): I asked them at the Stores if they were quite *sure* it would bear me, and they said it would take anything up to – I forget how many tons. I know I thought it was rather rude of them. (*Looking at it anxiously, and trying to get in, first with her right leg and then her left.*) How does one get in! So trying to be a sailor!

BETTY: I think you sit in it, ma'am, and then (*explaining with her hands*) throw your legs over.

BELINDA: I see. (*She sits gingerly in the hammock, and then, with a sudden flutter of white, does what* BETTY

suggests.) Yes. (*Regretfully.*) I'm afraid that was
rather wasted on you, Betty. We must have some
spectators next time.

BETTY: Yes, ma'am.

It was frivolous and fun and it ran for nine weeks. In New
York, where it opened a month later at the Empire Theater,
with Ethel Barrymore in the lead, it only lasted four weeks. It
was not an easy time for theatre on either side of the Atlantic.
There was a war on, and US troops were on their way to
Europe. The Germans were mounting one final, furious
offensive in the hope of securing victory before the arrival of
the Americans. They called the offensive the Kaiserschlacht.
It was brutal. In under three weeks, the Germans suffered
an estimated 240,000 casualties; the British 178,000 and the
French 77,000. In London, *Belinda*'s run coincided with
one of the worst air-raids of the war. 'In the circumstances,'
reflected its author, 'it was difficult to regard its ill-fortune as
a matter of much importance.' At least the play earned him
£311: the 2025 equivalent of £15,000.

Audiences had enjoyed the play; the critics had liked it
(one had even compared it favourably to *The Importance of
Being Earnest*); Alan and Daphne had enjoyed the experience. In a letter to Philip Agnew, whose family printing and
publishing business owned *Punch*, Alan wrote: 'I am glad you
like *Belinda*. I think our chief pleasure in it has been meeting
Irene Vanbrugh, who is as delightful off the stage as on it.'

Milne was writing to Agnew because Agnew had written
to him on a delicate matter. Throughout the war, *Punch* had
been paying Alan half his assistant editor's salary to help
supplement his army pay. Now that Alan had become a successful playwright and was contributing to the magazine only

rarely, the time had come to reconsider the arrangement. Alan protested that he had only had two plays produced to date – and that their runs had not been extensive – but he could see the firm's point of view and accepted their decision 'in perfectly good part': 'So let us say no more about it.'

That said, he did think a great deal more about it. He was not discharged from the army until February 1919. For his final year in uniform, given the Medical Board's decision that he was only fit for 'sedentary work', he was transferred from his battalion to the War Office in Whitehall where, wearing 'the green tabs of Intelligence', he 'wrote (horrible word) "propaganda"'. He was part of MI7b, a secret propaganda unit made up of authors charged with writing positive articles about the war for newspapers in Britain and overseas, as well as producing pamphlets and newsletters to be sent to troops. He had a room to himself, which he liked, and was allowed to write, he said, pretty much what he liked. 'If it were not "patriotic" enough, or neglected to point the moral with sufficient hardihood, then the Major supplied the operative words in green pencil.'

Later, in 1934, in *Peace with Honour*, he said, 'I want everybody to think (as I do) that war is poison, and not (as so many think) an over-strong, extremely unpleasant medicine.' He accepted the inevitability of the First World War (and the Second when it came), but the notion of war – and the cruel reality of it – appalled him. Loathing war as he did, he accepted that 'his' war, in its way, had been a good one. 'Really,' he wrote to a friend in the summer of 1917, 'I have found the Army very inspiring and I've done much more work in it (literary, I mean) than I ever did in peacetime.' Back from the front, behind a desk, he was safe, and in the evenings and at weekends, he had time to write what he wanted to write. And through the army he met all types and conditions of men in a way he had never done at Westminster School or at Cambridge or in pre-war literary London.

In 1918 Milne wrote a poem in honour of the Tank Corps that nicely illustrates his approach to propaganda. The Tank Corps was officially established in July 1917, with its origins in the tank companies of the Heavy Branch of the Machine Gun Corps. The Tank Corps' most famous victory was at the Battle of Cambrai on 20 November 1917, when nine battalions, with 386 Mark IV tanks, breached the German Hindenburg Line in the first truly combined arms attack in history. Milne in his poem – performed at a charity concert in aid of the Tank Corps Prisoners of War Fund organized by the music-hall comedian, Harry Tate, and featuring music from the bands of the Welsh Guards and the Scots Guards – begins by celebrating the tank itself, but ends like this:

> So remember, whenever you talk of the Tanks,
> The newest invention, the wonderful Tanks –
> The older invention – the men in the ranks;
> The wonderful men of all ranks.
> For they're just the same men, only more so, in Tanks.
> You'll remember them?
> THANKS!

A. A. Milne abhorred war, but was ever grateful to – and admiring of – the simple courage of the ordinary fighting man.

> 'Did I really do all that?' he said at last.
> 'Well,' said Pooh, 'in poetry – in a piece of poetry – well, you *did* it, Piglet, because the poetry says you did. And that's how people know.'

'Oh!' said Piglet. 'Because I – I thought I did blinch
a little. Just at first. And it says, "Did he blinch no no."
That's why.'

'You only blinched inside,' said Pooh, 'and that's the
bravest way for a Very Small Animal not to blinch that
there is.'

Piglet sighed with happiness, and began to think
about himself. He was BRAVE . . .

The House at Pooh Corner

The Tank Corps Prisoners of War Fund concert was
held on 7 November 1918, just four days before the signing
of the Armistice between Germany and the victorious
Allied powers. The Armistice was signed at 5.45 a.m. on
11 November, with the cessation of hostilities taking effect
at 11.00 a.m., the 'eleventh hour of the eleventh day of the
eleventh month'. The guns fell silent on the Western Front,
though fighting continued in other areas. The formal peace
treaty, the Treaty of Versailles, marking the official ending of
the war, was signed on 28 June 1919. By then, Alan Milne was
back in civvy street, wondering what the future might hold.

Duty, he felt, called him back to *Punch*. After all, the
magazine had been paying him a half-salary throughout the
war years. But inclination drew him towards this exciting
new life in the theatre. Could he make being a full-time
dramatist pay? Perhaps he should go back to *Punch* for a
year or two – maybe three. He had always assumed he would
go back to *Punch*. Daphne assumed it, too. He had promised
her he would be editor one day. Owen Seaman, her godfather,
was twenty-one years Alan's senior. He had been the magazine's editor since 1902. He would retire quite soon and Alan

could succeed him. The last two editors of *Punch* had been honoured with knighthoods. Perhaps Alan would get one, too. That would be nice.

On Armistice Day Alan abandoned his ambivalence. He was going back to *Punch*: 'Once more I should sit in that dusty little office sorting out good jokes from bad; once more have fun with the paragraphs, be (oh, so happily) bored at the Wednesday dinners; once more (on Thursdays) take Daphne with me as unofficial secretary to clear up the week's arrears of work. She loved it; I loved it . . . I was going back.'

Alan knew that demobilisation would be quicker if you could produce a letter from an employer saying how eagerly they longed for you to return to them. He hurried round to the *Punch* office for his letter. 'I burst in on Owen Seaman,' Alan recalled. Seaman looked up.

'Hello?' he said.

'I've come back,' announced Alan dramatically.

But he wasn't wanted any more. Seaman was surprised to see him. He did not think that Alan would want to return to the humdrum duties of an assistant editor having basked in the warmth of the bright lights of the West End, and, candidly, since Alan boldly raised the possibility (under cover of it being Daphne's ambition for him), Seaman saw no prospect of Alan becoming editor of *Punch* in the foreseeable future (Seaman did not retire until 1932) – or, indeed, ever. 'That settled it,' said Alan. He arranged to send in his resignation to the proprietors.

The truth was that Seaman and the proprietors had not been happy that Milne, while in their pay, had chosen to write plays rather than pieces for their magazine. The truth, too, was that Seaman and the proprietors were of a naturally conservative disposition and reckoned that radical Milne, with his pacifist agenda, was never going to be the man to edit the national institution that was *Punch*. They still wanted A A M to contribute to the magazine, of course. 'They were very nice about it,' Alan said. 'They told me to drop into dinner when I liked, and to drop in to the pages of *Punch* when I liked. For six months or so I dropped in occasionally. Then I dropped out.'

On the day of Alan's dramatic encounter with Owen Seaman, the Milnes were due to go out for dinner with friends. 'Daphne was dressing when I got back,' Alan recalled, 'and in no mood for conversation.' It was not until they were in the taxi that he told her his news. He was not going back to *Punch*. He was never going to be editor. You can forget about the knighthood. Daphne burst into tears. She was still crying quietly to herself when Alan paid off the taxi. 'I promised her that we shouldn't starve,' he said. 'I promised to make a success of the theatre.' He reflected that it was a little like telling a woman whose loved cottage has been burnt down that you will build a more expensive one on the ruins: 'It doesn't really comfort her at the time.'

The people they were going to dine with were Alan's sort of people: Mr and Mrs W. L. George. Walter Lionel George was Alan's exact contemporary and a fellow writer who shared Alan's radical, pacifist views. Though British, George had been brought up in France and did not learn English until he was twenty. He had moved to London in 1905 and become a freelance journalist like Alan. Unlike Alan, his fiction dealt unashamedly with the seamier side of life. In 1911, when Alan was still in denial about his own first novel, *Lovers in London*, W. L. George enjoyed a considerable success with his fiction debut *A Bed of Roses*, an account of a young woman's descent into a life of prostitution.

The only other guest at the Georges' dinner was another radical, the actress Lillah McCarthy, then forty-three, still beautiful (according to Alan) and on her own because she was between husbands. (She had been married to the actor-playwright-director Harley Granville-Barker. He left her during the war when he fell in love with a rich American.) McCarthy was internationally famous, known for her work in the classics (the Greeks and Shakespeare) and for appearing in several of the early plays of Bernard Shaw. Alan enjoyed her company – she was beautiful, she was a friend of Milne's mentor H. G. Wells, and she loved golf – and at the end of the evening, the Milnes and Miss McCarthy found they lived in the same part of town and travelled together from High Street Kensington to Sloane Square on the underground.

A few days later, Alan was more than a little pleased to receive a letter from her. She told him that she was just starting out in management and that J. M. Barrie (now Sir James: he had been knighted just before the war) had suggested that she should ask Alan for a play. Could he come and have tea with her on Tuesday to discuss it?

Surprised, excited, delighted – perhaps, he said to Daphne, they weren't going to starve after all – Alan retreated to his room to think of a play for Lillah McCarthy. This was Friday morning. His time was his own. Post-Armistice, he and the rest of the propaganda unit at the War Office had been given six weeks' leave before rejoining their regiments for demobilisation. By Tuesday afternoon, he had written the first act of a play he called *Mr Pim Passes By*. It was all about a beautiful and happily married woman in her forties who discovers, through a chance encounter with the mysterious Mr Pim, that when she married her second husband, she wasn't the young widow she thought she was. The play was going to be a drawing-room comedy about bigamy. He felt it would be just the ticket for Lillah McCarthy. He went round to tea with her, full of hope.

Miss McCarthy was charming. And still beautiful. Alan told her about his play. She asked him to send it to her manager as soon as it was finished. They talked, they laughed, they had tea . . . He said goodbye. She said how delightful it had been to meet him.

'Well, of course, we did meet last Tuesday,' said Alan.

'Oh – did we?' said the beautiful Miss McCarthy.

'Since then,' reflected Alan afterwards, 'I have never expected my name or my face to mean anything to anybody. It saves a lot of anxiety.'

For me, this anecdote is telling. It tells us something about the self-absorbed actress Lillah McCarthy, perhaps, but it also tells us something about the self-deprecating writer A. A. Milne. Alan Milne saw himself – and presented himself – as an author, always, never as a performer or a 'personality'. He was not a public figure like J. M. Barrie or Bernard Shaw or H. G. Wells. He chose to make his mark in print rather than in person. He was a delight to read, but not memorable to meet. His appearance was conservative and unassuming. His manner was courteous and unassertive. He encountered all the leading literary, journalistic and theatrical figures of his time – and quite a few politicians, too – but features rarely in their memoirs, diaries and correspondence. He was observing them (brilliantly), but they were not noting him.

Alan had older mentors – Barrie, Wells, Owen Seaman – and a variety of close acquaintances – with whom he played golf and cricket, had lunch at his club, and occasionally stayed with for the weekend – but beyond his marriage and outside his immediate family (his brother, Ken, and his two sisters-in-law) he does not appear to have had any profound friendships. People knew him, and liked him, but though they spent time with him, they would say, as the illustrator Ernest Shepard did, they 'never knew him intimately'. He was, according to Shepard, 'rather a cagey man'. He did not give much of himself away.

Alan was not easy to know and he was not always easy to be with, either. He may have claimed to have learned a useful lesson from Lillah McCarthy and, henceforward, to have never expected anyone to know who he was – but, in truth, he did want to be recognized. And admired. A lifelong friendship he made around this time was with W. A. Darlington, who was just beginning his long career as a drama critic on the *Daily Telegraph*. Darlington, eight years Alan's junior, often played golf with him. They had mutual golfing friends. It was from these, Darlington revealed after Milne's death, that he learned 'the disconcerting fact' that 'they all found him on occasion very difficult to deal with.' 'The trouble was,' according to Darlington, 'that he simply could not take any form of adverse criticism.' As a theatre critic, Darlington recognized it as not an uncommon trait in creative artists to need praise and shrink from censure, 'but Alan had it to an abnormal degree. The violence of his reaction against even a hint of blame had in it something pathological, as if he were short of a skin.'

Happily, as a theatre critic, Darlington liked Milne's plays. He especially admired his dialogue and, more than once, likened its wit and naturalness to the best of Oscar Wilde. Young Darlington particularly enjoyed *Mr Pim Passes By*. It was the very first play he reviewed on his appointment as drama critic for the *Daily Telegraph* (a post he held for more than fifty years) and his notice was adulatory. Most of the notices were. *Mr Pim Passes By* was A. A. Milne's first unalloyed hit.

In the event, the play did not star Lillah McCarthy. She and her manager took too long thinking about it and, while they pondered, the play was picked up by Dot Boucicault as another vehicle for him and his wife, Irene Vanbrugh. The Boucicaults opened it in Manchester, at the Gaiety Theatre, on 1 December 1919. It was a night to remember. 'I have attended many first nights in the miserable role of author,' Alan recalled twenty years later, 'but never one like that.' He gave the credit to Miss Vanbrugh: 'The house was so delighted to see its loved and lovely Irene back again that in sheer happiness it extended its favour to the play.' The Manchester audience cheered and cheered. There were cries of 'Speech!' – 'the author was pushed on and pushed off; and still Dot and Irene were bowing.' Alan sat in the wings among the stage-hands until he heard a weary voice behind him saying, ''Ere, go on and give 'em a speech, guv'nor, and let's all get 'ome.'

Alan imagined the stage-hand when he got home:

'Late tonight, Bill.'

'Yes, we 'ad a success.'

Mr Pim Passes By was probably A. A. Milne's greatest theatrical success. Alan and Daphne were never happier. It was during rehearsals for the play that Christopher Robin was conceived.

Chapter Sixteen

in which Christopher Robin and Winnie-the-Pooh enter the scene

Mark August 21st in letters of blood

1919 to 1920 was A. A. Milne's *annus mirabilis*. Professionally, the air was full of praise. Domestically, dreams were coming true. In August 1919, the Milnes moved into their new home – their first house, 'the prettiest little house in London', Alan called it. A year later, on 21 August 1920, Christopher Robin was born.

The house in Chelsea, close to the King's Road, at 11 Mallord Street (later renumbered to 13), was in a terrace built just five years before. It was not so small. It was narrow but tall, with three storeys and a basement. Alan loved it simply because it was a house and not a flat. He had not lived in a proper house since he had last lived with his parents at Streete Court twenty years before. His new home thrilled him: 'I have (imagine my excitement) a staircase of my own.' Best of all, for the first time in his life, he had a bathroom all to himself. Mallord Street was the Milnes' London home until 1940, when, with the bombing of the capital, they moved permanently to the country. They did not sell the house until after the Second World War. It gave them everything they wanted. It was light (built around an inner well), it was convenient (fifteen minutes by taxi into the West

End), it provided all the accommodation they required: a study for Alan, bedrooms for each of them, a drawing-room, a dining-room, a kitchen for Cook and a nursery suite for Nanny and Christopher Robin.

Christopher Robin was born in Mallord Street. It was not an easy birth. Daphne found the experience painful and confusing. Years later, a friend of Daphne's, Tatyana Peppé, told Ann Thwaite: 'It's difficult to believe, but until she was actually giving birth, she had no idea of the mechanics of it. It came as a thoroughly traumatizing shock and made her absolutely determined never to repeat the performance.' Becoming pregnant had not been easy, either. Daphne belonged to the generation where the average age for mothers at the birth of their first child was twenty-three. In the early summer of 1919, exactly six years after her wedding, and six months before her thirtieth birthday, Daphne spent some time in a nursing home. She was apparently there to have her appendix removed, but it may be that she was having a gynaecological procedure as well.

Happily, Christopher Robin was quite healthy when he was born. His mother was exhausted by the ordeal and over-whelmed. His father (who wasn't in the room for the birth, but heard it all happening as he paced about, anxiously smoking his pipe, on the floor below) was overjoyed. At once he began to spread the good news in letters to family and friends – among them the novelist and critic, Frank Swin-nerton, who was then working as an editor at the publishing house of Chatto & Windus:

A tremendous event has happened, unrecked of by
the minor novelist. THERE IS A JUNIOR MILNE!
This is a creation of my wife's (Daff – short for Daphne

or, as some say, Daffodil) . . . Locally this creation is known as Billy.

Sir, if you never grovelled before, grovel now in the presence of this miracle. When women can do these things, why do we go on writing, you and I? (You observe that I put us both on one level, but I am in a generous mood this evening.) Why do we continue to call ourselves lords of creation when we obviously are not? Why – but I must not overtax your brain!

Salute Chatto for me, slap Windus on the back. Tell them to mark August 21st in letters of blood on their calendars. And believe me to be, Sir,

Your mental superior

A. Milne

who shines equally as Husband, Father, Citizen and Author

As you can tell, Alan was thrilled to be a father, and his son, though officially named Christopher Robin, was called Billy from Day One. One of the first to respond to the infant prodigy's arrival was J. M. Barrie: 'May Billy be an everlasting joy to you. From what you say I gather he is already a marvel, but I shall decide about this for myself when I see him, which I hope will be soon.'

As we shall see, Billy was not to be an everlasting joy to A. A. Milne. Nor was Christopher Robin. But why this early confusion of Christian names? In his autobiography, Milne offered a rather unsatisfactory explanation. The Milnes had hoped for a girl: 'We had intended to call it *Rosemary*, but decided that Billy would be more suitable.' So far, so good, but then this: 'However, as you can't be christened William – at least, we didn't see why anybody should – we had to think of two other names, two initials being necessary to ensure him any sort of copyright in a cognomen as often plagiarized as Milne.' One of them thought of Robin, the other of Christopher – 'names wasted on him who called himself Billy Moon as soon as he could talk, and has been Moon to his family and friends ever since', Milne added, disingenuously (since he was writing this in the late 1930s, by which time he was well aware of his son's reservations about his name). 'I mention this because it explains why the publicity which came to be attached to "Christopher Robin" never seemed to affect us personally, but to concern either a character in a book or a horse which we hoped at one time would win the Derby.'*

When I first met him in the 1980s, I asked Christopher Robin Milne about his name. 'I've never been Christopher Robin,' he said, 'except when I was "being" Christopher Robin and out on show when I was small and I think I quite enjoyed it then. I've always been plain Christopher – or maybe Chris when I was at school or in the army. Sometimes C. R. My mother always called me Christopher. My father always called me Moon. And I called him Blue. That was his nickname – because he had blue eyes, I think. I don't really remember being called Billy. I think that died out when I was quite small. Moon started because of the way I tried to say Milne when I was little. Apparently, I used to say, "My name

---

* From the late 1920s, a number of race horses have been named Christopher Robin, most recently a Bay Gelding foaled in 2018. None has won the Derby. In 2007, Walt Disney Japan launched a sophisticated video game called *Winnie the Pooh's Home Run Derby*, but it was not about horse racing. It featured Christopher Robin, Pooh and friends playing baseball.

is Billy Moon." I quite liked being called Moon. By the time I was nine or ten, I hated being called Christopher Robin. I don't know where they got the names from. They're not family names. I'm afraid my parents were rather unsatisfactory in a number of ways.'

'I'm sure they meant well,' I said. Christopher did not respond to that.

On another occasion, he said to me, laughing: 'Of course, it could have been worse. I could have been Little Lord Fauntleroy. I believe Frances Hodgson Burnett's son had a terrible time of it.' Vivian Burnett was teased as a child because his mother dressed him in the style of the boy in her famous 1886 novel, *Little Lord Fauntleroy*. But in real life Vivian was not Cedric Errol, Lord Fauntleroy: he was simply the author's son. By several accounts, Hodgson Burnett was a difficult, domineering, self-obsessed lady and Vivian had a challenging childhood, but when, three years after her death in 1924, he published his biography of her – *The Romantick Lady (Frances Hodgson Burnett): the Life Story of an Imagination* – it was written with love as an act of homage. Fifty years later, in 1974, when Christopher Milne published his own childhood memoir, *The Enchanted Places*, his account of his parents was much more conflicted. 'If I cannot say that I loved my parents,' he wrote, 'it is only because, in those early days, I just didn't know them well enough.'

When Christopher's book was reissued a few years after his death, Lesley Milne wrote the introduction. Lesley's verdict on her husband's mother and father (who were also, of course, her aunt and uncle) was simply this: 'Mother was that distant woman who laughed a lot, and Father a large, remote, godlike being.' Lesley said, 'Christopher and Alan Milne had a curious relationship, as neither knew the other very well.' I am not sure she was right about this. Father and son were close, particularly during his adolescence and teenage years. Christopher told me: 'I was very close to my father – very close – until I left school, really, until the Second World War. I was close to him for longer than he was close to his father. Perhaps because we had once been so close, when we drifted apart we drifted further and farther apart than we might have done otherwise. Towards the end of his life he was all buttoned-up. He wasn't like that with me when I was a boy. Far from it.'

Lesley said, 'To Alan, the extraordinary event of acquiring a baby was at first a shock, and a breeder of dreams and memories.' I am not sure that is right, either. Alan was overjoyed when Billy was born and the boy remained his pride and joy for years. Almost every one of the letters Alan sent to family or friends that I read in the library in Texas features a proud and loving reference to Billy. Yes, Alan had high hopes for his boy – what new father doesn't? Lesley wrote, 'Christopher was expected to play cricket for England, but he inherited his mother's weak eyesight and never made it beyond the school team.' I doubt very much that Alan Milne ever seriously expected his boy to play for England (he knew his own limitations as a cricketer), but I am not surprised that Lesley put his failure to do so down to Daphne's poor eyesight. Lesley really did not like her aunt/mother-in-law. She made that clear every time I spoke with her. 'No, I did not like her,' she said to me. 'She wasn't likeable.'

Where I did agree with Lesley was in her reflection on the changing nature of parenting across the years. 'It is difficult to imagine these days,' she wrote in 1998, 'when families are so close, how children were raised in an affluent middle-class family between the wars. A small child saw his parents only occasionally, however much they loved him in theory. A little boy or girl was more a pet than a companion: well washed, brushed and dressed up to be brought out, cute and lovable, on special occasions. He might be asked to sing or recite for teatime guests to coo over. I doubt that Christopher's parents ever saw him throw a tantrum or encountered dirty nappies.'

That might be true about the nappies, but there is plenty of evidence to suggest that Daphne and Alan were very much present in Christopher's early childhood, playing with him, singing songs, reading stories, having fun. From the mid-1920s, when he was five or so, Christopher remembered one day in particular: 'My mother and I were in the drawing room . . . The door opened and my father came in.'

'Have you finished it?' asked Daphne.

'I have,' said Alan.

'May we hear it?'

'My father settled himself into his chair,' recalled Christopher. '"Well," he said, "we've had a story about the snow, and one about the rain, and one about the mist. So we ought to have one about the wind. And here it is.

'"It's called:

'"IN WHICH PIGLET DOES A VERY GRAND THING.

'"Half-way between Pooh's house and Piglet's house was a Thoughtful Spot . . ."

'My mother and I, side by side on the sofa, settled ourselves comfortably, happily, excitedly, to listen.'

Half-way between Pooh's house and Piglet's house was a Thoughtful Spot where they met sometimes when they had decided to go and see each other, and as it was warm and out of the wind they would sit down there for a little and wonder what they would do now that they *had* seen each other. One day when they had decided not to do anything, Pooh made up a verse about it, so that every-body should know what the place was for.

> This warm and sunny Spot
> Belongs to Pooh.
> And here he wonders what
> He's going to do.
> Oh, bother, I forgot—
> It's Piglet's too.
>
> *The House at Pooh Corner*

'Mark August 21st in letters of blood . . .' 21 August was also the day when the bear destined to be Winnie-the-Pooh came into the life of Christopher Robin. Bought from the toy department at Harrods of Knightsbridge, the beautiful brown cuddly toy teddy bear was a first-birthday present for Christopher, given to him on 21 August 1921, and, according to Christopher, from then on, until he went away to boarding school, 'my inseparable companion'. Christopher told me, 'I think he was called Big Bear or Edward Bear or Mr Edward at first, but I only remember him as Pooh. He was always Pooh to me.'

As with Christopher Robin/Billy Moon, there is some confusion over the bear's name, too. There is no dispute about the Winnie in Winnie-the-Pooh. Christopher, as both a baby and a little boy, was regularly taken to visit the animals at Regent's Park Zoo and a particular favourite was an American black bear (*Ursus Americanus*) named Winnipeg, or Winnie for short.

From 1914 to 1934, Winnie was something of a London Zoo celebrity. Canadian by birth, the bear was brought to

England by a handsome young soldier, Lieutenant Harry Colebourn. Colebourn (1887–1947), born in Birmingham, had emigrated to Canada aged eighteen and attended the Ontario Veterinary College, before moving west to Winnipeg. In August 1914, at the beginning of the First World War, as he was travelling by train across Canada to embark for Europe and war service as a member of the Royal Canadian Army Veterinary Corps, Colebourn came across a hunter who had a female black bear cub for sale. The hunter had killed the cub's mother. Colebourn bought the cub for twenty dollars, named her Winnipeg and took her with him across the Atlantic to Salisbury Plain, where she became the un-official mascot of the Fort Garry Horse, a Canadian cavalry regiment that had originated in Winnipeg in 1912.

When Colebourn was ordered to the front in France, he decided his bear should stay behind and left her in the care of the Zoological Society at Regent's Park Zoo. There she stayed, happily and much loved, for the rest of her life. Cole-bourn, promoted to Major, returned safely from the war and decided to let the zoo keep the bear.* Because Winnie had been hand-reared by Colebourn and the zoo-keepers, she was accustomed to humans and was allowed to interact with them freely in a way that seems almost incredible to us now. 'So when Christopher Robin goes to the Zoo,' A A M explained in the introduction to *Winnie-the-Pooh*, 'he goes to where

---

* In 1981, a bronze sculpture of Winnie as a young cub was unveiled at London Zoo by Christopher Robin, then sixty-one. When Winnie died of old age in 1934, her skull was then donated to the Royal College of Surgeons curator, Sir James Colyer, a dental surgeon with a keen interest in comparative den-tistry. He was the first to report on dental variations and diseases in bears. Winnie's skull shows that she had lost all her teeth and suffered from chronic periodontitis, possibly because of her diet, which included condensed milk. The skull is currently on display at the Royal College of Surgeons in London.

the Polar Bears are, and he whispers something to the third keeper from the left, and doors are unlocked, and we wander through dark passages and up steep stairs, until at last we come to the special cage, and the cage is opened, and out trots something brown and furry, and with a happy cry of "Oh, Bear!" Christopher Robin rushes into its arms.'

That may be a bit of an exaggeration, but possibly not much: see the photograph of Winnie and young Christopher together at the zoo and listen to the children's author, Enid Blyton, who went to interview A. A. Milne in 1926 and subsequently reported to her readers that 'the bear hugged Christopher Robin and they had a glorious time together, rolling about and pulling ears and all sorts of things.' 'Now this bear's name is Winnie,' A A M continued in his introduction to *Winnie-the-Pooh*, 'which shows what a good name for bears it is, but the funny thing is that we can't remember whether Winnie is called after Pooh, or Pooh after Winnie. We did know once, but we have forgotten . . .'

Some say the Pooh part of the name originated at London Zoo, too, when Christopher went to the zoo one day with a party of children celebrating a little girl's birthday and the smell of the bear prompted the little girl to cry 'Oh poo!' in disgust, while Christopher exclaimed 'Oh poo!' in delight. Christopher told me that version of events rang no bells with him, even though Daphne thought there might be something in it. 'I think my father's explanation is probably the correct one,' said Christopher. When he was very small, the family went to stay in a thatched cottage called The Decoy at Pooling, near Arundel, in Sussex. There there was a lake and a swan on the lake and Christopher fed the swan and, with his father's encouragement, decided to call the swan Pooh. 'This is a very fine name for a swan,' A A M explained in the introduction to *When We Were Very Young*, 'because if you call him and he doesn't come (which is a thing swans are good at), then you can pretend that you were just saying "Pooh!" to show how little you wanted him.' Milne added, 'I should have told you that there are six cows who come down to Pooh's lake every afternoon to drink, and of course they say "Moo" as they come,' – and Moo rhymes with Pooh, which is poetic and rather nice.

Milne explained that when he and Christopher Robin said goodbye to the swan on the lake for the very last time, 'we took the name with us, as we didn't think the swan would want it any more,' and when, later, Edward Bear decided he needed 'an exciting name all to himself, Christopher Robin said at once, without stopping to think, that he was Winnie-the-Pooh. And he was.'

And a 'he' is definitely what he was, too, whereas Winnie, the bear at London Zoo, was a 'she' without question. In the introduction to *Winnie-the-Pooh*, Milne faced the issue almost head-on:

When I first heard his name, I said, just as you are going to say,
    'But I thought he was a boy?'
    'So did I,' said Christopher Robin.
    'Then you can't call him Winnie?'
    'I don't.'
    'But you said—'
    'He's Winnie-ther-Pooh. Don't you know what "*ther*" means?'
    'Ah yes, now I do,' I said quickly; and I hope you do too, because it is all the explanation you are going to get.

And what about the other animals in Christopher's nursery? (They were kept in an ottoman, by the way, rather squashed in at night, and generally known as 'The Others'.) Eeyore arrived soon after Pooh, as a Christmas present in 1921. When he was new, according to Christopher, Eeyore held his head quite high, but by the time the stories came to be written his head had fallen forward 'and this had given him his gloomy disposition'. You just had to hug Pooh, but Eeyore was a donkey so you could swing him about by his ears and his legs and his tail. As Eeyore observed of his companions, 'They've no imagination. A tail isn't a tail to *them*, it's just a Little Bit Extra at the back.' Christopher acknowledged to me that Eeyore was almost as much loved as Pooh, but not quite. Pooh went everywhere with Christopher. Eeyore was often left squashed in the ottoman.

'Nobody tells me,' said Eeyore. 'Nobody keeps me informed. I make it seventeen days come Friday since anybody spoke to me.'

The House at Pooh Corner

Piglet came next, according to Christopher, 'a present from a neighbour who lived over the way, a present for the small boy she so often used to meet out walking with his nanny.' Christopher told me that while Pooh was his ally and best friend, Piglet was his alter ego. 'There was a bit of Pooh in me, of course,' he said. 'I was a boy of very little brain. I believe my kindergarten teacher thought I was so dim she got herself invited to tea at Mallord Street to see whether I was always like that or only at school.' But, claimed Christopher, he was more Piglet than Pooh, because, like Piglet, he was small and somewhat tentative. ('It is hard to be brave . . . when you're only a Very Small Animal.') Christopher said that, as a boy, he was 'very shy and un-self-possessed'. Alan used to reassure him that he had been shy, too, that on the whole shy people were nicest, 'and that it was better to be shy than boastful and self-assertive'. But, in retrospect, Christopher reckoned he had been too shy for his own good: 'When people asked me simple questions, like did I want another piece of cake, I really ought to have known the answer and not turned to the hovering figure at my side and said, "Do I, Nanny?"'

> Pooh is the favourite, of course, there's no denying it, but Piglet comes in for a good many things which Pooh misses; because you can't take Pooh to school without everybody knowing it, but Piglet is so small that he slips into a pocket, where it is very comforting to feel him when you are not quite sure whether twice seven is twelve or twenty-two. Sometimes he slips out and has a good look in the ink-pot, and in this way he has got more education than Pooh, but Pooh doesn't mind. Some have brains, and some haven't, he says, and there it is.
>
> *Winnie-the-Pooh*

Pooh, Piglet and Eeyore: they were the trio around which the famous stories began – and long before they were famous stories, they were simply stories that Alan told Billy Moon just for the fun of it. Daphne sat with her son and played with him and his toys. By playing with them, 'Daphne brought them to life,' according to Alan. Christopher acknowledged that. For all his later ambivalence about being 'Christopher Robin' and how the fame of the name affected him and his life, he did not – and did not want to – deny his central place at the beginning of the creation of the world of Winnie-the-Pooh. 'It started in the nursery; it started with me,' he said. 'It could really start nowhere else, for the toys lived in the nursery and they were mine and I played with them. And as I played with them and talked to them and gave them voices to answer with, so they began to breathe.' But alone, he knew, he couldn't take them very far: 'I needed help. So my mother joined me and she and I and the toys played together, and gradually more life, more character flowed into them, until they reached a point at which my father could take over.'

Alan always said that he 'described rather than invented' the characters who lived in the Hundred Acre Wood: 'My collaborator [Daphne] had already given them individual voices, their owner [Christopher], by constant affection had given them the twist in their features which denoted character.' Only Rabbit and Owl, said Milne, 'were my own unaided work'. According to Christopher, 'Owl was owlish from the start and always remained so. But Rabbit, I suspect, began by being just the owner of the hole in which Pooh got stuck and then, as the stories went on, became less rabbity and more Rabbity.' Kanga and Roo and Tigger were later arrivals, according to Christopher, soft toys bought from Harrods, 'presents from my parents, carefully chosen, not just for the delight they might give to their new owner, but also for their literary possibilities'.

Later in his life, there was a time when Christopher came to resent the way his father had exploited the 'literary possibilities' of his childhood toys – the time when he said, 'It seemed to me almost that my father had got to where he was by climbing upon my infant shoulders.' But that feeling came and went.

In my time I have written biographies of the late Queen Elizabeth II and her husband Prince Philip, Duke of Edinburgh, and I recall how there was a time in the 1990s when their son, Prince Charles, then in his forties, going grey and with a pained expression, let the world know that, as he was growing up, he felt 'emotionally estranged' from both his parents, craving 'the affection and appreciation' from them that they were either 'unable or unwilling' to offer. He recollected that he had felt lonely in his nursery and isolated in his pram. At least, that was his recollection in the 1990s when, personally, with his first marriage foundering, Charles was in an unhappy place. Ask him about his parents now, and King Charles III, personally in a much happier place, speaks of them quite differently, with love, admiration and respect. It was much the same with Christopher Robin. In his twenties and early thirties, he felt bitter about his childhood, but he was in a bad place then. Towards the end of his life, when I knew him, his views had mellowed, though not, I think, to the extent that King Charles's have done.

All that Prince Philip would say to me about his and his wife's parenting skills was, 'We did our best.' If asked, I imagine Alan and Daphne would have said much the same. In his childhood memoir, written in the 1970s, Christopher Milne looked back to the 1920s and concluded: 'Some people are good with children. Others are not. It is a gift. You either have it or you don't. My father didn't – not with children, that is. Later on it was different, very different. But I am thinking of my nursery days.' Of his mother, he wrote: 'I enjoyed playing with my mother. This was something she was good at. There were plenty of things that she couldn't do, had never been taught to do, didn't need to do because there was someone to do them for her, and she certainly couldn't have coped alone with a tiny child. But provided Nanny was at hand in case of difficulty, she was very happy to spend an occasional half hour with me, playing on the floor, sitting me on her lap to show me how the gentleman rides, reciting (for the hundredth time) Edward Lear's "Calico Pie".'

Nanny, happily, was always at hand in case of difficulty. Nanny was the beating heart of Christopher's childhood. 'She had me when I was very young,' he said. 'I was all hers and remained all hers until the age of nine. Other people hovered around the edges, but they meant little. My total loyalty was to her.' Her name was Olive Rand. Christopher called her 'Nou'. She was a traditional English nanny: experienced (she came to the Milnes in her mid-twenties, with excellent references: she had previously looked after the children of the Chilean ambassador to London), formal (she wore a grey nurse's uniform, with starched white collar and cuffs, a white nurse's cap indoors and a veil when out), devoted. She was engaged to an ex-soldier, Alf Brockwell, who had joined the Post Office as an electrical engineer after the war, but she would not marry him until Christopher went away to boarding school and she thought she could be spared. 'She was just a very good and very loving person,' said Christopher, 'and when that has been said, no more need be added.'

In 1974, four years before she died aged eighty-three, Christopher dedicated his first book to her:

> For Olive Brockwell
> 'Alice' to others
> But 'Nou' to me.
> To remind you of those enchanted places
> Where the past will always be present.

He never forgot her. She was part of his life, he told me:
'In my head,' he said, 'always – long after I'd stopped seeing
my parents, certainly.' Christopher felt completely safe with
his Nanny and loved by her, without reservation. He was at
pains to point out that she wasn't at all like Alice, the nurse
in A. A. Milne's famous poem, 'Buckingham Palace'.

They're changing guard at Buckingham Palace –
Christopher Robin went down with Alice.
Alice is marrying one of the guard.
'A soldier's life is terrible hard,'
   Says Alice.

They're changing guard at Buckingham Palace –
Christopher Robin went down with Alice.
We saw a guard in a sentry-box.
'One of the sergeants looks after their socks,'
   Says Alice.

They're changing guard at Buckingham Palace –
Christopher Robin went down with Alice.
We looked for the King, but he never came.
'Well, God take care of him, all the same,'
   Says Alice.

They're changing guard at Buckingham Palace –
Christopher Robin went down with Alice.
They've great big parties inside the grounds.
'I wouldn't be King for a hundred pounds,'
   Says Alice.

They're changing guard at Buckingham Palace –
Christopher Robin went down with Alice.

A face looked out, but it wasn't the King's.
'He's much too busy a-signing things,'
    Says Alice.

They're changing guard at Buckingham Palace –
Christopher Robin went down with Alice.
'Do you think the King knows all about me?'
'Sure to, dear, but it's time for tea,'
    Says Alice.

When We Were Very Young

Other nannies might give their charges a dismissive answer as Alice does in the poem – 'Sure to, dear, but it's time for tea,' – but as Christopher put it emphatically in his book, in capital letters: 'NOT MINE'.

Christopher and his nanny – Billy Moon and Nou – had their own floor at the top of the house: the nursery floor, with a day nursery to play in, a night nursery to sleep in, and a bedroom and bathroom for nanny. Their meals were served to them up in the nursery. Mrs Penn, the cook at Mallord Street when Christopher was born, and Mrs Gulliver, her successor (who was 'large, fat and jolly' according to Christopher), and Gertrude ('small and thin and solemn'), Daphne's lady's maid, were all good cooks, but the nursery meals were served before the dining-room meals and, according to Christopher, were not nearly so appetising.

As a little boy, Christopher reckoned he spent more time with the family servants than he did with his parents. 'That's the way it was in those days,' he said. 'When my father was a boy, he had his brother Ken as his closest ally. If he felt frightened at night, he could call out to Ken. When I was frightened at night – and I had a lot of night fears and bad dreams – I called out to Nanny. She was always there. Apart from her two weeks' holiday a year, she was always there. She never let me down.'

Until he was ten, Nou was Christopher's best friend and closest ally. He had friends of his own age as well, the children of his parents' friends and neighbours, notably a little girl called Anne, eight months his senior, who always announced her own arrival with a cry of 'Coooooo-eeeeee!' Anne was the daughter of Alan's friend, the admiring *Telegraph* drama critic W. A. Darlington. An only child, like Christopher, she lived a few streets away with her parents (and her nanny) in a flat in Beaufort Mansions. 'We were as close and inseparable as it is possible for two children to be who live half a mile apart,' said Christopher. 'It was a closeness that extended to my parents, for Anne was and remained to her death the Rosemary that I wasn't.'

A. A. Milne dedicated *Now We Are Six*, his second book of children's verses, to Anne, 'now she is seven', and wrote inside the copy that he gave to her:

> This book of songs
>> Dear Anne, belongs to you.
> It carries much
>> Of love and such from Blue.
> And for the rest
>> It says as best it can
> 'Be never far
>> From Moon, my darling Anne.'

'Blue' was Alan's nickname for himself. He and Daphne loved her dearly and hoped, off and on, that one day Moon and Anne, true childhood friends, might become husband

and wife. Had they, the Milne family story would have ended differently, and Alan and Daphne might not have become estranged from their son. Who knows? In 1939, the year Anne turned twenty, Alan called his autobiography *It's Too Late Now*.

> When Anne and I go out to walk
> We hold each other's hand and talk
> Of all the things we mean to do
> When Anne and I are forty-two.
>
> *Now We Are Six*

Anne was fun and funny, older than Christopher, bolder and cheekier. She was more robust, too. Christopher was a fussy eater (which Anne was not) and always small for his age. The doctor recommended some strengthening medicine, which Christopher quite liked, but it did not succeed in building him up. He was sent to a gym, run by two Scotsmen called Munroe and Macpherson. 'Christopher Robin, you look like a camel,' shouted Macpherson. 'Hold yourself up, lad.' They equipped him with child-sized boxing gloves, to no effect. Finally, Mrs Preston, a specialist masseuse, was called in. 'I lay on the ottoman in the nursery while Mrs Preston powdered me and then thumped and kneaded. But though I loved it, I remained resolutely underweight.'

Anne wasn't bothered about Christopher's size. She liked him looking like a camel. Anne had a monkey whose name was Jumbo ('as dear to her,' said Christopher, 'as Pooh was to me,') and a nanny who wore black-rimmed glasses and a black straw hat and who the children wickedly nicknamed 'Jam Puff' because 'she had so many chins'. Anne was knowing and daring. She 'always knew things before I did,' said Christopher. It was Anne who told him there was no such person as Father Christmas. When they were six, they went together every day to Miss Walters' school in nearby Tite Street (the street where Oscar Wilde and his family once lived) and sat side by side in class. Some of Anne's spirit rubbed off on Christopher:

'Christopher Robin, I'm afraid six from nine does not make five.'

'No, Miss Walters. I'm not very good at easy sums. I'm better at them when they are harder.'

Christopher's affection for Anne never faded, nor hers for him, though romance was never part of the mix. 'We were just the best of friends,' Christopher told me, 'and she was an easy friend for me to have because my parents loved her, too. She was the Rosemary they never had.'

Christopher wondered out loud to me whether, when he was small, his parents had him dressed as a girl because subliminally they wished he had been a girl. 'I had long hair and I was put into smocks and dresses,' he told me. 'At night, I used to have dreams and in my dreams I was usually a girl. I remember going out for walks with Nanny and people seeing me and saying, "Oh, what a pretty little girl." It was odd because I know how much my father hated being dressed up like Little Lord Fauntleroy when he was young. But I don't suppose my father got involved in how I was dressed. He left all that sort of thing to my mother and Nanny. When I was small, I don't think I saw a lot of him. He was very busy in those days.'

Chapter Seventeen

in which A . A . Milne hits the heights

The roaring twenties

The 1920s – 'the roaring twenties' – was A. A. Milne's golden decade. With plays, movies, novels, a murder mystery (that has not been out of print in more than a hundred years), and those four short children's books ('no more than 70,000 words in all' as he said so often), he was all-conquering: a household name and an international bestseller. F. Scott Fitzgerald – who made the phrase 'the roaring twenties' famous – published *The Great Gatsby* on 10 April 1925. The book sold 20,000 copies in its first year. A. A. Milne published *Winnie-the-Pooh* on 14 October 1926. It sold 150,000 copies before Christmas.*

The Milnes needed a nanny – and a lady's maid and a cook and a parlour maid and a chauffeur, and more besides when, in addition to their London house, they bought a place in the country in 1924 – because Alan was so busy – so busy! – and Daphne was still very much his collaborator.

Following the West End and Broadway success of *Mr Pim Passes By* in 1919/1920, he wrote play after play. Some

---

* Happily, both books have stood the test of time. *The Great Gatsby* is esti- mated to have sold 25 million copies worldwide to date; the Winnie-the-Pooh books have sold more than fifty million.

worked; some didn't. *The Boy Comes Home,* his one-act melo-drama about a young soldier returning from the war, became a vehicle for the popular young leading man, Owen Nares, as part of a variety bill at the Victoria Palace. *Make-Believe* was a children's play in the whimsical Barrie tradition that opened the actor-manager Nigel Playfair's tenure at the Lyric Theatre, Hammersmith, and had some success – though, as Milne acknowledged, 'The difficulty in the way of writing a children's play is that Barrie was born too soon . . . We who came later have no chance.'* *The Lucky One* did not live up to its name, possibly because it was a romantic comedy with a twist – the twist being that the wrong man gets the girl. No London producer wanted it, and its 1922 New York showing was brief. Looking back, Milne said, 'I used to think it was my best play; well, I suppose it was once; but I see that I just wasted a good idea. I wish I hadn't thought of it so soon.'

Two months after Christopher Robin was born, on 18 October 1920, *The Romantic Age* opened at the Comedy Theatre. Its central idea was a fun one. The young heroine, aptly named Melisande, is a true romantic. She is looking for love in the chivalric tradition, but her suitors are all dull young stockbrokers who propose to her wearing ludicrous golfing clothes:

MELISANDE: Oh, Bobby, everything's wrong. The
man to whom I give myself must be not only my

---

* I appeared in the role of 'The Princess' in a production of the play at my prep school, aged 12 in 1960. At my next school my best friend was a would-be actor, Simon Cadell, whose grandmother, Jean Cadell, had starred in the original production that opened in Hammersmith on 24 December 1918. At school I also appeared in *Miss Elizabeth Bennet*, Milne's 1936 adaptation of *Pride and Prejudice.* I had hoped to play Mr Darcy. I was cast as Mr Collins.

lover, but my true knight, my hero, my prince. He must perform deeds of derring-do to win my love. Oh, how can you perform deeds of derring-do in a stupid little suit like that!

The play is about romance versus reality. In London in the autumn of 1920, reality seemed to have the upper hand. The first night coincided with thousands of unemployed men and women marching on Downing Street and the play did its best to struggle on through a national coal miners' strike that led to street lighting restrictions and fuel and food rationing. The reviews were mixed and left Milne 'dispirited' but undeterred. It hardly mattered because hot on the heels of *The Romantic Age* came two big-hitters that proved to be not only protest- and strike-proof, but considerable income generators for Milne in the years to come. As well as playing in London and New York, Milne's plays were produced across the Empire: in Australia, Canada, India and beyond. From the 1920s to the 1950s, they were especially popular with amateur dramatic societies. By his own admission, in the mid-1920s, his earnings from amateur rights alone topped £2,000 a year – the equivalent today of more than £100,000.

The Truth About Blayds opened on 20 December 1921 at the Globe Theatre in London; *The Dover Road* opened at the New Bijou Theatre in New York two nights later. Within forty-eight hours, Milne was simultaneously the Christmas toast of both the West End and Broadway.

With *The Truth About Blayds* Milne was back with his most reliable producer, Dot Boucicault, and Boucicault's wife, the lovely Irene Vanbrugh. In the drama, the couple played the daughter and son-in-law of the eponymous Blayds, a grand old man of English letters, 'a very great

poet, a very great philosopher and a very great man . . .
simple as Wordsworth, sensuous as Tennyson, passionate as
Swinburne', who turns out to be an old fraud: he is not the
author of the poems that made his name. The opening night
was a glittering affair. According to the *Pall Mall Gazette*,
'The Princess Royal, accompanied by Princess Maud, was
in a box. Sir James Barrie and Mr Stephen Leacock, Mr
Somerset Maugham and Lord Latham were there . . .' Better
still, in the reviews Milne was compared favourably with
Barrie, Bernard Shaw and even Ibsen. A few weeks later,
when the play had settled comfortably into a long run, Milne
wrote to his friend, Turley: '*Blayds* is a success. I feel rich
and lazy.'

The *Dover Road*, which opened in London, at the Theatre
Royal, Haymarket, on 7 June 1922, was another palpable hit
– with another ingenious plot. A wealthy and eccentric Mr
Latimer (played by a noted Shakespearean leading man,
Henry Ainley: he was still playing Hamlet to acclaim in his
fifties) contrives to waylay eloping couples to his house on
the Dover Road, where they are brought face to face with
the reality of what they may be letting themselves in for. *The
New York Tribune* called the piece 'a quietly twinkling, adult
entertainment'. This time Milne was likened, among others,
to the great Restoration playwrights, Congreve and Wycher-
ley. *The Stage* described the play as 'one of the most notable
English comedies of modern times' and asked why Broadway
audiences had been allowed to see it first. In 1927, William
C. De Mille (brother of Cecil B.) turned it into a silent movie
called *The Little Adventuress* and, in 1934, it became a talkie,
Where Sinners Meet.

The 1920s, of course, was the heyday of the silent cinema
and, for a while, Milne was in on the act. He joined forces

with Leslie Howard, who appeared in the London production of *Mr Pim Passes By* in 1920 and the Broadway production of *The Truth About Blayds* in 1922, and Howard's friend, Adrian Brunel, a young director, ten years Milne's junior, to form Minerva Films – named after the Roman goddess and patroness of the arts and founded with high hopes. In the event, the company made just four two-reelers (*The Bump*; *Twice Two*; *Five Pound Reward*; and *Bookworms*), written by Milne, starring Leslie Howard and C. Aubrey Smith, and directed by Brunel. Howard and Aubrey Smith went on to greater things in Hollywood, and Brunel later made pictures with Ivor Novello and Buster Keaton among others, but Milne did not stay the course. He found story-telling for the silent cinema a wearisome business. It was all rather obvious, filmed action illustrating very few words set out in fleeting captions between scenes. Milne was always a dialogue man. Other companies made film adaptations of several of his plays, from a silent *Mr Pim Passes By* in 1921 to a talkie of *Michael and Mary* in 1932, but Milne preferred not to be involved – except in the matter of money. He took a keen interest in the negotiations for the film rights to his work and never rushed to accept the first bid on the table. Paramount Studios acquired the 'talking picture rights' to *The Dover Road* for $10,000, the equivalent of around $190,000 today.

The plays kept coming, tumbling out of him throughout the 1920s, dictated to Daphne, and presented, with varying degrees of success, in London and New York. He had high hopes for *The Great Broxopp*, written in 1918/19 and first produced on Broadway in 1921 and at the St Martin's Theatre in London in 1923. What is remarkable about the play is how strangely prophetic it is. The plot revolves around a young man, Jack Broxopp, who feels his life has been blighted by his father's commercial success manufacturing and marketing a baby food – Broxopp's Beans – using his infant son to advertise his product. The play anticipates with uncanny foresight exactly how his still-unborn son, Billy Moon, would one day feel about 'being' Christopher Robin:

> JACK: I'm simply *fed up with Broxopp's Beans*.
>
> BROXOPP (*surprised*): But – but you haven't had them since you were a baby.
>
> JACK (*seeing the opening*): Haven't had them? Have I ever stopped having them? Weren't they rammed down my throat at school till I was sick of them? Did they ever stop pulling my leg about them at Oxford? Can I go anywhere without seeing that beastly poster – a poster of me – me, if you please – practically naked – telling everybody that I love my Beans. (*Bitterly*) *Love* them! Don't I see my name – Broxopp, Broxopp, Broxopp – everywhere in every size of lettering – on every omnibus, on every hoarding; spelt out in three colours at night – B-R-O-X-O-P-P – until I can hardly bear the sight of it. Free bottles given away on my birthday, free holidays for Broxopp mothers to celebrate my coming of age! I'm not a man at all. I'm just a living advertisement of Beans.

In the play, Broxopp Sr sees his son's point of view, sells his business and changes the family name to Chillingham, his wife's maiden name. The Chillinghams retire to the country hoping to live happily ever after, but life, of course, doesn't work out as simply as that.

The Great Broxopp was well received in New York ('A

merry satiric fantasy . . . generally gorgeous comedy', Alexander Woolcott, *New York Times*), but less so in London. Almost inevitably, *Success*, which opened at the Theatre Royal, Haymarket, in June 1923, did not live up to its name. In retrospect, Milne accepted that the title was a hostage to fortune. When the play eventually made it to New York in 1931, it was called *Give Me Yesterday*. Milne had called the play *Success* quite simply because that was what it was about – or, rather, it was about the *price* of success, which might have been a less provocative title. The critics did not like the play, and it only survived six weeks, but J. M. Barrie thought it was the best thing Milne had ever done. And Milne thought so, too. He called it his 'masterpiece'.

On he went: *To Have the Honour* (London, 1924, with the celebrated Gerald du Maurier in the lead); *The Man in the Bowler Hat* (New York, 1924); *Ariadne* (New York and London, 1925); *Miss Marlow at Play* (London, 1927); *The Ivory Door* (New York, 1927; London, 1929); *The Fourth Wall* (London, 1928). *The Fourth Wall* (or *The Perfect Alibi* as it became when it was presented in New York) was different from Milne's customary cocktail of drama, romance and family secrets. This was a detective play with a twist – a twist that, forty years later, became the basis of the globally successful TV series *Columbo*, starring Peter Falk: we are shown the murder at the outset of the drama and we then follow the solving of the crime. In 1930, *The Fourth Wall* was another Milne play turned into a film: *Birds of Prey*, directed by Basil Dean and distributed by RKO.

Milne's golden decade culminated with two distinct theatrical successes: the first, *Michael and Mary*, which opened in New York on 10 December 1929 (and in London on 1 February 1930); the second, *Toad of Toad Hall*, which began its long life as a perennial Christmas favourite at the Liverpool Playhouse on 21 December 1929 and opened in London, at the Lyric on Shaftesbury Avenue, a year later, on 17 December 1930.

In many ways, the two plays give you the essence of A. A. Milne. *Michael and Mary* is a comedy, a romance and a drama all rolled into one, a three-generation family saga with a plot that involves bigamy (again) and a subtle exploration of what love and goodness mean – and involve. As well as the Michael and Mary relationship of the play's title, at the heart of the drama is the connection between a father and a son, between Michael and his clergyman Papa. Milne's father was still alive when Alan wrote the play, but the intimacy they had known until Alan was twelve was long gone. Christopher was coming up for ten when the play opened in London and there was still a decade or more to go before Billy Moon and Blue went their separate ways. But from his own adolescence onward, Milne was aware that the freedom and magic and trust and unspoken understanding that can bind a father and a son together is extraordinary, but it does not last:

> MICHAEL: It's awful cheek to say it, but however many other commandments I may break, I do *honour* you, father. There's something about sheer goodness that always gets me. Mind you, I disagree with you profoundly about everything under the sun, sometimes you irritate me intensely – and – and yet (*with a little ashamed laugh*) I believe I love you. Good-bye.

Toad of Toad Hall was A. A. Milne's adaptation of Kenneth Grahame's novel *The Wind in the Willows*. Originally published in 1908, Grahame's evocative account of the lives of the animals who live on the riverbank – the mole, the water rat and the badger: Moley and Ratty and Mr Badger – and of how they do what they can to save their impossible friend, Mr Toad, from himself and the scrapes he gets into, is now accepted as one of the classics of children's literature, but it was at first turned down by an assortment of publishers and received mixed reviews when it appeared. However, the public loved it. And A. A. Milne loved it, almost as much as he loved *Peter Pan*. 'One does not argue about *The Wind in the Willows*,' he said. 'The young man gives it to the girl with whom he is in love, and if she does not like it, asks her to return his letters.'

Daphne loved the book, too. Christopher told me that she read it to him often – and often with tears in her eyes. Daphne, according to Christopher, loved the less well-remembered parts of the book, such as the chapter (Chapter Seven) where the god Pan makes a surprise appearance on the riverbank to look after Otter's son, Portly. Christopher claimed his mother was moved by the parts of the book that explored human emotions, 'the emotions of fear, nostalgia, awe, wanderlust'. His father, Christopher maintained, having concentrated on Toad's adventures for his play, only allowed one emotion to creep in: nostalgia.

I told Christopher I did not entirely agree with him. I reckon Milne made Toad the focus of his play because Toad's adventures provide the action, the drama and the comedy. And Toad himself is an irresistible character, a beguiling rogue, in the tradition of Sir John Falstaff. You do not need to be nostalgic to love the world of the riverbank: you can be optimistic – it can be your ideal, to be celebrated and revelled in. Sir John Falstaff and the merry wives of Windsor and Mr Toad and his good friends on the river-bank – and, yes, Winnie-the-Pooh and his good friends in the Hundred Acre Wood – in their different ways belong to the tradition of Merrie England. It's not life as we know it necessarily, but perhaps it is life as we would like it to be. It's an aspiration that has moved and excited people for centuries. One Henry of Huntingdon coined the phrase *Anglia plena jocis* – 'England full of mirth' – sometime around the year 1150. If ever there was a Merrie England, idyllic and pastoral, full of good humour, good-heartedness and good cheer, it began to disappear with the advent of the industrial revolution and, to people of A. A. Milne's generation, it vanished finally in the horror of the First World War.

It was Curtis Brown, Milne's literary agent, who came up with the idea of Alan turning *The Wind in the Willows* into a play. That was in 1921. Milne was immediately taken with the idea. 'If Kenneth Grahame is willing,' he wrote to Curtis Brown, 'and if you feel pretty sure you can find the right manager for it (as I think you should be able to do), I will do it. And I shall love doing it.' He got on with it right away, and he did love doing it, but finding the right manager was not so easy. It was eight years before *Toad of Toad Hall* reached the stage.

When A. A. Milne wrote *Toad of Toad Hall* he had no idea he might one day write *Winnie-the-Pooh*. By the time *Toad of Toad Hall* was produced, he had become famous as a children's author. Critics inevitably saw a connection between Grahame's anthropomorphic animals on the riverbank and Milne's anthropomorphic toys in the Hundred Acre Wood. Milne had to live with that.

More annoyingly, from the moment of the success of his children's books, whatever he wrote, he reckoned he was seen entirely as a writer whose 'spiritual home is still the nursery'.

He went on writing plays for adults (*Other People's Lives*, New York and London, 1932; *Sarah Simple*, written in 1932, produced in New York in 1937; *Gentleman Unknown*, 1938), but now they were viewed through the prism of Winnie-the-Pooh. 'As a discerning critic pointed out,' he wrote with more than a touch of asperity in 1939, the year after the failure of *Gentleman Unknown*, 'the hero of my latest play, God help us, was "just Christopher Robin grown up". So that even when I stop writing about children, I still insist on writing about people who were children once. What an obsession with me children are become!'

The 1930s were tough for A. A. Milne, as we shall see. The 1920s were sweet. He was happy as a husband, as a father, as a writer. In the summer of 1922, on holiday in Devon with Daphne and Billy Moon, he wrote to a friend: 'When I return to London, I shall WORK; a constant stream of GREAT PLAYS and POWERFUL NOVELS will flow from my pen.'

In 1921 he published *Mr Pim*, a successful novelization of his successful play, *Mr Pim Passes By*. The year before, he decided to write a murder mystery. His agent and his publishers weren't sure that was such a good idea. A A M was known as a humorist and a playwright. Shouldn't he stick to humour and plays? As ever, Milne was obstinate. He did as he pleased, as he thought fit – and, in this instance, he reaped the reward. Apart from his four children's titles, *The Red House Mystery* was and remains A. A. Milne's most successful book.

It was published in the spring of 1922, when Milne had just turned forty, and dedicated to his father, who was now seventy-seven:

TO
JOHN VINE MILNE

MY DEAR FATHER,

Like all really nice people, you have a weakness for detective stories, and feel that there are not enough of them. So,
after all that you have done for me, the least that I can do
for you is to write you one. Here it is: with more affection
and gratitude than I can well put down here.

A.A.M.

A century on, when it comes to detective stories, I doubt
that anyone thinks there are not enough of them, but in 1920
the genre was still in its relative infancy. Detective fiction
in the English-speaking world is usually reckoned to have
begun in 1841 with the publication of Edgar Allan Poe's *The
Murders in the Rue Morgue* and the first appearance of Poe's
eccentric and brilliant sleuth, C. Auguste Dupin. In *Bleak
House* (1853), Charles Dickens gave us a detective, too, when
the lawyer Tulkinghorn is killed in his office late one night
and the crime is investigated by the nicely named Inspector
Bucket of the Metropolitan Police. Dickens's young friend
and mentee, Wilkie Collins, has been called 'the grandfather
of English detective fiction'. The poet and detective story
devotee T. S. Eliot described Collins's novel *The Moonstone* (1868) as 'the first, the longest, and the best of modern
English detective novels . . . in a genre invented by Collins
and not by Poe.' Dorothy L. Sayers called *The Moonstone*
'probably the very finest detective story ever written'.

Arthur Conan Doyle created Sherlock Holmes in
1887 and kept him going, off and on, for forty years. *The*

Case-Book of Sherlock Holmes was published in 1927 and contained Doyle's final twelve Holmes stories, originally serialized between 1921 and 1927. The so-called 'Golden Age' of detective fiction is the period between the two World Wars of the twentieth century when we saw the first flourishing of British writers like Dorothy L. Sayers, Agatha Christie and Margery Allingham. A. A. Milne was following the pioneers – Poe, Collins, Conan Doyle – and anticipating the Golden Age. In 1920, when word got out that he was working on a detective story, he said, 'The news spread all over the world.' He wrote to a friend at the time: 'The Emperor of China is already saving up for a copy. I hope I shan't disappoint him.' Years later, he reflected, 'The result would have passed unnoticed in these days when so many good writers are writing so many good detective stories, but in those days there was not so much competition.'

The Red House Mystery was published before *Whose Body?*, Dorothy L. Sayers's 1923 debut novel, and the book in which she introduced the character of Lord Peter Wimsey. *The Red House Mystery* was written before the publication of Agatha Christie's first book, *The Mysterious Affair at Styles*, the novel where we first encounter Hercule Poirot and Inspector Japp, and which Milne later described as 'the model detective story'.

When *The Red House Mystery* appeared in Britain and the US in 1922, it was immediately popular. In time, it was translated into a variety of languages, French, Japanese, Swedish and Serbo-Croat among them. The American critic, Alexander Woollcott, called it 'one of the three best mystery stories of all time', though Raymond Chandler, one of the founders of what became known as 'the hardboiled school' of detective fiction, reckoned Woollcott had gone too far. Chandler's verdict was more measured: 'It is an agreeable book, light, amusing in the *Punch* style, written with a deceptive smoothness that is not as easy as it looks.'

Given the book's success, and the quantity and quality of the dialogue in the novel, it is surprising that *The Red House Mystery* was not (and has not been) turned into a play or movie. Milne could have adapted it himself, of course, and toyed with the idea, but did not pursue it.* He was pleased with the book's success (especially as he had been advised against writing it) and rated his detective, Gillingham. In the mid-1920s, when the Milnes suffered a burglary from their London house, Alan reported in a letter to his brother Ken:

All they got was

    Two silver boxes
    Ciro-pearl necklace (which I hope they thought was
    genuine)
    Jade and diamond brooch
    Ear-rings
    My gold wrist watch
    My gold 'albert' [watch chain] (which I haven't
    worn since 1914)
    and
    Two pairs of cami-knickers and two chemises
    of Daff's! (You ought to have heard me describing the cami-knickers to two stolid policemen.)
    About £70 worth. Insured, of course. The visitors
    came in politely by the front door which they burst

---

* In 1922, while he was at school, at Repton in Derbyshire, the future novelist and screenwriter Christopher Isherwood, aged eighteen, had a go at turning it into a play as an end-of-term entertainment.

open with a jemmy. They did no damage whatever inside, owing to the lucky fact that not a single drawer, cupboard or desk is ever locked in this house. But bills, letters and clothes were scattered all over the rooms. Holmes (or Gillingham) would undoubtedly have said they were searching for the secret will or the compromising photograph.

Milne cast his man Gillingham in the Holmes tradition and acknowledged his debt to Conan Doyle. And just as Holmes has his Watson, Milne provided Gillingham with an amiable sidekick, too – together with other stock characters from the genre: a retired major, a widow and her wilful daughter, a good-looking young man-about-town and a long-lost brother who is the black sheep of the family.

'Once a writer of detective stories you inevitably return,' said Agatha Christie in an interview in 1922, the year that *The Red House Mystery* was published. With *The Fourth Wall* in 1928, A. A. Milne put a murder mystery on stage, but he chose not to return to detective fiction – despite handsome offers to do so. He explained his thinking towards the end of his autobiography: 'It has been my good fortune as a writer that what I have wanted to write has for the most part been saleable. It has been my misfortune as a business man that, when it has proved extremely saleable, then I have not wanted to write any more.'

At the start of the 1920s, he was writing detective fiction. At the end of the 1920s, he was writing children's stories. Having found both genres extremely saleable, he was immediately ready – anxious, even – to say 'goodbye to all that'. 'I wanted to escape from them as I had once wanted to escape from *Punch*,' he explained, 'as I have always wanted to escape. In vain. England expects the writer, like the cobbler, to stick to his last. As Arnold Bennett pointed out: if you begin painting policemen you must go on painting police-men, for then the public knows the answer – Policemen. If you stop painting policemen in order to paint windmills, crit-icism remains so overpoweringly policeman-conscious that even a windmill is seen as something with arms out, obvi-ously directing the traffic.'

Arthur Conan Doyle wanted to write books that were not detective stories – and did. But his public (and his publish-ers) demanded more Holmes and he felt obliged to oblige. Agatha Christie enjoyed writing romances, but she knew what her readers wanted – more Poirot! More Miss Marple! – and she did not disappoint them. A. A. Milne was made of sterner stuff. He did what he wanted to do, in his own way, for just as long as he wanted to do it, and then he moved on.

A. A. Milne was always his own man, which may be why some people, who in theory knew him well (like E. H. Shepard), felt they did not know him well at all. He was deliberately guarded; he could appear shy (especially in crowds); some people found him awkward company. Others found him quietly forbidding. He had definite opinions and, inherited from his father, a strict moral sense. 'He loves goodness,' one of his closest friends, Frank Swinnerton, said, 'He stands for virtue.' Swinnerton, who at Chatto & Windus had published Milne's first collection of plays in 1919, acknowledged: 'Those who disagree with him complain of his rigidity in argument and severity in outlook.' But that wasn't Swinnerton's experience: 'I have always found him overflowing with good spirits.'

If he liked you, he liked you. Over dinner with two or three friends, playing a round of golf with a familiar partner,

A. A. Milne, photographed by Howard Coster, 1926.

Daphne, Christopher Robin and A. A. Milne at Cotchford Farm, circa 1926.

Cotchford Farm in 2025.

A letter from A. A. Milne to his brother, Ken, where he encloses 'a little something, as Pooh says.'

The Milnes holidayed in Dorset in the summers between 1934–37. The first photo shows Anne Darlington, Christopher Robin and A. A. Milne. The second shows A. A. Milne with his arm around Angela Milne, who is standing next to her brother Tim. In the chair is Maud Milne (Ken's wife) with Christopher Robin in front.

Elmer Rice, photographed for *Vanity Fair* in 1931.

Leonora Corbett in *Sarah Simple* by A. A. Milne, featured on the cover of *Theatre World* in July 1937.

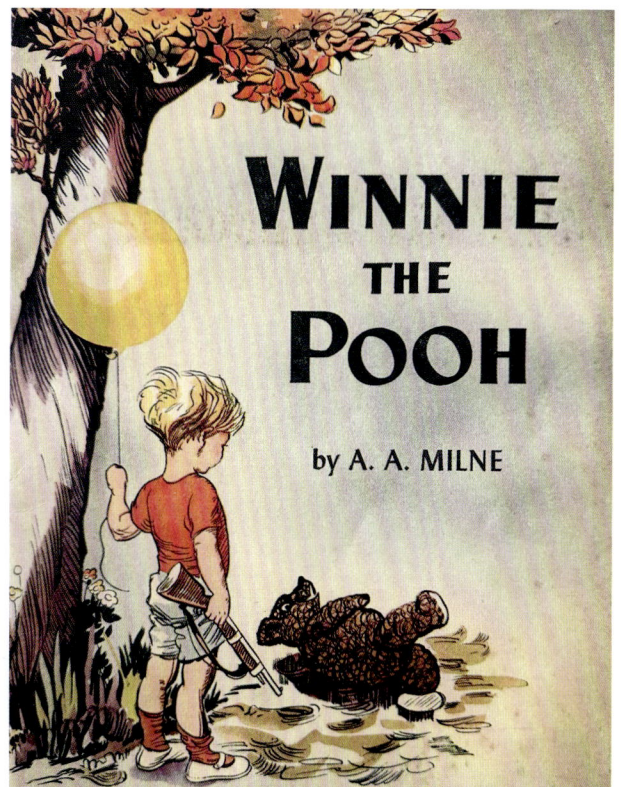

A letter from A. A. Milne to his literary agent Curtis Brown, 1925

Cover of an American edition of *Winnie-the-Pooh*, published in 1944, using an original illustration of Winnie-the-Pooh from J. H. Dowd.

Christopher Robin Milne serving in the British Army in World War Two.

Christopher Robin with his bride, Lesley de Sélincourt, on their wedding day, 1948.

Christopher Robin with his friend Anne Darlington at the memorial service for A. A. Milne, 1956.

Christopher Robin and Gyles Brandreth.

Gyles Brandreth's play *Now We Are Sixty*, first produced in 1986, with music by Julian Slade and starring a young Aled Jones as Christopher Robin.

Now We Are Sixty

This is a very special event: exactly sixty years after A. A. Milne introduced Winnie the Pooh to an unsuspecting public, the Cambridge Festival is presenting the World Premiere of a sparkling new comedy about Milne, one of the most successful writers Cambridge — and Britain — has ever produced.

There was very much more to Alan Milne than *When We Were Very Young* and *Winnie the Pooh*. He was a popular playwright, a *Punch* columnist, a comic writer of great flair and style, and *Now We Are Sixty* is a witty and intriguing play that reveals a remarkable man and his amusing world. There's nostalgia, high comedy, high jinks and marvellous music by H. Fraser-Simson and Julian Slade — his best score since *Salad Days*.

This special Festival production — destined for the West End after its premiere in Cambridge — is being directed by one of Britain's most distinguished directors, James Roose-Evans, whose most recent success was his multi-award winning production of *84 Charing Cross Road* which he directed in London and on Broadway and which is now being filmed.

Victorama Ltd and Adrian Gilpin for Artattack Ltd present the 1986

CAMBRIDGE FESTIVAL PRODUCTION

Now We Are Sixty

The World Premiere of a comedy with music based on the life and work of

A. A. MILNE

by
GYLES BRANDRETH and JULIAN SLADE

Music by
JULIAN SLADE and H. FRASER-SIMSON

Lyrics by A. A. MILNE

Directed by
JAMES ROOSE-EVANS

Designer
BRUNO SANTINI

Choreographer
GERALDINE STEPHENSON

Tue 22 July - Sat 2 August
ARTS THEATRE, CAMBRIDGE
Box Office Cambridge (0223) 352000

Gyles Brandreth   Julian Slade

Pamphlet for *Now We Are Sixty*.

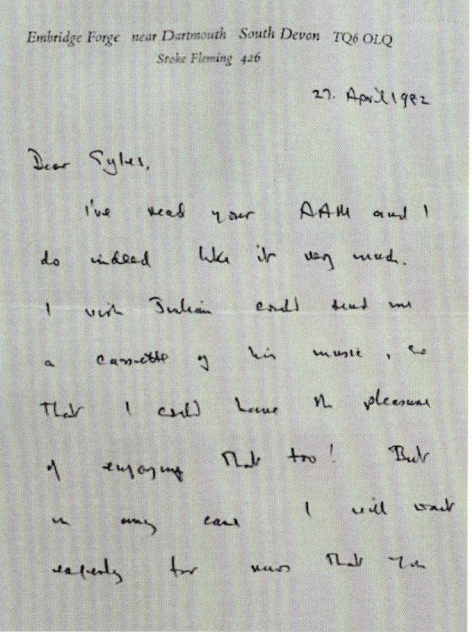

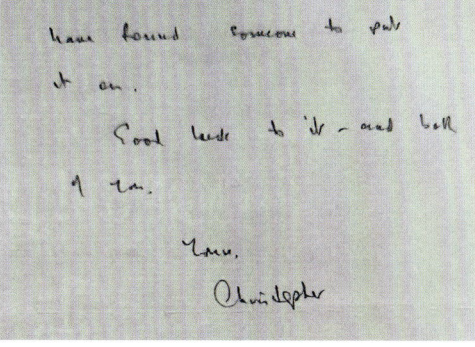

Letter from Christopher Robin to Gyles.

Gyles with the original inhabitants of the Hundred Acre Wood, at the New York Public Library, 2025.

Gyles on Pooh Sticks Bridge in the Ashdown Forest, Hartfield.

enjoying a game of cricket with other members of J. M. Barrie's Allahakbarries cricket team, he was a good companion, easy-going and likeable. At a party or confronted by strangers, he was more taciturn. He was probably happiest alone in his study, at work at his desk, or sitting in a deck chair in the garden, in the shade, smoking his pipe.

> I have a house where I go
> When there's too many people,
> I have a house where I go
> Where no one can be;
> I have a house where I go,
> Where nobody ever says 'No'
> Where no one says anything – so
> There is no one but me.
>
> *Now We Are Six*

Inevitably, Milne found himself surrounded by people quite often – and fabulously famous people, too, at his own first nights and those of others. Through the theatre and publishing, he encountered almost all the noted cultural figures of his time. He knew the great Arnold Bennett, the most financially successful writer of the day: 'We seemed to get on all right,' he said, while admitting they did not find much to say to one another. He worked with the great Gerald du Maurier, knighted in 1922 and reckoned the *nonpareil* of naturalist acting, and found him tiresome. In 1921, at one of H. G. Wells's house-parties, he met the great Charlie Chaplin, at the time, without question, the most famous man on earth. Milne seized the moment to get Chaplin's autograph to send to Ken and Maud's daughter, Marjorie, who was then fifteen.

In 1919, he was elected a member of the Garrick Club, named after the actor David Garrick (1717–79), and founded in 1831 as a gentleman's club for 'actors and men of refinement to meet on equal terms'. Situated on Garrick Street, between Covent Garden and Trafalgar Square, for Milne in the 1920s, and even more so in the 1930s, it was his home from home. It was a civilized safe haven in the heart of town, away from domestic distractions, where the food was reliable (and not too fancy) and the company generally agreeable. Dot Boucicault, J. M. Barrie, P. G. Wodehouse and H. G. Wells were all members. Milne told an interviewer in the mid-1920s: 'Mrs Milne encourages me to go to my club every day; she says it brightens me up and that I bring her back plenty of good stories.' His membership was proposed by his friend and mentor E. V. Lucas – the man who took him through the Stage Door of a theatre for the first time and would secure him a place in the Library of Queen Mary's Dolls' House and persuade him to have E. H. Shepard as the illustrator of his children's books. His application to join was signed by his actor-manager friend Nigel Playfair, and by a fellow novelist and playwright, Somerset Maugham, among others.

Later in the 1920s, Milne was invited to join the Athenaeum Club without having to put his name on the customary waiting list – an honour reserved for 'persons of distinguished eminence in Science, Literature, or the Arts or for Public Services'. He was chuffed: the Athenaeum was an older club, with grander premises on Pall Mall, less raffish than the Garrick, 'more intellectual'. He accepted the flattering invitation and when he went to the club, was pleasantly surprised to find the members (who included Rider Haggard and Rudyard Kipling) less stuffy than he had expected. The

Garrick was his club of choice (and, of course, the club to which he left that considerable share of his estate), but the Athenaeum gave him a recognition that he appreciated.

As he moved into his forties and through the 1920s, Milne was increasingly a public figure. He took his responsibilities seriously. He was actively involved in the work of the Society of Authors and the Royal Literary Fund, raising and giving money to both. He wrote letters to *The Times* on issues of the day. He was a public figure, yet he saw himself as a private man – and a family man. At his clubs he could meet up with other interesting men on friendly terms without the need (or expectation) of unnecessary intimacy. At home, he had Daffs and Billy Moon. Daphne was still very much his collaborator. As Celia Brice, she was still acting as his secretary; the manuscripts of plays like *The Truth About Blayds* are in her handwriting, with corrections and additions in his. Most importantly, she was still laughing at his jokes. When an interviewer asked him if his wife ever criticized his work as he dictated it to her, he said: 'No, she just praises.' 'Praise,' he said, 'is what an author really wants when he is actually writing.' And little Billy Moon was still his pride and joy – and his inspiration.

As we know, one evening in 1922, Alan, on the top floor in Mallord Street, was passing the open door to his son's nighttime nursery and caught sight of his two-year-old boy kneeling beside his bed under the watchful eye of his nanny, Olive Rand. Christopher Robin was saying his prayers. Alan described the scene in his poem 'Vespers' – the poem he sent to join the Library in Queen Mary's Doll's House, the poem he gave to Daphne that she sold to *Vanity Fair* for $50, the poem, it turned out, that started the whole Christopher Robin/Winnie-the-Pooh industry.

Coincidentally, Alan had received a letter from the children's author Rose Fyleman (1877–1957), asking him to consider contributing some verses to a new magazine she was editing, *The Merry-Go-Round*. Fyleman and Milne knew of one another because, over the years, they had both written poems for *Punch*. Alan's verses had been largely satirical; Rose's chiefly sentimental, chief among them the one that made her famous, 'There Are Fairies at the Bottom of Our Garden'. (She published more than a hundred books and plays, with fairies featuring in most of them.) Milne wrote back saying this really wasn't in his line. And then he had second thoughts: 'I did what I always do after refusing to write anything: wondered how I would have written it if I hadn't refused.'

The wondering led to working . . .

There once was a Dormouse who lived in a bed
Of delphiniums (blue) and geraniums (red)
And all the day long he'd a wonderful view
Of geraniums (red) and delphiniums (blue)

. . . and, fourteen verses later, 'The Dormouse and the Doctor' was finished. Milne sent it off to Rose Fyleman and went on holiday.

The holiday was in North Wales, in a rented house called Plas Brondanw at Llanfrothen near Portmadoc, and the Milne family (Alan and Daphne, and Billy Moon with his bear and his nanny) shared it with the family of Alan's friend, the actor-manager Nigel Playfair. This was the summer of 1923. I heard about it at first hand fifty years later, in 1973, from Giles Playfair*, one of the Playfair

---

* Giles Playfair (1910–1996) was an author and social reformer and the middle son of Sir Nigel Playfair (1874–1934). GP's many books included biographies

children, who was thirteen at the time but remembered the holiday vividly. He took photographs of it and later wrote about it in his biography of his father. It rained constantly and Playfair Sr did his best to keep everyone entertained, organizing parlour games, which the Milnes were obliged to take part in, but did not appear to enjoy. Giles had no recollection of Christopher Robin (he was mostly kept upstairs with the nannies and Giles's four-year-old brother Andrew) and what he remembered of Alan was chiefly how disapproving he was of everything. Mr Milne did not like music or dancing, or beer or spirits, or football or gambling. He was strongly against betting on horses and the notion of getting 'something for nothing'. He was most passionate when railing against militarism and those inclined to celebrate the so-called glories of war. The teenage boy found his father's friend prim, proper, strait-laced and sanctimonious. Giles acknowledged that the celebrated writer probably did not much take to him either.

'In a week,' Alan recalled later, 'I was screaming with agoraphobia.' He could not bear the other people, their chattering and forced jollity. According to Giles Playfair, Alan and Daphne kept themselves to themselves as much as they could and were 'very close' and 'lovey-dovey'. Fortunately for Alan, just as he thought he could take no more of the gaiety of the house-party, a letter arrived from Rose Fyleman, forwarded from Mallord Street and enclosing the proof of his poem, 'The Dormouse and the Doctor', for his correction, together with the suggestion from Miss Fyleman that he should sit down and write a whole book of verses in a similar vein.

---

of his father and of the actor Edmund Kean. I got to know him because he was an Oxford University contemporary and friend of my father.

As the rain continued to pour down (as it does, in my experience, on the Welsh riviera in August), Alan retreated to the summer-house in the garden at Plas Brondanw to review the proof. That done, he stayed in the summer-house and started work on a second poem. And then a third. 'There I was,' he recalled later, 'with an exercise book and a pencil, and a fixed determination not to leave the heavenly solitude of that summer-house until it stopped raining.' He was on holiday, of course, so 'there on the other side of the lawn was a child with whom I had lived for three years . . . and here within me were unforgettable memories of my own childhood.' What was he writing? 'A child's book of verses obviously. Not a whole book, of course; but to write a few would be fun – until I tired of it. Besides, my pencil had an India-rubber at the back; just the thing for poetry.'

A dozen days of downpour later, a dozen sets of verses had been completed. With the Welsh holiday over – Giles Playfair had a recollection of the Milnes leaving the house-party earlier than planned with his father playfully leading a chorus of 'The Milnes are going, hurrah, hurrah' to the tune of 'The Campbells are coming' as their car departed – and with A A M happily back in the solitude of his study in Mallord Street, he decided to write some more children's verses. By the end of the year, he had completed forty, enough for a book.

He despatched his slim manuscript to his publishers on both sides of the Atlantic. The publishers, of course, had been hoping for another Milne detective story as a sequel to *The Red House Mystery*. John Macrae of E. P. Dutton in New York was dismayed. 'Chagrin' and 'disappointment' were his immediate responses to the news of what Milne now had to offer. 'We are all aware,' he reflected with a sigh, 'that probably the most hopeless kind of manuscript a publisher expects to receive from his favourite author is that of poetry for children.' E. V. Lucas, Milne's friend and mentor at Methuen in London, was marginally more positive and came up with two ideas that he hoped would help the new book's prospects. One was to get E. H. Shepard on board to illustrate the poems. The other was to whet the public's appetite for them by persuading A A M's *alma mater*, *Punch*, to feature a number of them in the months running up to the book's publication.

Despite Milne's initial reservations about Shepard, the author quickly realized that the illustrator's 'decorations' for the poems were going to work a treat. Though of a similar age (Shepard was three years Milne's senior), and from not dissimilar English middle-class backgrounds (Shepard's father was an architect; Shepard went to St Paul's School and the Heatherley School of Fine Art in Chelsea before going on to win prizes at the Royal Academy Schools in Piccadilly), the two men had different temperaments. Shepard was easier company and more larky. A mischievous 'giddy kipper' as a boy, his family and friends knew him as 'Kipper' or 'Kip'. Like Milne, Shepard served on the Somme, but the artist was less conflicted than the author. In 1917, Shepard was awarded the Military Cross for 'conspicuous gallantry and devotion to duty'.

Milne dedicated his collection of poems to his four-year-old son:

TO *Christopher Robin Milne*
OR, AS HE PREFERS TO CALL HIMSELF,
BILLY MOON
THIS BOOK WHICH OWES SO MUCH
TO HIM IS NOW HUMBLY DEDICATED

Several of the poems were inspired by Christopher Robin, several featured him by name. ('You will have noticed,' Milne told his readers, 'that the words "Christopher Robin" come trippingly off the tongue. I noticed that too.') Others had their roots in Milne's recollection of his own childhood: 'As a child I had a mouse; probably it escaped – they generally do. Christopher Robin has kept almost everything except a mouse. As a child I played lines-and-squares in a casual sort of way. Christopher Robin never did until he read what I had written about it, and not very enthusiastically then.'

Toy teddy bears had not existed when Alan was a boy. Billy Moon's teddy bear had a poem all his own in Alan's book:

A bear, however hard he tries,
Grows tubby without exercise.
Our Teddy Bear is short and fat,
Which is not to be wondered at;
He gets what exercise he can
By falling off the ottoman,
But generally seems to lack
The energy to clamber back.

Milne invited Kip Shepard to Mallord Street to meet Christopher Robin and the teddy bear and to see the ottoman and the other toys. Milne said in his autobiography: 'Shepard drew them, as one might say, from the living model.' Not so, in fact, in the case of the teddy bear – who eventually became Winnie-the-Pooh. The drawing of the tubby bear we all now recognize as 'the original Winnie-the-Pooh' was not based on Billy Moon's British-made 1920s Pooh (the bear that now lives in the New York Public Library), but on Growler, an earlier, German-made Steiff bear that belonged to Shepard's son, Graham. Graham had been born in 1907 and was now seventeen, but his bear was still at home and much-loved and a more convenient model for Shepard to use.* Billy Moon wasn't to be parted from Pooh.

Today, if people think of the 'look' of Winnie-the-Pooh, it is likely to be either Shepard's drawing or the Disney version that appears in their mind's eye. Milne came to be very grateful to Shepard for his contribution to the Pooh books' success (and shared some of his author's royalties with the illustrator to show his gratitude), but the pair were not (as they are sometimes described) the 'joint creators' of Pooh. Milne described Pooh and his world and Shepard illustrated what Milne described. During the four years when Shepard was working on the four Milne books, he illustrated at least eight other books, none of which is remembered now.†

Milne could not decide on a title for his collection of verses. He wrote to Owen Seaman, the editor of *Punch*: 'I can think of none better than *When We Were Very Young*, but I am ready to be persuaded if you, or anybody, can suggest something. *Children Calling* was my only other idea . . . ' He did have other ideas – *A Nursery Window Box*, *Pinafore Days*,

---

* Shepard and his wife Florence had two children, Graham and Mary (born 1909), both of whom also became illustrators. Graham died in the Second World War serving in the Royal Navy when his ship was sunk by a German submarine in September 1943. Mary married E. V. Knox, who succeeded Owen Seaman as editor of *Punch*, and was best known as the illustrator of the *Mary Poppins* books written by P. L. Travers. Florence Shepard died in 1927 and in November 1943, two months after his son's death, Shepard married Norah Carroll, a nurse at St Mary's Hospital, Paddington. They remained married until his death, aged 96, in 1976.

† Shepard illustrated scores of books by sundry authors over the years. What are remembered best are the best books: the four by Milne and the new edition of Kenneth Grahame's *The Wind in the Willows*, which Shepard illustrated, post-Pooh, in 1931.

Swings and Roundabouts, Buttercups and Daisies – but nobody expressed any particular preference, so *When We Were Very Young* it was.

The first poems appeared in *Punch* on 9 January 1924. The collection of poems was published in book form in London on 6 November 1924 and in New York on 20 November. By the end of the year, A. A. Milne was the bestselling poet in the world.

Chapter Eighteen

*in which A. A. Milne publishes four
international bestsellers*

Tiddely pom

1924 was a notable year. It saw the publication of *A Passage
to India* by E. M. Forster, the first production of Bernard
Shaw's *Saint Joan* and the first performance of George
Gershwin's *Rhapsody in Blue*, as well as the unexpected and
extraordinary success of *When We Were Very Young*. For
Alan and Daphne Milne, however, 1924 was memorable for
another reason. It was the year in which they found for themselves their 'place in the country' – not as a new home, but as
a weekend and holiday getaway.

They had been looking for somewhere for a while.
Daphne, now thirty-four, wanted a proper garden of her
own: as a girl she had loved the garden at her parents'
country home in Hampshire. Alan, now forty-two, wanted a
place where he could escape from 'other people': his metropolitan safe havens, the London clubs he belonged to, were
closed at weekends. They found Cotchford Farm in the
East Sussex village of Hartfield, on the northern edge of
Ashdown Forest, seven miles south-west of Royal Tunbridge
Wells, the nearest proper town, and thirty-five from Chelsea.
Burnside, the family chauffeur, driving the new family car (a
handsome Fiat 501), could get them from Mallord Street to

Cotchford Farm in under two hours, with Alan and Daphne in the back, and Christopher Robin and Nanny alongside Burnside in the front.

Possibly late-fifteenth century in origin, Cotchford Farm wasn't a farm, or hadn't been for a very long time. When they bought it, Alan described it in letters to friends as 'a cottage' and 'more or less derelict'. Years later, after they had given up their London home, he wrote: 'The farmhouse wherein we live is a very old one. None can say exactly how old, but because it is still marked as a farm on the ordnance survey map, so it is still known. For ourselves, we have bred no more than goldfish.'

Christopher loved it: 'There we were with a cottage, a little bit of garden, a lot of jungle, two fields, a river and then all the green, hilly countryside beyond, meadows and woods, waiting to be explored; and Nanny and I set out at once to explore them, bringing back reports of our discoveries.' Christopher told me that 'Pooh's Forest and Ashdown Forest were the same place – they were identical.' He told me that he and his parents loved Cotchford Farm in different ways and for different reasons, but that he believed he was the one who loved it most completely.

Ashdown Forest is still there, waiting to be explored. I love it. In the sunshine, wandering down the lanes and through the woods, it is the best of England's green and pleasant land. In the rain (if you have an umbrella) it is mysterious and exciting. Thanks to Pooh, it is a little more crowded than it used to be. There are two car parks now for the convenience of visitors. One is near what is known today as Poohsticks Bridge, but was called Posingford Bridge when the Milnes arrived. The original bridge (dating from 1907) was built by a local farmer to get his cattle across the stream – hence its width. That bridge died of old age and was replaced in the late 1970s by a new bridge of similar design. (Don't worry: I have played Poohsticks on it: it feels like the real thing.) The Quarry car park is the one you need to walk the two-and-a-half mile loop that's now known as the Winnie-the-Pooh trail. Again, don't worry: Disney may have contributed to the cost of rebuilding the bridge, but there is no hint of a theme park in Ashdown Forest. It is all wonderfully unspoilt. You can picture Nanny and Christopher – Nou and Moon – out on their walk. You can find all the places that feature in the stories: Roo's sandpit, the North Pole, Eeyore's Sad and Gloomy Place, Gills Lap and the Enchanted Place. They are all there still, and they look today much as they did a hundred years ago, as the Milnes knew them, as Shepard drew them.

Alan and Daphne decided to spend a lot of money on Cotchford Farm. Thanks to Alan's plays and children's poems, there was an increasing amount of money available to spend. Alan sent his brother Ken a photograph of the farmhouse with details of the planned improvements, including a barn conversion to provide a proper garage (with flat above), extra servants' rooms in the attic in the main house, a servants' hall alongside the kitchen, with, above it, 'a dressing room for me next to Daff's bed-room', a family playroom (big enough to take a ping-pong table), and a huge family sitting room, 'the most lovely room in the world,' Alan told Ken, with an open fireplace and French windows opening out onto what would be the lawn leading down to a stream.

According to Christopher, Alan claimed that lawn 'as his own private preserve and laid it out for clock-golf.' The stream – originally a ditch, according to Christopher, but widened into a moat and called 'the stream' – was also allowed as part of Alan's territory. It was hardly a babbling brook: 'Brown scum congealed on its stagnant surface, and strange creatures moved in its depths.' Alan and Christopher – Blue and Moon – 'plunged nets and golf clubs into it' and, gradually, 'the various inhabitants would work their way up to the surface, flip-flapping if they were fish, wriggling if they were newts, crawling if they were dragonfly larvae.'

So, for Christopher's father, the garden 'was where you sometimes looked for newts, but mainly where you putted and where you admired my mother's labour.' The garden overall was Daphne's domain. She tended it with total commitment and loving care. Christopher told me he remembered her most vividly in the garden. She was at her happiest there and he was at his happiest with her when they were together there. She had help, of course. Tasker, the gardener, was ever present. And Christopher remembered a Mr Berrow appearing, with his horn-rimmed glasses, his plus fours, his bow tie, pencil and paper to sketch out 'proposed plans for terrace gardens, orchard, and summer house.'

To the end of his days, Christopher – who as an adult became totally estranged from his mother, barely seeing her during the last twenty years of her life – could picture her clearly in her garden: 'Trowel in hand, planting Darwin tulips by the hundred. Secateurs in hand, snipping at roses. Crouched down, weeding, weeding, weeding.' He remembered her teaching him the names of the flowers – 'lovely names like salpiglossis and spiraea Anthony Waterer, difficult names like eshscholzia which were fun to spell'. But mostly, he said, 'I remember her just quietly, happily, brooding over it all, alone in the half dark.'

Talking about this with Christopher in the 1980s, 'alone in the half dark', he told me, was how he saw each of them – the three members of the Milne family – at different stages of their lives. Alan, according to his son, sometimes seemed most alone when surrounded by other people: solitary in a crowd. Christopher said he thought his father was probably happiest in the 1920s and 1930s, alone in his study, alone in the garden playing a round of clock-golf, alone in a deck chair, sitting in the shade at the edge of the lawn, reading Jane Austen and smoking his pipe. It was later, he said, after the Second World War, that Alan was 'alone in the half dark': 'He had always been alone, I think, with his thoughts and with his work, but after the war, there was less work and his thoughts were gloomier. He was disappointed, regretful.'

According to Christopher, his mother was happy both alone in the garden and when out and about, socializing with friends. 'She enjoyed company, parties, shopping, buying a new hat – and she adored her garden. When she was working with my father, taking his dictation, acting as his secretary, that was a project they shared, but when the children's books came along and they bought Cotchford Farm that began to change. They began to develop their own interests, separate interests. At the end, they were still together, but they were together living alone in the half dark under the same roof.'

Christopher said that he, too, had felt unhappily alone in the half dark, especially immediately after the Second World War, when he was in his twenties, before he got married, before he had found his way in life, when he was feeling at his most disenchanted with his parents.

'But you had good times with them, didn't you?' I asked.

'Yes,' he said almost reluctantly. He would not concede that he had ever really loved his mother. In his memoir, *The Enchanted Places*, he said of his young place in her life: 'If I wasn't a full-time job, I was at least a part-time hobby.' She read to him; she played with him; she shared her joy in her garden with him. But she was happiest alone. 'Once,' Christopher recalled, 'when she was going for a walk, I asked if I could come with her. "No," she said, "but come and meet me on my way back. I like best being met." And so we spent a lot of time meeting her. She would walk to the village, and half an hour later my father and I would set off up the hill and hope that somewhere before we reached the top we would see her coming around the corner.' He did remember walks they took together, mother and son – after dark. 'It was different in the dark. You could be with someone and they would be there if you felt you wanted them, and if you didn't, you could forget them.' He remembered a walk in the dark when a car had roared past, with blinding lights, and Daphne and little Christopher had 'clung to each other, standing against the hedge'.

Christopher told me he remembered his parents individually rather than as a couple. 'I did different things with each of them,' he said. 'With my mother it was the garden. With my father it was playing games – throwing a ball, putting on the lawn, later playing cricket, playing golf, the things he enjoyed.'

'But you enjoyed them, too,' I said.

'Yes, we had some very good times, from about the time I was ten, I suppose, for a few years then. But not so much when I was smaller.'

'But that's when he told you the stories,' I reminded him. 'And not just the stories about Pooh, but stories about knights and dragons.'

'Yes,' said Christopher. 'I loved knights and dragons. I had a wonderful suit of armour that I was given for my fifth birthday. It was beautiful, with a helmet with a proper visor and a red plume. I think I loved that suit of armour almost as much as I loved Pooh.'

And when it came to the stories about Pooh, Christopher did not deny that it was he and his mother who played together with the toys and it was his mother who conjured up their voices and his father who read each story as he wrote it out loud to mother and son, sitting cosily side by side on the sofa.

But whatever the truth, each of us remembers our childhood in our own way. Daphne and Alan did not loom large in Christopher's recollection of his early years at Cotchford Farm. What did he remember? Taking his toys out into the garden and playing with them in the grass: 'I played in the hay, I played in the mud, played in the water, played with friends, played with Nanny, played alone, climbed trees, picked primroses in the spring and nuts in the autumn, went exploring, rode a donkey.'

Looking back, Christopher felt his parents were only 'half-interested' in him. I suspect that's unfair. They were busy. With plays and books and film scripts, with rehearsals and first nights, with negotiations for overseas rights in everything Alan was writing, with a house in London, a new house in the country, there was a lot going on. Alan – judging from all the correspondence that still exists from the time – adored his boy. He took him for regular walks around the streets of Chelsea; he played games with him in the country; he told him bedtime story after bedtime story – and not just the stories about Winnie-the-Pooh. There was a funny story about a rabbit who was really a prince and another about a princess who could not do what Daphne always did for Alan ('She laughed at my jokes'):

There was once a King who had an only daughter, the pride of his heart. She was sweet, she was good, she was beautiful, and the king would have said she was perfection itself, but for one thing. She never laughed. Nothing seemed to amuse her . . .

A. A. Milne thought of himself as a good family man: loyal to his collaborator, devoted to his son, considerate of his parents. Now so busy, he could not see his brother Ken – or Ken's wife and daughters – as often as he used to, but he wrote to Ken – and to Maud – on a regular basis. He kept in touch with Connie, his brother Barry's wife, too. Barry he neither trusted nor liked and simply did not wish to know, but he was very fond of Connie.

Did Alan neglect his own parents? Possibly, but not consciously. Letters from 1920 and 1921 suggest that Alan and Daphne did not rush to take little Billy Moon over to see Maria and J. V. Milne at Burgess Hill. Maria, now eighty, was increasingly frail: her eyesight and hearing were failing. She walked with difficulty, using a stick. Christopher told me that he knew his grandmother had seen him 'once or twice' when he was a baby, but, of course, he had no recollection of her. She died soon after his first birthday. Christopher showed me a letter JV had written to a family friend at the time: 'When she left me, a sword went through my heart and I was broken.' JV was five years younger than his wife and carried on alone, as best he could, being 'as cheerful as possible in company'. 'I think it is one's duty to bear one's own sorrow privately,' he said.

It seems JV spent his first Christmas as a widower on his own. 'Of course the boys cannot leave their families on that day,' he wrote to a friend. 'It would have been such a disappointment to their children.' JV was proud of all three of his sons and proud, too, of his own independence. He moved from Burgess Hill to a smaller house, in Purley in the London borough of Croydon, and lived on until 1932, always uncomplaining and ever grateful for visits and treats when they came his way, and always answering positively and proudly whenever anybody enquired about his famous son. He was delighted that Alan ('the same dear Alan', unspoilt by his success) sent a car to bring his father to first nights and take him home again. He relished every aspect of his son's growing fame through those roaring twenties, but, as a former teacher, he took especial pride in the success of Alan's children's writing. He kept press cuttings; he noted the sales figures as Alan reported them to him. Alan wrote in a letter to Ken: 'Father seems so terribly happy and excited that he makes me feel ashamed of not having made him happy before.'

At first, everyone was happy and excited at the success of the four famous children's books, which, over just four years, flowed quite naturally from one to the next. Just as the streets of London, Christopher Robin and his Nanny had been central to *When We Were Very Young*, so the Ashdown Forest, Christopher Robin and his toys were central to *Winnie-the-Pooh*. The Pooh stories are all set in the Forest and the Hundred Acre Wood: that was the Ashdown Forest and the Five Hundred Acre Wood in every particular. This was territory that Alan and Billy Moon explored together. They knew the Six Pine Trees where Pooh and Piglet decided to dig their Cunning Trap for Heffalumps. They knew the different trees where Christopher Robin, Pooh, Piglet and Owl each had their homes. Billy Moon had his own tree house in the garden at Cotchford Farm. It was an old walnut tree. 'It was,' Christopher remembered years later, 'the perfect tree house for a five-year-old. I could climb inside and sit on the soft, crumbly floor. In the walls there were cracks and ledges where things could be put and high above my head was a green and blue ceiling of leaves and sky. Pooh and I claimed it. It was Pooh's House, really, but there was plenty of room for us both inside, and here we came to play our small, quiet, happy games together.' There is a wonderful photograph of Billy Moon standing inside the hollow of the tree, with Pooh and Kanga at his feet. Alan invited Kip Shepard to come down to Cotchford Farm to see where all the scenes in the story were set so that he could 'draw them from life'.

Everyone was taken aback by the success of *When We Were Very Young*. Prior to publication, American book-shops had ordered just 385 copies. Quite soon, reorders were coming in by the hundred thousand. Even Milne was surprised by the scale and breadth of the book's appeal. 'It is all most odd,' he reported in a letter to Ken. 'Yellow-faced Anglo-Indian colonels, with no livers and a general feeling that somebody ought to be shot down dammit sir, tell me with tears in their eyes how important it is to avoid the lines of the street and thus escape bears.' Almost incredibly, the great Sir Arthur Wing Pinero, one of the most successful playwrights of the late Victorian era, now seventy, saw him at the Garrick Club, patted him on the shoulder and told him 'what a wonderful book' he had given the world. Milne was totally bemused: 'I don't suppose he has seen or read a play of mine in his life.'

A. A. Milne, the playwright and detective story writer, was now the children's laureate. His publishers, naturally enough, wanted more children's verses. Instead, they got *Winnie-the-Pooh*.

One day when Daphne went up to the nursery, Pooh was missing from the dinner table which he always graced. She asked where he was. 'Behind the ottoman,' replied his owner coldly. 'Face downwards. He said he didn't like *When We Were Very Young.*' Pooh's jealousy was natural. He could never quite catch up with the verses.

It's Too Late Now

'What about a story?' said Christopher Robin.
'*What* about a story?' I said.
'Could you very sweetly tell Winnie-the-Pooh one?'
'I suppose I could,' I said. 'What sort of stories does he
    like?'
'About himself. Because he's *that* sort of Bear.'
'Oh, I see.'
'So could you very sweetly?'
'I'll try,' I said. So I tried.

Winnie-the-Pooh

As we know, the very first story about Winnie-the-Pooh appeared in the London *Evening News* on 24 December 1925, illustrated by J. H. Dowd. At 7.45 p.m. on 25 December, 'as part of the Christmas Day wireless programme', it was broadcast across the country by the BBC, read by the actor (and scion of the Boucicault family) Donald Calthrop. People liked what they heard and read. This was a children's story about a boy and a bear and bees and balloons and a search for a pot of honey, but it contained puns and nonsense, as well as a touch of poetry, and immediately it appeared to appeal not just to children, but to adults as well. As the months went by, Milne produced more stories, serialized in *The*

Royal Magazine, a popular publication, founded in 1898, and specializing in short fiction. (Agatha Christie's Miss Marple made her first appearance in print in the magazine the following year.) Milne brought Shepard on board to provide the illustrations, writing to him in March 1926: 'I think you must come on Thursday, if only to get Pooh's and Piglet's likeness, (and I want Piglet quite small – as you will see when you read the sixth story).'

It was Milne's idea to give a share of his royalties to Shepard. As a rule, illustrators would get a flat fee for their work, paid for by the publisher. That had been the arrangement for *When We Were Very Young*. From *Winnie-the-Pooh* onwards, Milne shared his children's book income with Shepard and, 'by agreement with the author', Shepard also got his share of the revenue from the merchandise – the spin-off books, the toys, the calendars, the stationery, the wallpaper, the crockery, the linen and all the rest.

Alan reported to Ken at the time: 'Shepard and I are having a joint agreement, dividing in the proportion of 80 to 20. Actually he did all the WWWVY illustrations for £200, and as on this book we are getting £1000 in advance from England and £1000 from America, he gets £400 straight off. And, of course, should eventually get much more.'

Milne was happy to share his royalties with Shepard because he was happy with Shepard's 'decorations', as they were described on the book's title page. He was also grateful to Shepard for his collegiate approach to the enterprise, visiting the toys in Mallord Street, coming to Cotchford Farm to catch all the detail of the local topography. The drawing of Pooh himself, inspired by Christopher Robin's bear, modelled more on the Shepard family teddy bear, really looked like neither. 'Shepard's drawing of Pooh looks like the

Pooh in the stories,' Christopher said to me. 'I think I look rather girlish in the drawings, but that's the way my hair was at the time.' In his memoir, Christopher wrote of Shepard's portrait of Pooh: 'What is it that gives Pooh his particular Poohish look? It is the position of his eye. The eye that starts as an elaborate affair level with the top of Pooh's nose and ends up as a dot level with his mouth. And in that dot all of Pooh's character can be read.'*

The contract for *Winnie-the-Pooh* was signed on 15 March 1926. The book itself, running to just ten chapters and around 20,000 words, was published on 14 October 1926 in London and on 21 October in New York, and dedicated to Daphne – though not by name:

TO HER

Hand in hand we come
    Christopher Robin and I
To lay this book in your lap.
    Say you're surprised?
    Say you like it?
    Say it's just what you wanted?
        Because it's yours –
        Because we love you.

Daphne loved the book. Billy Moon was happy with it, too. And A. A. Milne was content, despite finding two

---

* Christopher was quite particular about Pooh's appearance. For our stage production of *Now We Are Sixty* in 1986, we used the composer Julian Slade's childhood Winnie-the-Pooh, given to him in the early 1930s. Christopher did not approve of the stitched mouth on the bear. There was too much of a smile. At Christopher's insistence, the bear, which, since the 1980s, has been on show in the Brandreth teddy bear collection (first in Stratford-upon-Avon and now at Newby Hall in North Yorkshire), has his face firmly turned to the wall.

mistakes in the first edition: one a typo (Milne had Piglet saying it was time 'to spleak painly' and an over-zealous copy-editor had corrected it to 'speak plainly') and the other an oversight of his own: Milne had originally made Kanga a male kangaroo and then, possibly realizing Kanga had a pouch for Roo, which was a bit of a give-away, had firmly crossed out the words 'his' on the manuscript when referring to Kanga, but inadvertently let one 'his' slip through.

On both sides of the Atlantic, *Winnie-the-Pooh* was widely and warmly acclaimed. 'There are not so very many books that, sitting reading all alone, you find yourself laughing aloud,' said the *New York Herald Tribune*. 'This is one of them.' The paper reckoned Milne had produced 'nonsense in the best tradition', with the added dimension of a 'high seriousness about it that children and other wise people love'. The reviews were generous; the sales were generous, too, though initially not quite as good as they had been for *When We Were Very Young* – one of the reasons Milne accepted that his next children's book, for the following Christmas season, should be a second collection of children's verses.

Now We Are Six (dedicated to Billy Moon's friend, Anne Darlington, 'now she is seven and because she is so speshal') was published on 13 October 1927. Alan wrote inside the personal copy he gave to his son:

> For my Moon
> From his Blue
> Now I am 45

Soon after publication, Alan wrote to Ken: 'The reviews have been poor in England but much better in America. If I were a critic I should loathe A. A. Milne. How could one help wanting to say that he was falling off, or taking success too easily or whatnot? However this is the end of the verses; and then, after one more Pooh book, I must think of something else. In fact, it's time I tried a novel.'

Despite the mixed reviews, the sales were more than satisfactory. Before Christmas, in a letter to a friend, proud JV was able to share the English sales figures to date supplied to him by his son:

Now We Are Six	94,000
Winnie-the-Pooh	80,000
When We Were Very Young	169,000

There was 'one more Pooh book', as promised, the following year, 1928: *The House at Pooh Corner*, regarded by many, including Milne, as his best. He particularly relished the review in the London *Evening News* that declared that, a century hence, of the books and authors whose work would still be alive, the two certainties were 'Conrad and A. A. Milne's *House at Pooh Corner*.'

Inevitably, not every critic was so enthusiastic. Dorothy Parker (1893–1967), the American poet and founding member of the celebrated Algonquin Round Table, who had already poured scorn on *Now We Are Six* in her 'Constant Reader' column in the *New Yorker*, returned to the fray, announcing that it was at page five of Milne's new book – the page where we are introduced to 'a special Outdoor Song which Has To Be Sung In The Snow' and features a variety of 'tiddely poms' – that 'Tonstant Weader fwoded up'. 'Sic, if I may,' Milne added when quoting Parker in his autobiography a decade later. Like many an author (and actor), Milne was sensitive to criticism and remembered the detail of poor reviews long after he had forgotten the good ones.

The House at Pooh Corner was again dedicated to Daphne
– and fulsomely:

> You gave me Christopher Robin, and then
> You breathed new life in Pooh.
> Whatever of each has left my pen
> Goes homing back to you.
> My book is ready, and comes to greet
> The mother it longs to see –
> It would be my present to you, my sweet,
> If it weren't your gift to me.

Other than Kanga, there is no mother in the Pooh stories,
but Daphne was grateful to be acknowledged for her contribution to the creation of the world of Pooh. Billy Moon, too,
knew that he had played his part in the genesis of the stories.
'It is difficult to say which came first,' he reflected half a
century after the first appearance of Pooh in print. 'Did I do
something and did my father then write a story around it?
Or was it the other way about, and did the story come first?
Certainly my father was on the look-out for ideas; but so too
was I. He wanted ideas for his stories, I wanted them for my
games, and each looked towards the other for inspiration. But
in the end it was all the same: the stories became a part of
our lives; we lived them, thought them, spoke them. And so,
possibly before, but certainly after that particular story, we
used to stand on Poohsticks Bridge throwing sticks into the
water and watching them float away out of sight until they
re-emerged on the other side.'

The House at Pooh Corner is the book where we are introduced to the game that is now universally known as 'Poohsticks'. Pooh claims it as a new game, but, of course, it is a

very old game indeed. *Pooh Corner* is also the book where we meet a new character:

> 'I'm Pooh,' said Pooh.
> 'I'm Tigger,' said Tigger.
> 'Oh!' said Pooh, for he had never seen an animal like this before. 'Does Christopher Robin know about you?'
> 'Of course he does,' said Tigger.

Tigger was based on Billy Moon's toy tiger, a later addition to the Milne menagerie, another soft toy bought from the Harrods' toy department. 'Tiggers can do everything' and Milne's Tigger first bounced onto the scene in a story published in 1927 in a book called *Sails of Gold*, a children's anthology edited by Lady Cynthia Asquith, daughter-in-law of the British prime minister Asquith, novelist, diarist, friend of D. H. Lawrence and L. P. Hartley, and secretary to Milne's mentor, J. M. Barrie.*

In his childhood memoir in 1974, Christopher Milne vividly recalled happy times on the Poohsticks Bridge and playing with Pooh and Tigger and his other toys. He also remembered two girls, each a little older than him. One, of course, was Anne Darlington. The other was a girl called Hannah, who he used to meet on the lane leading to the Poohsticks Bridge. Her father kept a chicken farm nearby. 'Probably we just happened on each other on one of our walks up the lane,' he said, 'and Nanny – who was good at

---

* When he died in 1937, Barrie left her his literary estate, other than the rights in *Peter Pan*. Among her incidental claims to fame was taking part in the ITV quiz show, *The $64,000 Question*, in 1957, three years before she died aged seventy-two, winning the top prize of £3,200 answering questions on the works of Jane Austen.

talking to the people we met – talked to her, and that was how it all started.' Hannah and Christopher Robin never visited each other's houses. When they were together it was always out of doors: 'We played in the woods and in the fields. We climbed trees and pretended to be monkeys. We paddled in the river and dug a hole in the riverbank and called it the Channel Tunnel. We played in the barn and in the stables that had once been part of Cotchford. We helped with the haymaking and rode home on top of the hay cart. We helped with the apple picking and were allowed to eat the windfalls.'

The happiness of these childhood days stayed with Christopher all his life. In the mid-1980s, when he was in his mid-sixties, he told me that 'Cotchford, the wood, the forest, the Poohsticks Bridge,' these were his 'enchanted places'. 'I loved Pooh and Nanny best,' he told me, 'and I realize now that I loved Anne and Hannah, too. They were my special friends and they were perfect friendships – free, easy, completely comfortable, innocent and unspoilt.'*

Christopher resented being Christopher Robin in the 1940s. In the 1920s, he admitted to me, he quite enjoyed it. 'Even though I was shy, I think I quite liked the attention.' He was photographed at home, in London, in the country, in a studio, at London Zoo – alone, with Pooh, with his parents, with cheering strangers, with Winnie, the Canadian bear who had given Pooh half his name. He received fan mail from

---

* For several years I have hosted a podcast called Rosebud, in which I interview high-profile people about their first and early memories. I always ask the guests (and there have been scores) about the first friend they can remember outside their own family. Invariably, they recall that first friend's name instantly – and, intriguingly, I have noticed that the first friend is usually a little older than they were and more often a girl rather than a boy. (The first friend I remember was called Sarah-Jane Dorothea Hoos. I think I was five and she was six at the time.)

around the world – and presents, too. He particularly remembered getting a large cuddly toy pig he called Poglet that he said 'was much more handsome, indeed much more appealing and lovable' than his own little Piglet who had become 'rather dog-bitten' over the years.

When either Alan or Daphne was interviewed by the press, Christopher Robin was brought out on parade. He did not mind because he wasn't expected to say very much – and the stammer that bedevilled his teenage years didn't begin to appear until he was eight or nine. He knew he was different – 'An only child, oddly dressed, odd hairstyle, odd name, the hero of a nursery story. "Hullo, Christopher Robin! Still saying your prayers?"' – but he knew no different. He accepted his fate. He went with the flow.

In 1928, the idea came up that Christopher Robin might make a record. He enjoyed singing. He had a good voice. And the composer Harold Fraser-Simson, celebrated for his operetta, *The Maid of the Mountains*, a friend and Chelsea neighbour of the Milnes, had set quite a number of Milne's children's verses to music. They had become popular songs. Why not get Cicely, Mrs Fraser-Simson, to teach them to Billy Moon and then HMV could record them?

Alan did not favour the idea. He reported the domestic row about it in a letter to Ken:

Me (when it was first suggested): Bah!

Daff: It will be a Wonderful Thing to Have!

Me: Who *is* Moon? . . . I'm the only important person in this house. Christopher Robin doesn't exist. He is a pigment-figment of the imagination. Why should a small unimportant boy –

Daff: It would be a Wonderful Thing to Have
– Afterwards.

And so the row continued, until Alan admitted defeat:

Me: I think the Whole thing is Perfectly Disgusting;
I'll have Nothing to do with it. You can do what you
like about it. I wash my hands of it. (Exit to bathroom.)
So Daff went to the gramophone Co., they all fell on
her neck –

And two records were made. I got the impression from
Christopher that, while embarrassed by the idea of the
recordings in retrospect, he was happy to sing the songs at the
time. He remembered being driven to the HMV recording
studio in the Fraser-Simsons' car, with the Fraser-Simsons'
dog ('Mr Henry Woggins') on the back seat with him for
company. He hated 'Vespers', as we know, but he loved music
– all sorts of music – all his life. And he didn't have to sing
the songs perfectly. He knew that. 'I was a small boy not
a professional. A little wobbling on the long notes, a little
breathlessness at the end of the line wouldn't matter, might
even add to the charm . . .'

And the fact that Milne and Fraser-Simson, in 1926, had,
with gracious royal permission, dedicated their collection of
songs to the infant Princess Elizabeth, seemed somehow to
put Pooh's owner on a par with the future Elizabeth II. Certainly, by the end of the 1920s, Princess Elizabeth was the
most famous little girl in the world and Christopher Robin
was the most famous little boy.

Then, in 1929, everything began to change. Ken died.
Dot Boucicault died. Alan had a theatrical flop in the West
End with what he had once believed was 'the world's greatest

play, somewhat in the Shakespearean style'. And Christopher Robin was sent to a new school – a more grown-up school. Pooh, he realized, 'was moving into the shadows. For seven and a half years he had been my constant companion: now our paths were beginning to part.' The little boy was growing up: 'I was now living in two worlds. In one we could perhaps still meet for a little longer, but in the other I was on my own.' Soon he would go to boarding school and have to say goodbye to Nanny. She was going to leave Billy Moon and marry Alfred Brockwell: 'Alfred! My rival! "Nanny, don't marry Alfred. Marry me."' But she married Alfred and together Olive and Alfred bought a bungalow and called it 'Vespers'. Billy Moon was bereft. 'She had me when I was very young,' he said. 'I was all hers and remained all hers until the age of nine. Other people hovered around the edges, but they meant little. My total loyalty was to her.'

Chapter Nineteen

in which the tide begins to turn

Triumph and disaster

Kenneth Milne had not been well for years. He had been diagnosed with consumption in 1923, when he was barely forty-three, and in those days consumption – sometimes nick-named 'the white death' – was a killer. Known as tuberculosis now, there were no antibiotics then to treat the life-threat-ening bacterial lung infection. The disease was called 'con-sumption' because as it progressed it appeared to 'consume' its victims. The only remedy the doctors could suggest was 'fresh air' and plenty of it.

Ken – Alan's beloved Ken – was obliged to give up his job at the Ministry of Pensions, leave Croydon and resettle himself, his wife and his four children away from London. They chose to go to Shepton Mallet in Somerset and found themselves a house with a garden in which they installed a revolving wooden and metal cabin to serve as Ken's bedroom to allow him to sleep overnight out of doors. His civil service pension amounted to a third of his salary, but Alan was ready, willing, and fortunately able to come to the rescue. He offered to provide whatever supplementary income was necessary, starting with £400 per annum to help with the children's education. Alan also suggested that Ken should now try to fulfil the ambition they had once shared – to be a writer. Years before, you will recall, when Alan had become editor of *The Granta* at Cambridge, Ken had written to him in mock-bitterness. He had always thought that he, Ken, would be the writer of the family: 'And now you have taken that too. Well, damn you, I suppose I must forgive you. My head is bloodied but unbowed. I have got a new frock coat and you can go to the devil. Yours stiffly, Ken.'

In 1924, Alan wrote to Ken urging him to consider book-reviewing, but he was anxious not to be misunderstood:

> For God's sake don't think I mean by all this: 'You've got to jolly well set to, and earn some money' – You know I don't; but I do mean, old boy, that you're only 43, and that it's no good regretting the brilliant service career which has been denied you, when there's another sort of career still open and waiting for you. There are dozens of good novels and plays waiting to be written, and hundreds of articles; but a little regular reviewing would be a great help meanwhile, not only financially, but artistically. And you know that if I can help in any way, I will. My love to dear Maud. In a sneaking sort of way I envy you both going to live in the country!
>
> Yours ever affectionately,
>
> Alan

Ken did do some writing. *Punch*, among others, published him. And Alan got him additional freelance work as a reader for Methuen & Co, his own publishers. But Ken was seriously ill and his condition gradually worsened. Alan visited him at Shepton Mallet when he could and wrote to him regularly, ever urging him to 'Get well, please' and trying to make him smile. In December 1928, soon after the publication of

The House at Pooh Corner, Alan was laid low for a few days and wrote from his own sick-bed to Ken in his:

Here is my day (a sample):

8.30 am	Moon and Nan come in, bringing me an early cup of tea, letters and *The Times*.
9.00 am	Daff brings me *her* letters and the *Daily News*.
9.30 am	Gertrude brings me breakfast.
10.00 am	Nan brings me evening paper.
10.30 am	Burnside brings me detective story.
11.00 am	Dr Blackie brings me thermometer.
12	Mrs Gulliver brings me egg beaten up in lemon.
1 pm	Moon brings me bunch of violets.
1.30	Daff brings me lunch.

And at half-hour intervals somebody rings up and Daff says she's very sorry but whatever Mr Milne may have promised he can't do it *now* because he's *ill*. Which is a great comfort.

Nan was Moon's Nanny, Olive Rand; Gertrude was the maid; Burnside was the chauffeur; Mrs Gulliver was the cook. Tasker, the gardener, was not mentioned in despatches, but he was another key member of the Milne household. Thanks to the books and the plays, Alan was a wealthy man. And Daphne had her own family money, too. Beyond her garden and her wardrobe (everyone agreed that Daphne was no beauty, but she was always impeccably groomed), she was not especially extravagant. She spent more than he did, but he spent very little. All he wanted was to write, smoke his pipe, enjoy a round of golf and, when in town, watch the cricket at Lord's and have lunch at one of his clubs. He took an active interest in his own financial affairs (1929 was the year he agreed to license the commercial exploitation of all the characters in his four children's books*) but more because he was conscious of his own worth – he wanted to be valued – than because he was driven by a desire for money. He was always generous – generous in voluntarily sharing his royalties with E. H. Shepard, generous to good causes (he supported the leading authors' charities; he gave money to help war veterans; he raised funds for hospitals and for the Children's Country Holiday Fund), generous to Ken's family always. Whatever Ken and Maud and their children needed, they should have: 'CVSD' ('*Ça va sans dire*'), as Alan often noted in his letters to his brother.

Ken died on Tuesday 21 May 1929 at his home in Shepton Mallet. He was forty-eight. He had hoped to be buried beside his mother in the graveyard of the church, St Peter and St John the Baptist, at Wivelsfield in Sussex, near where his parents had once lived. As we know, due to 'bureaucratic confusion', he wasn't: he was buried nearby. As we know, too, Alan blamed his solicitor brother Barry for the confusion. Alan could not bear to stand alongside Barry at

---

* The agreement, signed on 6 January 1930, was between A. A. Milne and Stephen Slesinger (1901–53), a New York comic strip cartoonist and literary agent who created, managed and developed a number of authors, cartoon and literary characters from the late 1920s onwards, among them Tarzan, Charlie Chan and Buck Rogers. Essentially, Slesinger acquired the sole and exclusive right in the United States and Canada to commercially exploit 'in any and every manner' all four of Milne's children's books, creating, over time, the first Pooh soft toy, record, board game, puzzle, US radio broadcast (with NBC), animation and motion picture film. In the 1950s, after Slesinger's death, his widow took over the business and launched her own nation-wide licensing campaigns. In 1961 and 1983, Stephen Slesinger Inc. licensed certain of its Pooh rights to the Walt Disney Company.

the graveside. Instead, he watched the burial from the edge of the graveyard, alone.

Ken had been everything to Alan always – his brother, his closest ally, his best friend; if you like, Christopher Robin to his Pooh, or even Pooh to his Piglet.

> So wherever I am, there's always Pooh,
> There's always Pooh and Me.
> 'What would I do?' I said to Pooh,
> 'If it wasn't for you,' and Pooh said: 'True,
> It isn't much fun for One, but Two,
> Can stick together,' says Pooh, says he.
> 'That's how it is,' says Pooh.
>
> *Now We Are Six*

Of course, Alan was not alone. He had his work and he had Daphne – and he had Billy Moon. Except work wasn't quite what it had been: ideas weren't coming to him as easily now he was in his late forties as they had done once upon a time. And his relationship with Daphne was changing, subtly, almost imperceptibly. Daphne turned forty in 1930. She was no longer acting as Alan's secretary, replying to the fan mail as 'Celia Brice', taking his dictation. She still laughed at his jokes and lavished his work with praise, but – so Christopher told me – she was now 'more interested in her garden than her husband'.

Christopher told me that it was around this time that he began to notice that his parents had quite separate interests. His mother cared about her house and garden, and her clothes, and having lunch with her girlfriends. She wasn't interested in playing golf or going with Alan to watch the cricket at Lord's. 'There were really very few things that they did enjoy doing together,' he said, but they seemed happy enough: 'Together but separate, if you know what I mean.'

'This meant,' Christopher wrote in his first memoir in 1974, 'that when, in 1930, I came downstairs to join them, I found that I was either doing things with my mother or doing things with my father . . . It all seemed quite natural: I wasn't expecting my mother to bowl to me at our net in the meadow, or come looking for birds' nests. And if she or I were engaged on some sort of redecoration in the house or work in the garden, I wasn't expecting more than just admiration from my father when it was done.'

Christopher told me that later, particularly after the Second World War, he sensed that his parents were living separate lives though still together: 'Two people alone under the same roof.' While he was still at home, Christopher did his best to be a good companion to each of them. He enjoyed doing practical things with his mother (he always enjoyed using his hands); he enjoyed helping her in the garden; later he discovered he and his mother shared a love of classical music – something that did not interest Alan at all. As a family, they never listened to music on the wireless, which Christopher regretted; in the evenings, they might sit together, listening to the news or a play on the radio. Daphne would fall asleep, while Alan and Christopher sat quietly, half-listening, half-reading their books.

When Christopher lost Nou and Alan lost Ken, each found a replacement in the other. His father now became essential to him. As Christopher put it, 'For nearly ten years I had clung to Nanny. For nearly ten more years I was to cling to him, adoring him as I had adored Nanny, so that he too became almost a part of me.' Visitors to Cotchford Farm in the 1930s, and his cousins when they saw him on holiday, noticed how the only person shy Christopher ever seemed to speak to was his father. 'We were so close,' Christopher told me, 'until I left school and beyond, until after the war, really.' Father and son had sport, nature and mathematics in common. Alan delighted in his boy as once he had delighted in his brother.

Christopher did well at his London prep school (Gibbs in Chelsea) and then as a boarder at Boxgrove, another prep school, near Guildford in Surrey. In the summer of 1934, Alan proudly reported: 'Moon left his prep school in July, being then top of the school, leader of the choir, captain of cricket and in the football XI.' He went on to Stowe, now an established English public school, but then quite young (founded in 1923), though already noted for its cricketing prowess. Christopher was not happy at Stowe. He never liked going back to boarding school:

> On the last day of the holidays, the pattern was always the same. We were back in London. My father went to the Garrick Club in the morning. I lunched alone with my mother. After lunch she read aloud to me in the drawing room. At about three o'clock, my father returned. Burnside came in for my trunk and loaded it onto the car. I changed into my school clothes and said goodbye to my mother. She never came with me. The journey to school was always with my father alone. We did *The Times* crossword, then sat silent . . . These journeys, three of them every year for nine years, were as sorrowful for me as the three annual journeys in the opposite direction (by train) were blissful.

At school, he was conscious of being 'Christopher Robin', the character from his father's famous books, and, having once rather liked it (except when what he considered an unflattering picture appeared in the press or an interviewer misquoted him), now he loathed it. He was teased by the other boys. His shyness increased; his stammer worsened. He did not share his unhappiness with his father who, in 1936, blithely wrote to tell a friend that his son was 'The most completely modest, unspoilt, enthusiastic happy darling in the world. In short, I adore him.'

Just as Alan had written regularly to his brother Ken – long, newsy letters, full of jokes – so Alan now wrote regularly to his son. He visited the boy at school whenever possible. Daphne rarely came. Alan did his best to sort out problems when he heard about them. There was a draughty classroom at Gibbs and an overcrowded changing-room at Stowe: Alan took up each matter with each school and got it sorted. He was protective of his son, caring of him, admiring of him. In short, he did indeed adore him.

And Christopher adored his father. They were 'so close' – he said it repeatedly – but reading Christopher's childhood memoir it is clear than when father and son were together, they were often silent. When Alan took Christopher back to school each term, 'We said our goodbyes while still in the car and while there was still a mile or two to go. We said them looking straight ahead. It was easier that way.'

A. A. Milne believed he had begun to say goodbye to his own father when he was twelve: 'Farewell, Papa, with your brave, shy heart and your funny little ways: with your humour and your wisdom and your never-failing goodness: from now on we shall begin to grow out of each other.' Christopher did not grow out of his father until he was in his twenties. Blue had Moon until then.

At the start of each school term, Christopher recalled, 'The goodbye I said to my father was different to the one

I had said an hour earlier to my mother. Hers was goodbye until the next holidays. His was only a partial goodbye; for part of him would be remaining with me, hovering over me, lovingly and anxiously watching me, throughout the term.' The complete goodbye did not come until later. For now, father and son were close. But between them a lot was left unsaid. The 1930s were not easy for C. R. Milne. They were not easy for A. A. Milne either. At the time, neither of them quite knew what the other was going through.

When *When We Were Very Young* was first published in 1924, the *New York Herald Tribune* had extravagantly compared A. A. Milne with Lewis Carroll, Robert Louis Stevenson and Rudyard Kipling. Kipling himself, then sixty and regarded as one of the giants of English letters, had sent Milne a fan letter at the time – probably the letter in his life Milne was most proud to have received. Milne, of course, was familiar with the most famous line in Kipling's most famous poem, 'If': 'If you can meet with Triumph and Disaster and treat those two imposters just the same . . .' 1929 was A. A. Milne's year for taking Kipling's advice seriously.

Ken's death in May 1929 was a tragedy. The death, a month later, of his friend and most reliable producer, Dot Boucicault, aged seventy, was another blow. The disaster of that summer, however, was the failure of his play *The Ivory Door*. It was a drama set in a castle about an old king and his young son: it mixed fantasy and romance, talked of love and faith, and had (at least in Milne's mind) echoes of late Shakespeare and early Ibsen. Written, pre-Pooh, in 1925, it enjoyed a healthy run in New York in 1927 (302 performances), but in London in 1929 it flopped – badly. According to Robert Whelan, the official historian of the Theatre Royal, Haymarket, 'It was such a disaster that, after reading the reviews, Horace Watson, the manager, picked up the phone and cancelled the photographer who was coming to take the production photographs. He knew it would be throwing good money after bad.' The play had survived mixed notices in New York – the *New Yorker* had called it 'a lethal combination of whimsy and lethargy' – but in London the critical reception proved fatal. '*The Ivory Door* is damned and slammed not by the public but by the critics,' Milne said, bitterly. In his introduction to the published edition of the play he highlighted the problem he felt he now faced: 'I have the Whimsical label so firmly round my own neck that I can neither escape from it nor focus it . . . it seems to me now that if I write anything less realistic, less straightforward than "The cat sat on the mat," I am indulging in a "whimsy".'

The failure of *The Ivory Door* did not stop him writing plays – there were eight more to come – but it confirmed him in his determination to write no more children's verses and no more stories about Christopher Robin and Winnie-the-Pooh. His four children's books amounted to an undoubted triumph – they brought him greater fame and a considerable fortune – and he had enjoyed their success, but enough is enough.

As J. M. Barrie told him after the success of *Mr Pim Passes By* a decade before, 'You will have a fine time now (till you get tired of it).'

He was tired of it, tired of being a children's author, weary of the kind of attention that came with it, and anxious that if he wrote more Pooh books he would run the risk of repeating himself. He wanted to do something different.

That said, in 1929 he approved *The Christopher Robin Calendar*, and in 1930 was ready to compile *The Christopher Robin Birthday Book*. He kept a beady and interested eye on the development of Pooh merchandise, turning down an invitation for Christopher Robin to endorse Wolsey underwear for boys, but agreeing to a range of Christopher Robin crockery. And in 1929–30, the public perception of him as a writer for children was consolidated with the first productions of what would prove to be one of his most enduring plays: *Toad of Toad Hall*, his adaptation of Kenneth Grahame's *The Wind in the Willows*. The play, written in 1921, pre-dated Pooh, but because it was produced post-Pooh, and with music by H. Fraser-Simson, 'the Christopher Robin composer', it was inevitable that some critics (including Milne's friend, W. A. Darlington) saw Grahame's Wild Wood and Milne's Forest as being 'only a mile or two away' from one another.

Milne was happy with the success of *Toad of Toad Hall*, but he was adamant he was not going to write anything more for children. In 1929, still smarting from the disaster of *The Ivory Door*, he wrote another play, *Michael and Mary*, which turned out to be something of a triumph, on stage and screen. The play opened in New York in December 1929 and in London in February 1930, running for 246 and 159 performances respectively. The West End cast included Margaret Scudamore (mother of Michael Redgrave and grandmother to the Redgrave theatrical dynasty) and two film stars, aged forty and thirty, in the title roles: Herbert Marshall and Edna Best, who in real life, in 1928, had divorced their first spouses to marry one another, and who went on in 1931 to star in the equally successful film version of the play.

There is very little whimsy in *Michael and Mary*. It begins as a melodrama might: Michael and Mary find a dead body in their drawing room: it is the body of the man who has been blackmailing them, the man who was once married to Mary

. . . So when Michael married Mary, some twenty years ago, was she still married to someone else? Does this mean their son, David, is illegitimate? It does – and that was a shocking thing in 1930. Even more shocking, in the play, in the third act, David forgives his parents and, as the stage direction has it, kisses 'the joined hands of Michael and Mary'. This moment – where a young man is seen kissing the hand of his father – caused a stir in the stalls (and the odd giggle in the gallery) and wide-eyed amazement from some of the critics.

Milne was not dismayed. He was amused. As he reflected in his introduction to the published edition of the play: 'David kisses "the joined hands of Michael and Mary", so that Michael's hand only gets, so to speak, half a kiss; but . . . "I mean to say, dammit, a fella, public school and all that, kissing half the hand of another fella . . ." No, I shall not apologize. I shall just congratulate the many who have stood it so well.'

Many, of course, both stood it and were touched by the moment. It is a touching play: an exploration of romance and reality, marriage and morality, and of a father's feelings towards his son, and vice versa. Essentially, it is a play about the nature, the importance and the power of love. At the end of the play, David departs with his own wife, and Michael turns to Mary and says: 'I suppose you do know, Mary, that, much as I love him, I love your little finger – your funny little finger, more than all of David.'

In Daphne's own copy of the book of the play, published in 1930, Alan wrote:

> For my darling
> from her Blue
> 'I suppose you do know – '

The year before, while he was working on the play, he had written to his father, who had asked how things were between him and Daphne. 'We have been, and are, terribly happy together,' he said. 'She is a perpetual joy to me and I think I am to her.' They had been married sixteen years. Alan was forty-six, Daphne was thirty-eight. Was he protesting too much? Was he secretly anxious that he was beginning to lose her?

Certainly, marriage was very much on his mind. Having finished *Michael and Mary*, he began work almost at once on a new novel. This was *Two People*, the novel I talked about in Chapter Seven, the novel P. G. Wodehouse said he was ready to re-read every six months, the novel all about love – young love, married love, extra-curricular love . . . This is the novel where Milne has the beautiful actress Coral Bell say at one point, 'It's terribly difficult marriage, isn't it?' – before adding, 'The really difficult thing is knowing when and how to fall *out* of love.'

To which Milne provides the proper response: 'Oh, come! There *are* people who stay in love with each other all their lives.'

'Of course,' says Coral Bell, 'and we all hope that's what our own marriage is going to be like.'

In October 1931 Alan and Daphne Milne made their first trip to America. They sailed on the famous four-funnelled Cunard liner, *Aquitania*. Daphne was excited to be going. Alan, less so. He had been invited to New York before but hadn't fancied it. This time he agreed to go, chiefly to promote *Two People*, but also to support the Charles Hopkins Theater (his loyal New York producers) who were planning to stage his latest play: *They Don't Mean Any Harm*. The play, when it happened, was a bit of a disaster, running for just fifteen performances. The novel, happily, was something of a triumph. Alan was delighted to see a book of his aimed at adults in the bestseller lists but disconcerted to find that each and every interviewer he met in New York only really wanted to talk to him about Christopher Robin and Winnie-the-Pooh.

The Milnes were given some time to themselves: Daphne went shopping on Fifth Avenue; Alan played some golf at the Westchester Country Club; they both went to the theatre, night after night. As well as dinner parties (far too many for Alan's liking), his publishers, E. P. Dutton, arranged an assortment of gatherings in honour of their celebrated British author, including a tea-time reception for four hundred guests at the Waldorf Astoria. Eleanor Roosevelt, the wife of the Governor of New York, was there. The great and the good of New York's social, literary and theatrical worlds turned out to welcome the Milnes – among them a noted American playwright both Alan and Daphne were especially pleased to see again.

Elmer Rice (1892–1967) is best remembered for his 1923 expressionist drama, *The Adding Machine*. The Milnes had met him when he came to London for the British premiere of his 1929 Pulitzer Prize-winning play about New York tenement life, *Street Scene* (later turned into an opera by Kurt Weill). Alan had liked Rice because he admired his craftsmanship and was in sympathy with his political thinking. They had talked about Rice's childhood (he was brought up in the tenements of New York), about socialism, about pacifism, about H. G. Wells. Daphne had liked Rice because he was charming – notoriously so. Married three times (divorced twice), he was not a believer in monogamy. He viewed sexual fidelity as 'a personal, pragmatic matter' and,

like H. G. Wells, had many affairs over the years. Rice liked
to think these relationships were discreet, but not furtive.
Some – like his dalliance with Dorothy Parker – were brief
flings. Others – like his relationship with Daphne Milne –
went on for years.

Elmer Rice was ten years younger than A. A. Milne and
just two years younger than Daphne. Rice was not just more
her own age, he was more outgoing, more sociable, more
exciting than AAM. (He was also a great art collector, owning
works by Picasso, Braque, Rouault, Klee and Modigliani,
among others.) Daphne met him first with Alan in London
in 1930 and next in New York in 1931. Their affair probably
began in 1932, when Daphne returned to New York without
Alan. She then went back to New York once or twice a year
for what she called 'my annual vacation from my husband'.
In October 1937, the *New York Post* reported that 'Auburn-
haired Mrs A. A. Milne' had arrived on the *Aquitania* and,
smiling, had told reporters enquiring after her husband:
'Sometimes I act as his secretary and do all sorts of tasks
for him – so he thinks I ought to have a rest from him once
a year. I'll stay a month, go to theatres – and see his producers! Still working for him, you see!'

The Milne marriage went on as ever, if not quite as before.
Daphne's relationship with Elmer Rice lasted until the beginning of the 1940s, when the Second World War made the
regular trips to New York impossible, when Daphne turned
fifty and when Elmer Rice, now forty-eight, had fallen in love
with the actress and soon-to-be film star, Betty Field, who
was twenty-four. Rice married Field in 1942 and, at least for
a while, found the 'complete emotional satisfaction in each
other' that means 'fidelity becomes a matter of course'.

As Alan knew, 'There *are* people who stay in love with

each other all their lives,' and, of course, 'we all hope that's what our own marriage is going to be like.' But life can't always be what we hope for.

After that first visit to New York in 1931, Alan never went back to America. Back in England, he formed an extra-marital friendship of his own. He first met Leonora Corbett (1908–1960) when she was twenty-two and playing the daughter in a revival of his play, *Belinda*. He got to know her properly when she was cast as one of the leads in *Other People's Lives* – the play that had flopped in New York when it was called *They Don't Mean Any Harm*. The new title did not help the play (about 'bright young things' and how cruel they can be) become much more successful in London than it had been in New York. Alan's consolation was Leonora's company for lunch. And since Daphne had set off for the first of her solo vacations from her husband in New York, there could be post-show suppers with Leonora, too. The play ran at the recently opened Arts Theatre in Great Newport Street, less than a hundred yards from three of Alan's favourite haunts: The Ivy, Sheekey's fish restaurant and the Garrick Club.

Leonara Corbett appeared in another of Milne's plays, *Sarah Simple*, another matrimonial comedy-drama, written in 1932 but not performed until it was produced at the Garrick Theatre in May 1937, in the run-up to the coronation of George VI. The play – like Milne's next, *Gentleman Unknown*, the last of his plays to be produced in the West End – got a luke-warm reception. But Leonora Corbett, as the young wife, gave what the critics seemed to regard as her customary performance: she was bright, brittle, amusing. By all accounts, she was that off-stage as well: fun to be with, good mistress material. During the Second World War she had a huge success on Broadway playing Elvira in Noël

Coward's *Blithe Spirit*. Before and after the war, she had a number of relationships (including one with a Member of Parliament that began before his marriage and went on after it) and a reputation as both a charming actress and what used to be termed 'a bit of a goer'. When she died, aged only fifty-two, in 1960, the obituarist in *The Times* deftly summed it up like this: 'She had a style of her own in elegance and gaiety, well suited to the more sophisticated comedy of the thirties. Her charm and wit were as effectively employed off the stage as on it, and she found and gave much amusement in London society and later in Paris.'

Alan Milne enjoyed dining, tête à tête, with attractive young actresses, who laughed at his jokes – it's always fun to find a new audience – and who, in turn, entertained him in their own way. Neither Alan nor Daphne let these outside relationships in any way rock their marriage, but inevitably the 'perpetual joy' Alan had told his father he and Daphne found in one another in the 1920s was no longer what it had been.

Which of the pair fell into infidelity first? The evidence, such as it is, is inconclusive.* What is established is that both affairs began at some point in 1932 – the year in which both Daphne's mother, Mabel de Sélincourt, and Alan's father, John Vine Milne, died. It may just be coincidence, of course,

---

* According to Dr Ann Thwaite, who got to know all of Ken's children when she was working on her Milne biography in the 1980s: 'The family definitely thought Daphne's infidelity with Elmer Rice came first, before Alan's with Leonora Corbett.' Dr Thwaite's main source for the contrary suggestion was 'a long conversation I had in 1988 with Fabia Drake, the actress, who was a friend of Leonora's.' I know there is nothing about either relationship in the Milne papers now in Texas, nor, I am told (I did not go through them myself) in the more than one hundred boxes of Elmer Rice material also housed at the Harry Ransom Center in Austin.

or it may be that there is something in the research that shows there is a tendency for people to embark on affairs when a parent is dying or has died, both as a means of assuaging grief and running at life and its possibilities in the face of death.

John Vine Milne, born in Clarendon, Jamaica, on 4 March 1845, died in Purley, Surrey, on 11 June 1932, aged eighty-seven. Alan was fifty; his parents had gone; Ken had gone; Barry had long been dead to him. Moon was away at school for much of the year, but he saw him whenever he could. Daphne was in the garden, or in town, or in America. He had occasional English family holidays with Moon and his sisters-in-law and their children: Daphne rarely came. In London, he had lunch at one of his clubs with some of his literary and theatrical friends – men who knew him well (but not that well), found him genial and amusing, and accepted that he wasn't a great mixer or especially interested in meeting new people. In restaurants, he dined with old friends, like Irene Vanbrugh, Dot Boucicault's widow, or new ones, like Leonora Corbett. He played golf, he watched the cricket, he smoked his pipe. And he worked.

The popularity of his plays was waning, which was frustrating, but he carried on regardless. (He wrote three plays that were never produced professionally, but were published in French's Acting Editions for amateurs to put on.) The popularity of his children's books kept growing (a million copies of them had been sold in America by 1932), but, perversely, he did not allow himself to get much satisfaction from that. As a writer, he wanted to go forward not back.

In 1933, he published a new novel, a fun one, a spoof murder mystery called *Four Days' Wonder*. It was a romcom (turned into a movie by Universal Studios in 1936), with a definite erotic charge (there is naked bathing), outrageous drug-taking actresses ('Snow in Large and Increasing Quantities'), and a blithe acceptance of adultery in the theatrical world. This is Milne at his most romantic: 'As they drove back . . . Jenny was singing. From time to time Derek's hand left the wheel and found hers, and said to hers "I love you, I love you, I love you". . . But Jenny thought of nothing. She was enfolded in a dream of happiness, and hardly knew that she was singing.'

This is Milne the realist, too: 'Mrs Waterson sighed and said nothing. She had been married for fifty years, and knew that men would always go on being children. This accounted for War and Politics and Sport, and so many things.'

War and Politics were on A. A. Milne's mind alongside murder and romance. In 1934, he published *Peace with Honour*, his passionate plea for pacifism, the book he regarded as his most important, the book his American publisher came to believe 'will have the greatest influence of any book in modern times'. If only.

In 1934, Milne believed that all war is wrong. Always. Unequivocally. By 1939, Hitler had forced him to change his mind. Six years after *Peace with Honour*, with a heavy heart, A. A. Milne published *War With Honour*, a smaller book that argued that, in certain circumstances, war is justified, when there is no alternative means of ensuring that Good conquers Evil.

As the Second World War itself began, in the autumn of 1939, he published his *Autobiography*. That was what it was called in America. In Britain, he called the book *It's Too Late Now*, not, he said, because he was full of regret, but because 'heredity and environment make the child, and the child makes the man, and the man makes the writer' and it's too late now to change any of that. 'One writes in a certain sort of way because one is a certain sort of person; one is a certain sort of person because one has led a certain sort of life.'

'This is the life,' he said. He devoted most of the book to his childhood and early years. Pooh barely gets a look-in. Ken is there on every other page. The book, published ten years after Ken's death, was dedicated to him:

1880–1929
TO THE MEMORY OF
KENNETH JOHN MILNE
WHO
BORE THE WORST OF ME
AND
MADE THE BEST OF ME

Chapter Twenty

in which Christopher Robin grows up and goes to war

The beginning of the end

J. V. Milne, Alan's father, died in June 1932, aged eighty-seven. Kenneth Grahame, Alan's friend, the author of *The Wind in the Willows*, probably Alan's favourite book, died a few weeks later, at the beginning of July 1932, aged seventy-three. Sir Owen Seaman, Alan's first boss and the man who introduced him to Daphne, died in February 1936, aged seventy-four. J. M. Barrie, Sir James Barrie OM, Alan's lifelong hero and mentor, died in June 1937, aged seventy-seven. *Peter Pan* was certainly Alan's favourite play.

In 1911, Barrie published his novel telling the story of Peter and Wendy. The novel, which Alan also loved, has a memorable opening paragraph, starting with a striking sentence and ending with a startling one. The book begins: 'All children, except one, grow up.' Children, Barrie explains, get to know they must grow up in different ways at different times. Wendy got to know when she was just two years old. She was playing in the garden and picked a flower and showed it to her mother, who looked at her little girl and cried, 'Oh, why can't you remain like this for ever!' That was the moment Wendy realized she must grow up: 'You always know after you are two. Two is the beginning of the end.'

For Alan, the beginning of the end did not begin until he

was about twelve. For Christopher Robin – the real Christopher Robin: Billy Moon, Moon, Christopher, Chris – the beginning of the end – the break with his father – did not begin until he was in his twenties.

Forty years later, in the 1980s, when he was in his sixties, Christopher told me that the rift between him and his parents did not occur until after the war – 'And was it a rift,' he wondered, 'or did I simply choose to follow a different path?'

'When do you think you began to grow up?' I asked him.

'I can give you a precise date for that,' he said. 'I've thought about it. September 3rd 1939, the day war was declared. Until then, my parents made all the decisions. They chose all the schools I went to, for better or worse. I played cricket because that was what my father wanted me to do. I went to Cambridge to study mathematics because that's what he had done. I went to Trinity, his old college. But the war changed everything. I remember I was with my father, in the sitting room at Cotchford. We were hunched together over the wireless listening as Chamberlain said, "This country is at war with Germany." We'd just been on holiday together, just the two of us, on Dartmoor, bird-watching, going for long walks, playing golf, but my father decided to cut the holiday short. He saw the war coming. He hated the idea of it. In his heart, he remained a pacifist all his life, but in his head he knew the war against Hitler had to be fought and won. He did his bit during the war, serving in the Home Guard. My mother was back from one of her trips to America. They decided to give up the house in Mallord Street and spent the war together at Cotchford Farm. I don't think they were much safer there. They were on the German flight path to London. On the way back, German bombers would drop bombs they hadn't used in the London raids on them. Several landed quite nearby. The war started and I grew up.'

Christopher arrived at Trinity College, Cambridge, in October 1939. He had rooms in Whewell's Court, as his father had done before him. In his 1979 memoir, *The Path Through the Trees*, Christopher noted: 'There are three small things that distinguish the grown-up from the boy: he can drive, he can drink, and he can smoke.' According to Christopher, while nothing was expressly forbidden to him, nothing by way of encouragement was given to him in the matter of growing up. 'My father,' he recalled, 'drove, safely, unenthusiastically, and in total ignorance of what went on under the bonnet. When on one occasion my mother asked if I, sitting next to him, was ever allowed to change gear, he said no – and the subject was dropped. But he sometimes let me hold the steering wheel while he lit his pipe.'

According to Christopher, his father drank in moderation and without much discrimination: 'He liked a glass of cherry brandy before lunch and a cocktail before dinner, and he celebrated special occasions with a bottle of hock.' Christopher discovered these weren't the drinks enjoyed by his fellow undergraduates in 1939. They drank beer. A. A. Milne did not like the taste of beer, so C. R. Milne accepted that he would not like the taste of it either. He stuck to bottled cider.

This left smoking. Alan, of course, was an inveterate pipe-smoker. Christopher recalled going for a swim with his father on one of their Dorset holidays, when having got out of the water and dressed, and being about to settle down for an idle hour on the beach, Alan felt in his pocket. 'My God!' he cried. 'I've left my pipe behind. Quick. We must go home *at once*.' According to Christopher, he set off *running*.

At Cambridge, to be different, possibly to assert his

independence, Christopher decided against a pipe. He bought himself a packet of Capstan cigarettes. He smoked about six and then gave up on the experiment, and never smoked again. Cigarettes were not to his liking. Quite quickly, he discovered that mathematics was not to his liking, either.

He completed his first year at Cambridge, took and passed the end-of-year exams and decided he would not come back for his second year. He would join the army instead. It was not as easy as he might have hoped. Because he was good at using his hands, because of his love of carpentry and things mechanical, he applied to join the Royal Engineers.

He had always resented his father's poem, 'The Engineer', which appeared in *Now We Are Six* alongside a Shepard drawing of the young Christopher Robin holding a toy train he couldn't make work. The poem ended:

It's a good sort of brake
But it hasn't worked yet

Christopher protested: 'I may have been a bit undersize. I may have been a bit underweight. I may have looked like a girl. I may have been shy. I may have been on the dim side. But if I'd had a train (and I didn't have a train), any brake that I'd wanted to make for it – any simple thing like a brake – WOULD HAVE WORKED.'

In 1940 he was so anxious to join the Sappers (the nickname for the Corps of Royal Engineers) that on the day of his medical examination he was overwhelmed by hyper-anxiety and failed it. He turned to his father for help. Alan was glad to do what he could. He wrote a few letters (one, about Christopher's need for a second medical, to Lord Horder, personal physician to the King – and H. G. Wells, among others); he pulled some strings. Alan was immensely proud of his son, proud of his academic achievement (he had won a scholarship to Cambridge), proud of his determination to serve his country.

In the first year of the Second World War, A A M made his own contribution to the war effort, both by signing up as a Local Defence Volunteer and by returning to the pages of *Punch* with a series of humorous and patriotic poems about life on the Home Front. The verses were collected in a book called *Behind the Lines*, published at the start of the London Blitz in the autumn of 1940 and dedicated to Christopher – in rhyme:

> To my affinity:
> C. R. Milne: Mathematical scholar of Trinity:
> And: By the time this appears:
> With any luck a Private in the Royal Engineers.

Thanks to his father's intervention, Christopher got a second crack at joining the Royal Engineers. At the second medical, he passed. He passed a trade test, too. At last, he received his commission and, in due course, was sent first to Kirkuk in Iraq, then on to Tunisia and eventually down into Italy. Christopher reckoned that his time in the army provided him with 'a foundation stone, strong and lasting, on which to build my adult life'. His wife, Lesley, said, 'A less warlike man than Christopher it would have been hard to find: he was gentle, sensitive, and kind.' That is certainly how he appeared to me when I knew him: you could not imagine a sweeter soul than Christopher Milne. Lesley said the Royal Engineers introduced him to the real world 'outside that highly artificial middle-class enclave within which he had been raised'. In the army, fighting overseas, he met all classes and conditions of men: 'He found a lot of good friends with whom he shared both pleasures and horrors. Nobody out there cared about Christopher Robin, in spite of Vera Lynn, "the Forces' Sweetheart" whose syrupy rendition of "Vespers" was a favourite on the radio among the troops. He was simply Chris, the young officer who swapped his cigarette ration for chocolate and could be trusted to dismantle a land mine or organize construction of a Bailey bridge under fire.'

And he did come under fire. At the beginning of October 1944, he was wounded near Sant' Arcangelo, in what is now the Province of Rimini, hit in the head by a piece of flying shrapnel. The War Office sent word to his parents at Cotchford Farm that their son had suffered 'a penetrating shell wound in the right occipital region' and was 'seriously ill'. In the 2017 film, *Goodbye Christopher Robin*, presumably to heighten the drama, you were given the impression that Christopher was reported 'missing in action, presumed dead'. Not so, but nevertheless the War Office communication caused dreadful anxiety for the Milnes, especially when a second communication arrived saying Christopher had been seriously wounded. 'We have had the hell of an anxious time,' Milne reported to his publisher, 'the news being conveyed by the W.O. in the most frightening way possible.' It turned out the wound had not been so serious after all. Alan wrote indignantly to *The Times* to complain about the way the War Office had handled the matter, causing 'unnecessary suffering' to the next-of-kin.

Throughout the war Milne wrote regularly to *The Times*. Taciturn with strangers, uncommunicative at parties, he was not shy when it came to putting his head over the parapet in print. He had definite opinions and he expressed them trenchantly. In the matter of the 'P. G. Wodehouse affair', some felt he went too far.

In 1934, 'Plum', as his friends called him (and Alan was a friend, if not a close one), having made a lot of money with his comic novels, Broadway shows and Hollywood scripts, moved to France for tax reasons; in 1940 he was taken prisoner at Le Touquet by the invading Germans and interned for nearly a year. After his release, he was given 'full freedom within Germany', placed in a Berlin hotel and persuaded to broadcast five talks from Berlin, aimed, he believed, at his many readers in the USA, and designed, he hoped, to reassure them that, though he was in Germany, he was alive and well and still amusing. 'Of course,' he admitted later, 'I ought to have had the sense to see that it was a loony thing to do to use the German radio for even the most harmless stuff, but I didn't.'

Unsurprisingly, in 1941, when the Wodehouse talks were broadcast in Britain, they provoked a storm. The Foreign Secretary (Anthony Eden), the Minister of Information (Duff Cooper), the *Daily Mirror* (among others), weighed in against him. Members of the public burnt and destroyed copies of Wodehouse's books. The talks may have been intended to be playful and apolitical, but here was a British subject (a world-famous one) talking to America (a country that had not yet joined the war) and giving the impression that these German fellows weren't that bad really. A. A. Milne joined the fray – and not on Plum's side. In a letter to the *Daily Telegraph* Milne accused his fellow humorist of being a man who, throughout his life, had shirked responsibility, who had avoided the responsibility of fatherhood, who had contrived to be safely in America during the First World War (when others had fought on the Somme), who had sought sanctuary in France to avoid paying taxes in his home country, and who was now pleading his innocence because he had 'never taken any interest in politics'. 'Irresponsibility in what the papers called "a licensed humorist" can be carried too far,' thundered Milne; 'naïveté can be carried too far. Wodehouse has been given a good deal of licence in the past, but I fancy that now his licence will be withdrawn.'

It was a profoundly personal attack and a lot of Milne's friends – who were also friends of Wodehouse – did not like it. 'Odd chap, Milne,' said Wodehouse many years later. 'There was a curious jealous streak in him which doesn't come out in his writing. I love his writing but never liked him much.'

Both Wodehouse and Milne were odd chaps in their way. They were near contemporaries, born a few months apart, who had enjoyed parallel careers. If not close friends, they had certainly been collegiate in younger days: they both wrote for *Punch*, they played cricket together, they both belonged to the Garrick Club; Milne had invested in one of Wodehouse's plays; Wodehouse was unstinting in his praise of Milne's novels. But they were different: one was politically unaware, the other was politically passionate. Was Milne jealous of Wodehouse? Possibly. Though chiefly remembered for creating Jeeves and Wooster, Wodehouse was recognized for the range of his work. Milne knew that, in the end, he was only really known for Christopher Robin and Winnie-the-Pooh. He was bitter about that.

And by the time the war ended, Christopher Robin had become bitter, too. Throughout the war he had remained close to his father, writing regular letters home and looking forward to the ones his father sent him, coming home to Cotchford whenever he was on leave, but by the end of the war, when he was in his mid-twenties, something had changed.

When, years later, I asked Christopher what it was that had changed, he said he couldn't exactly say, but he wondered tentatively – he could be quite tentative – whether it was, in part, because towards the end of the war, in Italy, in Trieste, he fell in love for the first time.

'Her name was Hedda,' he told me. 'She was a year younger than me, partly Austrian, mostly Italian.' She was studying English at the University of Venice. 'She was lovely.' She was one of a group of girls who became friendly with some of the young British officers from 221 Field Company who were stationed in Trieste. 'We were both quite shy, but we hit it off straightaway.' He laughed: 'I felt sensations with Hedda I had never known before.' He knew that he had loved Pooh and Nou, but this was different. 'We were young for our ages, and very innocent, but it was wonderful. I loved her completely and it was loving Hedda that began to set me free. She loosened the bond that had tied me to my father.'

'It didn't last, of course,' Christopher added – but it did last a couple of years. He wanted to announce their engagement. She thought, 'wisely' said Christopher, 'Better wait.' Hedda had to finish her studies in Venice; Christopher went back to Cambridge. They met for the last time in March 1947, in Venice – 'in the Piazza San Marco,' said Christopher, 'I could show you the exact spot,' – and went on to Trieste to meet her family. The visit was a happy one. 'And although when I said goodbye to her,' Christopher remembered, 'we were outwardly as confident about the future as we had ever been, I think inwardly we both wondered if we would ever meet again.'

They didn't. For another six months they continued to write to each other: 'Then, without too much heartbreak and with no ill-feeling, it came to an end.'

At the end of the war, after five years in the army, Christopher returned to Cambridge University, as was his right. He no longer wanted to read mathematics. He wanted to switch to English. Well, his father was a writer, so that was understandable. The college authorities agreed. He read English – and got a Third. He had first thought 'I want to be a writer' when he was about eight. He thought it again in Trieste when he was twenty-five. When he graduated from Cambridge, he moved to London, found himself a bed-sitter and sat at his typewriter: 'I tapped away at airy nothings, sent them off, and got them back.'

He needed to earn a living. He wanted to be a writer, but his father was a writer, and a famous one. 'C. R. Milne? Interesting name . . . Are you by any chance related to A. A. Milne? Oh my goodness, are you Christopher Robin?'

> In pessimistic moments, when I was trudging London in search of an employer wanting to make use of such talents as I could offer, it seemed to me, almost, that my father had got to where he was by climbing upon my infant shoulders, that he had filched from me my good name and had left me with nothing but the empty fame of being his son.

He tried all sorts. He got a job at the Central Office of Information, researching statistics, drafting speeches. (He had studied mathematics and English: he was qualified for the job.) It did not last. He joined the John Lewis Partnership. He was there for eighteen months, starting out in the Lampshade Department at Peter Jones in Sloane Square. He quite liked selling lampshades: 'I enjoyed the companionship of my fellow assistants: they were a cheerful, friendly lot.' He liked the practical things he learned to do at John Lewis:

'I learned how to upholster a sofa. I learned how to make slipcovers . . . I learned how to French-polish, how to make curtains, how to paint straight lines . . .'

'I was doing what I was doing,' he told me, 'because I had to do something, I needed to earn a living. I wasn't very happy. I didn't really know where my life was leading. And then I met Lesley and everything changed.'

Christopher Robin Milne met Lesley de Sélincourt on Thursday 5 February 1948, at seven o'clock in the evening. Christopher was twenty-seven, Lesley was twenty-two. They might have met long before: they were first cousins, after all. But Christopher's mother, Daphne, had never liked her younger brother, Aubrey, despised Aubrey's wife, Irene, and had never taken any interest in her brother's daughters, Lesley and her older sister, Anne. Daphne had barely spoken to her brother in thirty years.

Christopher got to meet Lesley because their joint grand-father, Martin de Sélincourt, had a younger, second wife called Nancy, and Nancy thought it might be nice for the young cousins to get to know one another. It might help heal the family rift.

Nancy gave Christopher Lesley's address. He was living alone in a small flat on Chancery Lane. Lesley was sharing with a girlfriend in Claverton Street in Pimlico, working in the showroom at the Cambridge University Press. He invited her for supper. She came: 'We had dried-egg omelette and chips. I made the omelette. She made the chips.' They met again a week later, on Thursday 12 February, when she made him supper in Claverton Street. On Sunday 15 February they went to Kew Gardens for the day. On Monday the six-teenth, they went to a play. On Thursday the nineteenth, they met for lunch. (Christopher noted all this in his pocket diary. He showed it to me. It was an Italian pocket diary – a present from Hedda.)

For Friday 19 March, the diary entry read: 'W'loo Platform 7, 6.15.' This was Christopher's first visit to the Isle of Wight, to meet Lesley's parents: 'My first meeting with Uncle Aubrey.' On Sunday 11 April he wrote in the diary: 'Got engaged!'

The wedding took place in London, on Saturday 24 July 1948, at Holy Trinity, Brompton, a stone's throw from Harrods, with a reception afterwards at Brown's Hotel in Albermarle Street, off Piccadilly – where Alan and Daphne liked to stay after they had sold their house in Mallord Street. It was quite a grand affair and quite a family gathering: so many brothers and sisters, so many cousins and aunts. Uncle Ken, of course, had died in 1929, but Ken's son, Tony, was there as Christopher's best man. The question of whether or not to invite Uncle Barry did not arise because Barry had conveniently died six years before, in 1942, aged sixty-three.

Aubrey and Irene, Daphne and Alan, as parents of the bride and groom, were there and did their best to remain civil through the day. It was the first time Aubrey and Daphne, brother and sister, had been in the same room together for many years – and it would be the last. Barry had hoped for a reconciliation with Alan before he died. Alan was not interested. Years later, in 1962, when Aubrey was dying of cancer, he wrote to Daphne looking for a reconciliation. She looked the other way.

Alan never lost his fondness for Barry's widow, Connie, and her children. He never lost his love for Ken and Maud and their children. Those deep affections stayed with him to the end. But in the final ten years of his life, gradually but definitively, he lost the love of his own son: Blue lost Moon.

A week or two before Christopher and Lesley announced their engagement, Alan wrote to Ken's widow, Maud, as he often did, bringing her up to date with family news. Moon had been to stay with his parents at Cotchford Farm: 'He is (apparently) in love again, and "thinking of 'er" all the time. We see little of him save at meals, and get nothing from him then except an affirmative, negative or non-committal grunt (it is difficult to distinguish between them) in answer to a direct question.' Was this delayed adolescence? Christopher was twenty-seven. What was going on? Alan did not pretend to understand. 'All very trying,' he concluded, 'but I suppose it will pass.'

It didn't. Hedda had loosened the bonds between Christopher and his father. Now Lesley severed them. Alan could not bring himself to like his daughter-in-law. She was not Anne Darlington. Worse, she was Aubrey's daughter. Worst of all, she and Christopher were first cousins. Alan believed it would be a dangerous match.*

From the time of their wedding, Christopher and Lesley saw less and less of Alan and Daphne. After Alan's death in 1956, they did not see Daphne at all. In 1951, Christopher and Lesley left London. 'London was the scene of my

---

* According to Alison Shaw, professor of social anthropology at Oxford University, the child of first cousins carries approximately double the risk of inheriting a serious disorder than the child of unrelated people. Health consequences can include: recessive disorders such as Tay-Sachs, cerebral palsy and cystic fibrosis; an increased susceptibility to cancer and infectious pathogens such as hepatitis; birth defects including facial clefts and cardiovascular conditions; an increased risk of many illnesses, including schizophrenia and Alzheimer's; and higher infant mortality. First-cousin marriage is illegal in some countries (and in thirty out of fifty states in the USA), but has been allowed in Britain since 1540. In 2024, at Westminster, Richard Holden MP introduced a Private Member's Bill to prohibit the marriage of first cousins.

father's successes,' said Christopher, by way of explanation, 'London was the scene of my failures.' They moved to Dartmouth in Devon and opened a bookshop. As Christopher recalled, Daphne was amazed:

'I would have thought,' said my mother, who always hit the nail on the head no matter whose fingers were in the way, 'I would have thought that this was the one thing you would have absolutely hated. I thought you didn't like "business". You certainly didn't get on at John Lewis. And you're going to have to meet Pooh fans all the time. Really it does seem a very odd decision.'

But it worked, and for Christopher and Lesley, for thirty years, it worked wonderfully well. Yes, Pooh fans did make their way to the Harbour Bookshop and, if they wanted, Christopher signed copies of his father's books for them – and did so with a good grace, in return for a small donation to a local charity.

Lesley loved Christopher: she had no time for Christopher Robin – or Winnie-the-Pooh. When I asked Lesley what she felt about her parents-in-law now, she said crisply: 'I didn't like them. They weren't likeable. It's as simple as that.' How did she find Alan? 'Cold, closed, ungiving.' And Daphne? 'She loved London and New York,' replied Lesley tartly, as though nothing more need be said. Then she added: 'She was flighty, very actressy and superficial. She laughed a lot.'

Perhaps Lesley's antipathy has made me more sympathetic to Daphne. Looking through the boxes in Texas, and listening to the tapes from the 1970s of conversations Ann Thwaite had with people who had known her, the verdict is mixed. Some perceived her very much as Lesley did; others liked her, thought her stylish, found her good company, lively and amusing.

What is clear is that, after the war, as Daphne and Alan lost Christopher, they found one another again. At home, at Cotchford, they were comfortable together: she had her garden, he had his pipe. Once a week she would go to London to do some shopping and have lunch with friends. Once a week, on a different day, he would go to London to have lunch at his club. Occasionally, they would go together to catch a play and stay the night at Brown's. To the end, she never criticized his work: she only offered praise. To the end, she laughed at his jokes.

Chapter Twenty-one

in which we lose Alan and we meet Clare

The honeypot at the end of the rainbow

In 1946, A. A. Milne published his last contribution to *Punch*. It was a tribute in verse to his wife Daphne's dog, a young cocker spaniel bitch who had been killed running out into the road near Cotchford Farm:

> She was yours to guard and love . . . While she's weeding,
>   there you sit,
> In your mouth, a garden glove
> 'Just in case she's needing it.'

Also in 1946, Milne published his last novel, *Chloe Marr*. It's the story of an actress – 'The Beautiful and Notorious Miss Marr' – and of the unhappy men who want and woo her. Chloe is perfection. She has a cocker bitch and she always understands your jokes:

> That was what was so wonderful about Chloe. She never let you down. There was no flaw in her body, no flaw in her mind. Think of all those girls one met in May week. All looking very pretty and well dressed; all gay and charming; and then you sit close up to one and talk to her, and it's all no good. Something's wrong. She was

341

right from the front, and now she reminds you horribly of somebody else; or there's a bit of superfluous hair about; or there's a spot coming on the corner of her mouth; or she's perspiring; or her hands are ugly; or you try one of the three best jokes in the world on her, and she laughs mechanically. Something. But you were safe with Chloe. No matter how close you were to her, she would never let you down.

Of course, Chloe is unattainable. It's a muddle of a world. Life isn't easy. Love is complicated. Women! At least there's always a pipe . . . and cricket . . . and work . . .

He touched her cheek with his lips, and said, 'Here's your drink,' thinking, the only thing that matters in the world is one's work. Thank God I've got some work to do.

None of the men who love Chloe can pin her down, and the wisest of them accept the fact:

It's a muddle of a world, but I like living in it. I even like being unhappy, it's all part of the muddle, part of the plan, I suppose you must call it. I like being outside my unhappiness and looking at it. What a muddle I've made of my life. How interesting to look at it, and think what a muddle I've made of it.

On both sides of the Atlantic, *Chloe Marr* was a critical and commercial success. Milne was happy with that – though, beyond the 1920s, he never seemed wholly happy with anything in his life. 'Like all happy men,' he wrote of one of his characters in *Chloe Marr*, 'he would lie awake at night sometimes, imagining that disaster had fallen on him. Only one real disaster could fall; he might lose his son.'

By the end of the 1940s, Blue had lost Moon for good. As Christopher and Lesley Milne set out on their new and separate life in Devon, Alan and Daphne Milne went on with theirs, much as before, two hundred miles away, in Sussex. Alan's final novel, *Chloe Marr*, was financially rewarding; though his plays were no longer being produced in the West End or on Broadway, they were still popping up in the provinces and providing a tidy sum with the royalties from amateur productions; his principal income, of course, continued to derive from the worldwide success of his four small children's books.

On 18 January 1952, Alan reached his biblical three score years and ten. In June, he published his last book: *Year In, Year Out*. It was a collection of essays on quite unconnected topics presented across the twelve months of the year – everything from a study of the railway timetables featured in *The Importance of Being Earnest* to his thoughts about gardening, novel-writing and the personality of George Bernard Shaw. The critics liked it. The *New York Times* called it 'delightfully surprising, witty and graceful'. The book was reflective and autobiographical:

> Some years ago an actor friend of ours, who had disappeared from our lives by retiring into Devonshire, surprised us with a letter. It began:
>
> 'I am seventy today. It is an extraordinary age for a young man to be.'
>
> By the time this book appears I shall be seventy; and I feel as bewildered as he was. It is indeed an extraordinary age to be: an age at which, without conscious effort, one should be clothed with dignity and authority; and here am I, invested with neither.

In truth, he was invested with fame and fortune – his birthday was featured in magazines and newspapers around the world – and with the affection of many: grateful readers, fond sisters-in-law, nephews, nieces, Tasker the gardener and his wife, old friends. Of course, as time went by, there were fewer old friends: E. V. Lucas died in 1938; Charles Turley Smith in 1940; H. Fraser-Simson in 1944; H. G. Wells in 1946; Irene Vanbrugh in 1949. Happily, Frank Swinnerton and W. A. Darlington were still alive, and still in touch. But his world was shrinking and his health was deteriorating, and he was conscious of both.

On 15 October 1952, not long after *Year In, Year Out* was published in New York, Daphne wrote to Ken's widow, Maud:

> Share most terrible news. My darling Alan is very very seriously ill and was taken last night to East Grinstead Hospital in an ambulance. He had a stroke.
>
> I have just come back from the Hospital and he is expected to live two or three days perhaps.
>
> It was so frightfully sudden. I still find it impossible to believe.
>
> My love to you,
>
> Daff

Alan survived. In the event, he lived more than three more years, but they were not happy ones. He could still read and write and talk, but everything was a struggle. In December he had an operation on his brain. 'I think it made matters worse,' Christopher told me, 'It affected his personality. It made him cantankerous and irritable. It brought out the worst in him.' Christopher saw his father only twice during those three years. 'We had said goodbye long ago.' Alan knew it, too. In a letter to Maud he wrote, 'I lost him years ago, but I still have Daff. Thank God, though I give her a rotten time.'

Discharged from hospital, Alan was confined to a wheelchair and, back at home, looked after by a succession of male nurses. He got on better with some of them than others. Daphne did her best. At least there were no money worries and there were always people in the house, so once a week, and sometimes more often, she could go to London for lunch – or tea at the Ritz – and a bit of shopping. To the end of her life, she treated herself to a new wardrobe every spring and every autumn.

Alan made his last visit to London in February 1954, soon after his seventy-second birthday. According to *The Times* (he was still newsworthy), he was brought by ambulance from Cotchford Farm to Brown's Hotel in Albermarle Street:

> Mr Milne in 1952 underwent a severe operation on the brain; he has since been partly paralysed and unable to walk. This year he wished to repeat for his friends the party he used to give annually. Mr Milne received the guests in a chair and was later driven back to his home in Hartfield, Sussex.

He died on Tuesday 31 January 1956, a fortnight after his seventy-fourth birthday. His body was cremated at Downs Crematorium in Brighton and his ashes scattered in the Upper Memorial Gardens there. Ten days later there was a memorial service in London at All Hallows-by-the-Tower. The theatre was represented by the actor Nicholas Hannen, a friend and contemporary of Milne's, who had appeared in the original London production of *The Dover Road* in 1922. Hannen read the famous passage from the Book of Ecclesiasticus: 'Let us now praise famous men, and our fathers that begat us.' Christopher told me that he liked that reading because JV had been so important to his father. *Punch* was represented by the cartoonist Fougasse (real name: Kenneth Bird) who had first contributed to the magazine in 1916 and became its editor in the late 1940s. He read another famous passage, from St Matthew's Gospel: 'Suffer little children, and forbid them not, to come unto me: for of such is the kingdom of heaven.' Christopher was less comfortable with that. 'My father was anything but sentimental when it came to children,' he said.

> How sweet to be a Cloud
> Floating in the Blue!
> It makes him very proud
> To be a little cloud.
>
> *Winnie-the-Pooh*

Finally, Norman Shelley, celebrated for playing Winnie-the-Pooh in BBC radio adaptations of the stories, sang Pooh's song 'How Sweet to Be a Cloud' and then, to a sonorous organ accompaniment, recited 'Vespers'. 'Well,' sighed Christopher, 'you can imagine how I felt about that – and what my father would have felt about it, too. It was all my mother's choosing. I wasn't involved at all.'

Daphne lived another fifteen years. She died in London on 22 March 1971, aged eighty-one. After his father's memorial service on 10 February 1956, Christopher never saw his mother again.

Lesley Milne did not attend her father-in-law's memorial service. She had a good excuse: she was pregnant. But the truth was, of course: she did not wish to be there. She did not like her father-in-law. Christopher was in attendance, he said, 'almost as a matter of form'. To him his father was 'already dead'. The brain operation designed to save him had made him 'a different person'. Christopher said, 'It had made my mother a different person too. And it had made Cotchford a different place.'

When Daphne died in 1971, for Christopher 'There was little sadness, little sense of bereavement. How could there be?' He had not seen his mother in fifteen years and they had barely written to one another since his father's death. When he learned that she had sold Cotchford and disposed of all his father's papers and possessions (his golf clubs, his pipes, his books), he felt 'a sudden surge of anger and a stab of sorrow. My poor father, that she should have treated him like this!'

He knew that in due course he would inherit part of his father's estate – but he did not want the money. He valued his independence. He was a bookseller now: he could earn his own living. He did not need 'a free ride' from his father: 'I didn't welcome the offer of a lift. No, thank you. I prefer to walk.' In time, he came to think differently. In time, he came to understand why his mother had acted as she did: she could not live in the past, she had to move on. In time, too, he was grateful for his father's money. He needed it – for Clare.

Clare Milne, Christopher and Lesley's only child, was born in 1956, a few months after Alan's death. 'The one question we always used to dread,' said Christopher, 'was "And do you have any children?" In the early days I became adept at steering the conversation onto safer ground. Now I find it better to make the matter quite plain from the start: it saves later embarrassment. "Yes, a daughter. She has cerebral palsy." There follows a momentary pause; then "Oh . . . I'm sorry to hear that." And then, after a few more words, we move to another subject.'

When I knew Christopher Milne in the 1980s the subject that he seemed happiest to talk about was Clare. He said that his daughter had taught him 'a philosophy that parents don't usually expect to learn from their children' and he was forever grateful for it. 'Once we had accepted Clare's disability,' he said, 'there were plenty of other things we could be happy about, plenty to enjoy, plenty to be grateful for. And at the top of the list was her own very evident zest for life, her high spirits, her sense of fun, her cheerful acceptance of all she couldn't do, her delight in what little she could. She set us an example. We tend to think that, if someone is deprived of a blessing that we ourselves possess, their life is sadder. But in fact the man who has less than his neighbour is only unhappy if he had been hoping for more and chooses to feel jealous.'

Christopher told me that his chief delight in life – greater by far than any satisfaction he derived from his own successful writing (four widely acclaimed books published in the 1970s and 80s) or any pleasure he got from his hobby of studying insects and caterpillars and weeds – had been using his hands to adapt and make everyday things for Clare: a chair, a tricycle, an unbreakable plate, a fork and spoon, a special egg whisk to help her make a cake. He had a fantasy that one day they might launch a business together: 'C. R. Milne & Daughter – Makers of Furniture for the Disabled'.

Christopher and Lesley Milne loved their daughter and, on their own resources, would have struggled to give her the support and care she needed. Thanks to Winnie-the-Pooh, they did not have to.

As we know, on 6 January 1930, the American cartoonist and licensing entrepreneur Stephen Slesinger had acquired US and Canadian merchandising, television, recording and other trade rights in Milne's children's books for an advance of a thousand dollars against sixty-six per cent of Slesinger's revenue. Slesinger marketed Pooh & Co successfully for more than thirty years,* and after his death in 1953, his widow, Shirley, continued to develop the Pooh brand. Walt Disney (1901–66) had shown interest in Pooh as far back as 1938, but did not pursue Pooh seriously until 1961 when Walt Disney Productions acquired full film rights from Daphne Milne and merchandising rights from Shirley Slesinger.†

Walt Disney took personal charge of the Pooh project, changed the look of Pooh, gave him an American accent, and dropped the hyphens from his name. Pooh's appearance became more Slesinger than Shepard. The voice of Pooh had no echoes of Norman Shelley, celebrated as much for recreating the wartime speeches of Winston Churchill as for

---

* Slesinger, as an artist himself, added his own touch to Pooh in 1932 when the stories were published with illustrations in colour for the first time. Slesinger gave Pooh a red shirt to wear. In the US – with *A. A. Milne's Winnie-the-Pooh* board game launched by Parker Brothers in 1933; the plush toy Poohs designed by Agnes Brush in the 1940s; and the Disney version of Pooh from the 1960s onwards – the red shirt became a permanent feature of the Pooh 'look'.

† Later, in the 1990s, Slesinger embarked on a lengthy legal battle with Disney over allegedly under-reported royalty revenue. Private detectives were hired to sort through Disney's waste paper as Slesinger alleged the company had destroyed thousands of documents. Shirley Slesinger died in 2007, aged eighty-four. The case was finally settled in 2009, with the Slesinger company denied the $2 billion in damages they had been looking for.

being Pooh on the wireless. Disney chose one of his favourite voice actors for the part of Pooh: Sterling Holloway, who
had started his Disney career playing Mr Stork in *Dumbo* and
whose finest hour was as Kaa in *The Jungle Book*.*

The first of the Disney animations, 'a featurette', *Winnie
the Pooh and the Honey Tree*, appeared in 1966, not long
before Walt died. Ernest Shepard was appalled by it: 'It's a
travesty,' was his verdict. Christopher Milne was similarly
dismayed. But audiences, especially in America and Japan,
were charmed. More short films followed (initially based on
the original Milne stories), then feature-length films, then
several TV series, then video games, then computer games
– and the rest, including Pooh characters on parade in the
Disney theme parks, theatre shows and, eventually, a musical.

In *Winnie the Pooh and the Honey Tree*, Disney added
a new character to the cast: a friendly, folksy, all-American
gopher, a well-meaning burrowing rodent, helpfully called
Gopher. Sibilant consonants are his vocal trademark: he
whistles as he speaks. 'I'm not in the book, you know!' he
explains when he first appears. The plan was to replace
Piglet with Gopher, but happily Piglet survived the Disney
development process and Gopher became an occasional guest
player rather than one of the stars of the show. In the 1980s,
he did not feature in the Disney Channel live-action life-
size-puppet series *Welcome to Pooh Corner*, in which actors
played the characters in animal costumes (with the exception

---

* Sterling Holloway voiced Pooh for Disney for more than ten years. He was
succeeded, first, by Hal Smith, formerly the voice of Owl, and then by
Jim Cummings, who played Pooh, and Tigger too, in assorted Pooh TV
series, films and video games from 1988 up to, and including, the 2018 live-
action-and-animation Disney movie *Christopher Robin*, which starred Ewan
McGregor in the title role.

of Roo, portrayed by a glove puppet), but he was back in cartoon form in the 1990s and 2000s in such television specials as *A Winnie the Pooh Thanksgiving*, *Winnie the Pooh: A Valentine for You* and, for Hallowe'en, *Winnie the Pooh: Boo to You Too!*

Disney exploited the Pooh brand every which way they could, but aimed, they claimed, to stay true to the characteristics of Milne's original characters and to the endearing ethos of the original books. That they succeeded, after a fashion, is evidenced by the number of 'quotes' from Disney versions of Pooh that are attributed to A. A. Milne on quotation websites around the world, from Goodreads to BrainyQuote. For example, in 2025 the most popular 'Pooh quote' appearing on the internet is this: 'You are braver than you believe, you are stronger than you seem, and you are smarter than you think.' Everywhere the line is incorrectly ascribed to A. A. Milne. In fact, the line made its first appearance in the Disney movie *Pooh's Grand Adventure: The Search for Christopher Robin* in 1997, so the credit belongs not to Milne but to the film's screenwriters, Karl Geurs and Carter Crocker.

On 11 April 2006, Winnie the Pooh was honoured with a star on the Hollywood Walk of Fame, the fourth Disney character to receive one, following Mickey Mouse, Snow White and Donald Duck. According to the show-business newspaper *Variety*, ninety years after A. A. Milne first published *Winnie-the-Pooh*, Winnie the Pooh had become the third bestselling franchise in the world, after Disney's own Disney Princess and Star Wars. Pooh was generating *billions* – $5.5 billion in global merchandising sales in the mid-2010s according to the *New York Times*.

When A. A. Milne died in 1956 his literary estate, you will remember, was divided four ways: a quarter each going to his family, his old school (Westminster), his club (the Garrick) and the Royal Literary Fund. When Daphne died in 1971, Christopher did not want to inherit anything for himself: 'To take money from my fictional self would have been the final insult.' But Christopher and Lesley needed to think about Clare's future so, in the early 1980s, they sold half their share in the Milne Estate to the Royal Literary Fund for £150,000 and used the other half to set up a trust to benefit Clare.

That meant that twenty years later, in 2001, when Disney came along with $350 million to secure their rights in Pooh until 2026 – the date when Milne's copyright would expire seventy years after his death – Clare's trust got a chunk worth many millions, but Christopher's widow got nothing. How did she feel? The world wanted to know. Lesley was disinclined to tell them.

I was working for the *Sunday Telegraph* at the time. Because he knew I knew the family, my editor insisted I call her.

'I have just got rid of the *Daily Mail*,' Lesley informed me with some satisfaction. 'I don't read the *Daily Mail*. I particularly dislike the *Daily Mail*.' There was a pause. 'Who are you writing your piece for?' she asked.

'The *Sunday Telegraph*,' I murmured, feeling I was offering the ultimate reassurance.

'That's no better,' she snapped. 'I am a lifelong *Guardian* reader. So was Christopher.'

'Talk to me anyway,' I said. 'Look on it as missionary work.'

She laughed. It was a small, throaty chuckle, cynical but warm. She talked to me, I think, both because I had known Christopher and, more so, because she wanted to set the record straight. 'I am being portrayed as some sort of penniless widow who has been left out of the will,' she said. 'It's ridiculous.'

'About twenty years ago,' she explained, 'we decided to sell half of our share to the Royal Literary Fund.'

'For just £150,000?'

'Yes, that was what it was worth at the time.'

'But now it's worth thirty million. You must regret that?'

'Not for a moment.' She took a deep breath and repeated the phrase distinctly, 'Not for a moment.' She wanted me to understand that there are still some people in this world for whom money isn't everything. 'I am entirely comfortable. When we were first married we were hard up, we had to count the pennies then, but now I've got everything I could possibly want. Please make that quite clear.'

'I will,' I promised.

'The other half of our share was put in trust for Clare.'

'How is Clare?' I asked.

'Clare is very well, thank you.' Clare was forty-four then. 'She's cared for in a home now. She has been for years. She is beautifully looked after.' Lesley sensed I wanted more. 'Clare is lovely,' she went on. 'Clare is happy. She comes to visit me regularly. She likes nice clothes. She loves shopping. And she likes good food. And wine. She particularly enjoys wine.'

Clare, of course, could have had anything she wanted. Her annual income from assorted royalties was around £500,000 and the final Disney windfall was going to net her £30 million. 'What does Clare think of all this money that's coming to her?' I asked.

'She's rather vague about that sort of thing,' said her mother. 'She doesn't know the difference between £1,000 and £1,000,000.

'That's rather nice, don't you think? I think that's very nice, really very nice.'

We talked about families and how odd they can be. I told Lesley about two of my sisters who did not speak to one another for more than forty years. (I am still not sure what it was all about, but I do know these things can run in families. One of those sisters and her daughter did not speak to each other for years either.) Alan loved his brother Ken, but despised his brother Barry. Lesley's father and Christopher's mother, brother and sister, Aubrey and Daphne, hadn't spoken to one another for thirty years. 'Mine was a very peculiar family,' said Lesley in a matter-of-fact way. 'They were cut out of my grandfather's will because they wouldn't go into the family business. They were deprived of all their money. There was lots of falling out, lots of rows and long silences. My father became a teacher. He was lovely. My aunt wasn't, of course.'

I did not argue with Lesley about Daphne. She had known her and I hadn't. She was not going to change her mind.

Just before I said goodbye, Lesley said: 'Have I told you the news?'

'No. What? Tell me.'

'We are going to create a special charity to help disabled people. It will be called The Clare Milne Trust. It will be launched this autumn. Isn't that marvellous? What do you think?'

I told her I did think it was marvellous. I still do: the Disney mega-millions surplus to Clare's care requirements went in their entirety into a fund to help others with physical and mental disabilities. 'A happy ending to the story,' I said, 'a honeypot at the end of the rainbow.' Lesley gave a brittle laugh and I left her – with her telephone answering machine back on and her front door firmly shut: a clear-eyed widow who spoke her mind, who enjoyed her garden, and her glass of wine, who wanted neither fame nor fortune, who certainly didn't want her photo in the paper ('thank you very much') or another penny in the bank, who remembered her husband for who he was and not what he was called, who loved her daughter for what she was and not what she might have been.

Clare Milne died on 27 October 2012. She was fifty-six. Her mother died two years later, on 3 October 2014, aged eighty-nine.

In 2026, a century after the publication of *Winnie-the-Pooh*, The Clare Milne Trust is thriving. To date, the Trust has given away well over £12 million to help enhance the everyday lives of people with disabilities. 'My dream,' said Lesley, 'is to know that my girl will be remembered for something that brings happiness where it is most needed.'

Chapter Twenty-two

in which we look for a happy ending

There's always Pooh

21 May 2025: Brown's Hotel, Albermarle Street, London SW1

They're changing guard at Buckingham Palace – right now, as I am writing this. Today it's the Coldstream Guards who are on parade (Number 7 Company), with musical support from the Band of the Scots Guards and the Band and Bugles of The Rifles. Impressive stuff. I have just walked from the Palace across Green Park to Albermarle Street. I was at Buckingham Palace seeing the Queen. The King was there, too. I didn't see him: he was much too busy a-signing things.

I was meeting Queen Camilla to talk about the Queen's Reading Room. She loves books. I know she would love to welcome Christopher Robin's own Winnie-the-Pooh to Windsor Castle for a holiday in 2026 – to mark his centenary, and Elizabeth II's centenary, and the 250th anniversary of American independence. But I'm not sure it's going to happen. I took my friends from the New York Public Library to Windsor a few weeks ago and I think they were impressed by where he would be put on show – probably the Waterloo Chamber, a huge room dedicated to the defeat of the Emperor Napoleon at the Battle of Waterloo in 1815.

(When Queen Elizabeth II hosted a dinner there in 2004 to celebrate the centenary of the Entente Cordiale, with the French President, Jacques Chirac as guest of honour, the Waterloo Chamber was renamed the Music Room – for one night only.) It is the room where the Knights and Ladies of the Garter, the members of England's oldest and most senior order of chivalry, gather for their annual lunch. The problem is Pooh is very precious to the New York Public Library – he's their principal attraction – and while he's in England, they would like something to put in his place in New York. I think they really do want a royal crown or the Magna Carta and I am not sure how realistic that is.

> By the time it came to the edge of the Forest, the stream had grown up, so that it was almost a river, and being grown-up, it did not run and jump and sparkle along as it used to do when it was younger, but moved more slowly. For it knew now where it was going, and it said to itself, "There is no hurry. We shall get there some day."
>
> *The House at Pooh Corner*

There is no hurry. We shall get there someday. And if we don't, does it matter? When Christopher Robin was sent away to boarding school, Pooh and the other toys stayed in the nursery in Mallord Street. A glass case was made for them and it was fixed to the nursery wall. 'And there they lived,' said Christopher, 'sometimes glanced at, mostly forgotten, until the war came.' After the war, when Alan packed them off to America, Christopher was content to see them go.

They have been back home for a couple of visits over the years, once for Pooh's fiftieth birthday in 1976, and, before that, in 1969, to mark E. H. Shepard's ninetieth birthday. On that visit, the BBC took Christopher's nanny, Olive Brock-well, to see them. Nou, now seventy-four, thought the toys looked well. Pooh had a lot of bumps on his nose: 'He had so many tumbles from the ottoman,' she explained. And Roo was missing. He had been missing for years. 'We took him out one day to the apple orchard along the lane,' she said, 'and we lost him. When we came back, he wasn't there.'

Some people believe that Roo was never lost. They say that, with Moon's permission, Nou took Roo with her when Christopher went away to boarding school and she went away to get married. She did not take Roo as a sentimental souvenir. She took him with a purpose: so she could give him to another special little boy one day and make him as happy as Christopher Robin had been. It's a lovely idea, but there is no evidence to back it up. Roo was lost, Pooh's nose took a pummelling and Piglet looked a bit battered, too. According to Christopher, 'Piglet's face was a funny shape where a dog had bitten him.'

Christopher's toys inspired the stories, but the model for the drawings of Christopher Robin's teddy bear wasn't Moon's Pooh, but E. H. Shepard's son Graham's bear, Growler. What happened to Growler? 'He was passed on to my grand-daughter, Minette,' Shepard told my friend and fellow Pooh-enthusiast Brian Sibley, 'a little worse for wear, but still the Best Bear in the World. Minette took him to Canada during the war, and poor Growler came to an untimely end, worried to bits by a Scottie dog in a Montreal garden.'

E. H. Shepard died in 1976, aged ninety-six. Olive Brock-well died in 1978, aged eighty-three. In 1964, seven years before she died in 1971, Daphne Milne sold Cotchford Farm and moved to London. Christopher remembered the garden at Cotchford best – his mother's garden: 'The penstemons, the bergamots, the phloxes, the heleniums, the rudbeckias, the dahlias, and even the solitary coreopsis that had seeded itself so cleverly in the paving stones by the sundial . . .' He remembered the sunshine of his boyhood at Cotchford Farm, with Nou in the 1920s and Blue in the 1930s. In the 1950s, when Christopher had gone to Devon with Lesley, and Alan and Daphne were at Cotchford alone, the garden was still beautiful, but the house – according to those who knew it then – had become 'cold, dead, lifeless, meticulously kept, run by the staff.'

In 1968, Cotchford Farm became the home of Brian Jones, the singer-guitarist founder of the Rolling Stones. The following year, at around midnight on the night of 2–3 July 1969, Jones was discovered motionless at the bottom of the swimming pool that had been built at the side of the farmhouse. His Swedish girlfriend Anna Wohlin was convinced he was alive when he was taken out of the pool, insisting he still had a pulse. When he reached the hospital, he was pronounced 'dead on arrival'. Some thought (some still think) he was murdered. The coroner's verdict was less dramatic: drowning, 'death by misadventure', with a mention of the fact that the victim's liver and heart were greatly enlarged by past drug and alcohol abuse.

I had thought of finishing my book at Cotchford Farm. It is available to let nowadays.* It is a comfortable house (with

---

* Cotchfarm.com: 'A Symphony of Natural Splendour and Historical Charm – Cotchford Farm promises a tranquil retreat replete with all the modern comforts nestled in nature's embrace. This 16th century farmhouse has been lovingly restored seamlessly melding the charm of the past with the comfort of the present. With six meticulously curated bedrooms, three elegant reception rooms, a cosy family farmhouse kitchen, and enchanting gardens with

a lovely garden), but it has been refurbished and lived in by many others, besides Brian Jones, since Milne died in 1956. I can picture Alan in the garden still, but I don't think you feel his presence any longer in the house. Perhaps I should end the book here, where I am now, writing this, at Brown's Hotel in Albermarle Street, off Piccadilly. He liked the hotel because of its literary associations. Kipling, Mark Twain and Joseph Conrad stayed here. This is where A. A. Milne made his last appearance in public in February 1954. He would like you to remember his work in the round, as a playwright and novelist, as a humorist and essayist, as well as a children's author.

By all accounts, he cut a sad figure on that final outing, sitting in his wheelchair in the corner of the room where I am sitting with my notebook now. 'Not my A. A. M. any more,' said Ken's daughter, Angela, seeing him then, old and ill and unhappy. Somerset Maugham, a near-contemporary and a rival playwright, became a Companion of Honour in 1954. No honours came Milne's way during his lifetime.

This is a story full of regrets ('It's too late now') and sadnesses: Alan's break with his brother, Barry; Daphne's break with her brother, Aubrey; Christopher's break with both of his parents; Lesley never accepted by either of her parents-in-law and never able to accept them; Clare, their only grandchild, not known by Alan, not acknowledged by Daphne. For Alan, of course, the greatest sadness, the deepest loss, came with the death of Ken in 1929.

---

wildflower meadows, this estate is a sanctuary of tranquillity on the edge of Ashdown Forest. Indulge in a game of tennis, stroll to Pooh Sticks Bridge and the Hundred Acre Wood, or take a dip in the swimming pool.'

I have just realized – just this very minute realized – that today, the day on which I happen to be writing this, is 21 May, the day on which Ken died. I do not think that Alan was ever wholly happy again after the death of his beloved brother.

'But you'll need a happy ending, won't you?' Christopher said to me.

'Yes,' I said. 'But I also want the truth.'

'You can have a happy ending,' said Christopher. 'That's not a problem.'

This was in the mid-1980s and Christopher was not talking about this book, of course. He was talking about *Now We Are Sixty*, the play about his father that I was writing with Julian Slade. When I knew Christopher, during the last fifteen years of his life, the pain and anger he had once felt had eased and dissipated. He had made his peace with Pooh. As he said, the writing of his own book about his family and childhood – and its reception when it was published in 1974 – had combined to lift him 'from under the shadow of my father and of Christopher Robin, and to my surprise and pleasure, I found myself standing beside them in the sunshine able to look them both in the eye.' The stammer that had bedevilled him for much of his life all but disappeared. In 1979, he cut the ribbon at the official opening of the newly restored Poohsticks Bridge and unveiled a memorial to his father and E. H. Shepard on a mound in a clearing in Ashdown Forest. In 1981, he unveiled a bronze statue of the original Winnie as a bear cub at London Zoo. In 1986, he came to a talk I gave in Chelsea about his father and his family and, very kindly, said to me afterwards: 'You seem to understand it all.'

21 May 2025: Garrick Club, Garrick Street, London WC2

I am not ending the book at Brown's Hotel. I have walked down Piccadilly, across Leicester Square, to the edge of Covent Garden. I have come to the Garrick Club to look A. A. Milne in the eye.

I am not a member of the club, though my father was and my son is, so I know it well. Milne loved it here. This is where he could meet his peers – fellow playwrights, fellow theatrical folk, fellow authors – and give as much of himself as he chose, but never more. He wanted his work (and his worth) to be recognized, but he guarded his privacy. 'Even now,' he said at the height of his fame, 'when I see my name in the paper, I feel that the world is intruding on my privacy. I ought to be anonymous: we all ought to be anonymous. When I give my name in a shop, I give it with an ill-grace.' He could be awkward in public. He was at ease at the Garrick. At the Garrick, the members knew the rules.

Milne showed his gratitude to his club, you will remember, by leaving it a quarter of his literary estate. The club has used Milne's munificence to restore and extend its magnificent art collection and improve the club's facilities. The club has also named a room in Milne's honour and, in 2018, commissioned a life-sized bronze bust of their benefactor from a young, London-based sculptor, Margot Roulleau-Gallais. I am looking at the bust now. I like it. Looking at it, I like *him*. He looks very English, and handsome in an undemonstrative way. The hair is swept back, the features clear-cut, the mouth enigmatic. Yes, this is A. A. Milne and I think he would like to be commemorated by this bust, especially knowing, as he did, that the Garrick also has on display busts of William Shakespeare, David Garrick and Sir Henry Irving.

I have just noticed that the sculptor, who has certainly caught Milne's likeness, has also included a little figure of Winne-the-Pooh sitting just behind Milne's right shoulder. It's an amusing touch. I like it. What would Milne have made of it, I wonder?

As Lesley Milne said to me, 'Pooh made him rich, but did not make him happy.'

'I suppose,' A. A. Milne acknowledged in 1926, 'that every one of us hopes secretly for immortality; to leave, I mean, a name behind him which will live for ever in this world, whatever he may be doing, himself, in the next.' I have come to the Garrick Club to look Alan Milne in the eye and confront him with the reality of his achievement. Never mind the fun pieces in *Punch*, the novels and the plays, it is those four small children's books that will one day earn him a memorial in Poets' Corner at Westminster Abbey, alongside Edward Lear, Lewis Carroll, Jane Austen, Kipling, Shakespeare – and P. G. Wodehouse.

In the 1920s and early 1930s, Milne's two books of children's poems sold even more copies than did his two books about the adventures of Winnie-the-Pooh. Writing in 1933, Compton Mackenzie saw a special significance in Milne's first collection of verses. '*When We Were Very Young* marks an epoch as positively as any children's book has ever marked one,' said Mackenzie. He reckoned that one small book captured the very essence of a comfortable and civilized English childhood: 'It is not extravagant to surmise that a distant posterity may find in that volume of children's verse a key with which to unlock the present more easily than with any contemporary novel, or poem, or play.'

When We Were Very Young and *Now We Are Six* are more than memorable collections of brilliantly crafted light verse; they are literary time-capsules that have stood the test of time. I read them to my children and my children are reading them to their children. They go on working as poems because, whether you are an adult or a child, they still ring true.

Independence

I never did, I never did, I never *did* like 'Now take care,
   dear!'
I never did, I never did, I never *did* want 'Hold-my-hand';
I never did, I never did, I never *did* think much of 'Not
   up there, dear!'
It's no good saying it. They don't understand.
                              When We Were Very Young

Thinking now about *Winnie-the-Pooh* and *The House at Pooh Corner*, I reckon that it is not too extravagant to surmise that their continuing global popularity (selling in their millions in every language, including Latin*) and their place in our shared psyche (we all know an Eeyore; the British prime minister was likened to Tigger in a newspaper headline only this week; the last two weddings I attended both included readings from *Winnie-the-Pooh*) is, in part, because many have found – and find – in those two volumes of children's stories both comfort and joy (sales soared during the darkest days of the Second World War: Methuen could

---

* *Winnie ille Pu*, the Latin translation of *Pooh* by Alexander Lenard, was published in 1958 and became the only Latin book ever to make it onto the *New York Times* Best Seller List.

not secure enough paper to keep them in print) and a simple key with which to unlock the secrets of the human heart.

Milne's Hundred Acre Wood is as distinct and vivid as Lewis Carroll's Wonderland or J. M. Barrie's Neverland, but, overall, the characters we meet with Milne are more lovable – more 'relatable' to use the modern jargon – than those we find in *Alice* or *Peter Pan*. The characters Milne created are immediately recognizable. There is only one human being in the stories, Christopher Robin, but, somehow, all human life is there. The stories themselves are funny and exciting, full of surprises and nonsense, with moments of sadness, moments of joy, moments of danger, moments of delight. There is wit; there is wordplay; there is wisdom, too. The philosophy of Pooh is profound.*

> 'Well, we must be getting home,' said Kanga. 'Goodbye, Pooh.' And in three large jumps she was gone.
>
> Pooh looked after her as she went.
>
> 'I wish I could jump like that,' he thought. 'Some can and some can't. That's how it is.'
>
> *Winnie-the-Pooh*
>
> 'Supposing a tree fell down, Pooh, when we were underneath it?'
>
> 'Supposing it didn't,' said Pooh after careful thought.
>
> *The House at Pooh Corner*

---

* In 1982, *The Tao of Pooh* by Benjamin Hoff saluted the simple, open, instinctive wisdom of Pooh Bear and used Milne's stories to explain the principles of philosophical Taoism. The book stayed on the *New York Times* Best Seller List for forty-nine weeks. Hoff later wrote *The Te of Piglet* and other writers over the years, in books and blogs, have gone on to explore and anatomize the wisdom on offer in the Hundred Acre Wood.

'When you wake up in the morning, Pooh,' said Piglet at last, 'what's the first thing you say to yourself?'

'What's for breakfast?' said Pooh. 'What do *you* say, Piglet?'

'I say, I wonder what's going to happen exciting *today*?' said Piglet.

Pooh nodded thoughtfully.

'It's the same thing,' he said.

Winnie-the-Pooh

15 June 2025: Poohsticks Bridge, Hartfield, East Sussex

This is Fathers' Day. This feels like the right day for finishing my book. And where I am standing now, notebook in hand, halfway across Poohsticks Bridge, feels very much the right place to be bringing the story to a close. I have walked here through the Ashdown Forest, with the sunshine from a cloudless sky breaking through the trees. It is a beautiful English summer's day. This is an enchanted place. A hundred years ago, A. A. Milne and Christopher Robin – Blue and Moon – played games of Poohsticks here.

I have been thinking of my own father today, of course. I suppose I have thought of him every day while writing this. He was a good man (Charles Brandreth, 1910–81), to me the best. I loved him unconditionally from first to last and he loved me in just the same way. (He never said so, of course. He did not need to. And men of his generation didn't.) He was a sweet man: good-hearted, good-humoured, courteous, kind, decent – very much, I imagine, in the mould of J. V. Milne. And like JV (like us all really), my father had his disappointments. He was a successful solicitor, but he would rather have been a barrister or an actor or an author or a member of parliament. He had a go at being each of those. Whatever I have tried to be or do in my life is because of him. When one of my children became a K.C. and another became a member of parliament, I thought only of my father and of how happy and proud he would have been to see them fulfilling his dreams.

My wife often reminds me that both my father and my remarkable mother (Alice Brandreth, 1914–2010) have been dead for many years and I do not need to keep striving to please them any more. I tell her I can't help it. I want to please them still because I owe them everything. They gave me an idyllic childhood and that childhood, for better or worse, has formed – and defined – my entire life, up to and including writing this book about A. A. Milne.

I have had a happy life and a lucky life. Of course, it's had its ups and downs. Most lives do. Before my parents died, I don't think I had given much thought to what they had been through in their time. They never talked about their travails, but looking through old letters and diaries since their deaths I have discovered the detail of all sorts of things I never knew about: the challenges they faced during the Second World War, their money worries, their mental instability (both had bouts of serious depression), the baby they lost in the 1950s and the reason they adopted my younger brother, Ben. My father had an older brother, also called Ben. I know nothing about him because my father never mentioned him. Was he a bad hat like Alan Milne's older brother, Barry? I do not know. Beyond the fact that he was a scientist (he taught at Cambridge) and was killed in the Second World War, I know nothing about him. My father adored his two older sisters (we saw a lot of my aunts when I was a boy), but though my father was talkative (very) he never mentioned his brother – or his own parents.

Perhaps he did not mention his parents because, like Alan and Daphne, they did not approve of their son's choice for a bride. My parents ran away together and were married in secret, without either of their parents' knowledge or approval. I am sharing this because thinking about it I am realizing that the Milne family story is perhaps not so unusual after all.

Before walking down here to the bridge, I had tea (and scones) in Hartfield High Street, at Pooh Corner, the teashop next door to the village pub. (Fifteenth century in origin, the pub used to be called The Anchor. It is now called The Bear, of course.) I know Pooh Corner because, in 2019, its owners, Neil Reed and his partner, Sam, did me the honour of inviting me to conduct the official opening of their Milne museum. They are a lovely couple. He was in the music industry. She worked for the royal stockbrokers, Cazenove. Now they curate a unique collection of Milne memorabilia (the best I know) and serve tea (with honey) to eighty thousand visitors a year. They have never been happier.

'Pooh is all about happiness,' says Neil. 'Pooh Corner is a happy place, it's as simple as that.' There is so much violence in the world – in the real world, and on TV, in the cinema, in video games, everywhere. There is no violence in the Hundred Acre Wood. 'In the world of Pooh, you find simple friendships,' says Neil, smiling, '– beautiful friendships without compromise.' Sam says, 'I am on the shop floor every day, in the museum and in the tea room, and everyone who comes has their own story, their reason for coming.' Many are adults who lost a parent when they were young and that parent used to read them *Winnie-the-Pooh*. 'Pooh is often quoted at funerals when a child has died or been still-born,' says Neil. He remembers getting a call from a father who had floated a little boat bearing his young child's ashes under the bridge on which I am standing now. He telephoned Pooh Corner the day after sending the ashes on their way, anxious that the little boat might have got stuck among the reeds and weeds beneath the bridge. Neil went to investigate and assured him that the little boat was not stuck. It had been safely swept from the stream to the river Medway, from the Medway to the Thames and on out to sea.

Neil and Sam have scores of stories to tell of Pooh pilgrims coming to Pooh Corner from all over the world. 'We don't have a right to comprehend their stories,' says Neil. 'For so many people, their reason for having a special place for Pooh in their lives is too personal. We don't pry.'

Interestingly, for Neil the hero of it all is not AAM: 'He was a professional writer – a brilliant one, but he did his job and then moved on.' For Neil, the hero is Christopher: 'Can you imagine being the real Christopher Robin? He lived through it. He survived it. He came out of it ultimately as a truly happy, decent human being.'

I agree. Christopher Milne was remarkable. He and Winnie-the-Pooh had something very special in common. Both the boy and the bear believed in 'living gratefully'. By the time I knew Christopher the bitterness he had once felt towards his father had quite disappeared. Moon talked to me about Blue with affection and admiration. He recalled the best of their good times together, when Christopher was in his teens, going for long walks, playing cricket, jointly solving *The Times* crossword, sharing their love of algebra, and Euclid, holidaying together in Dorset when Daphne had escaped to New York or the Mediterranean. Those were the days. He remembered them as vividly and gratefully as Alan remembered his childhood days with Ken.

Famously, the French poet, Baudelaire, said: 'Genius is no more than childhood recaptured at will, childhood equipped now with an adult's ability to express itself, and with the analytical mind that enables it to bring order to the sum of experience, involuntarily amassed.'

'Your father was a bit of a genius, wasn't he?' I said to Christopher Milne.

'Yes, I suppose he was,' said Christopher. 'I didn't think so when he was alive. The quality I most associated him with then was nostalgia.' (In his last novel, *Chloe Marr*, Milne has a character feel a deep 'ache of remembrance for those happy days'.) 'I felt he spent the second half of his life looking back on the first with regret. I now realize that life is too short for regrets. We have to make the best of each day the best we can. My father's childhood, my childhood, your childhood, Clare's childhood – our childhood is whatever our child-hood was. It's made us who we are. We cannot change it. We should not try to live in it once it's over. But we can visit and revisit the best of it whenever we want. And be grateful.'

Christopher then quoted one of his own books to me: 'For us, to whom our childhood has meant so much, the journey back is short, the coming and going easy.' I know what he means. I am standing in the evening sunshine on Poohsticks Bridge remembering playing Poohsticks with my mum and dad. What is the happiest memory of your childhood, I wonder? Catch it again if you can.

Alan Alexander Milne was a witty columnist, a prolific and popular playwright and a fine novelist. What makes him unique is that in his two books about Winnie-the-Pooh he created a world unlike any other – a world of good humour and good heart, a world of warmth and kindness and generosity. Those two books are our passport to that world.

'You want a happy ending?' asked Christopher.

'Yes,' I said.

'Well,' he said, 'it's there at the end of the stories. There's always Pooh . . .'

Yes, there's always Pooh. There's always Pooh and me. 'Let's go together,' says Pooh, says he. 'Let's go together,' says Pooh.

That's the point. Winnie-the-Pooh: he's always there. He will never let you down. You can visit him whenever you want.

The Hundred Acre Wood: it's always there, too. You can come and go as you please. It's where you can go when you want to feel happy, when you need to feel sad, when you long to feel safe. It's an enchanted place. It's somewhere, where a little boy and his Bear will always be playing.

Always.

'Pooh, promise you won't forget about me, ever. Not even when I'm a hundred.'

Pooh thought for a little.

'How old shall *I* be then?'

'Ninety-nine.'

Pooh nodded.

'I promise,' he said.

Still with his eyes on the world, Christopher Robin put out a hand and felt Pooh's paw.

'Pooh,' said Christopher Robin earnestly, 'if I – if I'm not quite – ' he stopped and tried again – 'Pooh, *whatever* happens, you *will* understand, won't you?'

'Understand what?'

'Oh, nothing.' He laughed and jumped to his feet. 'Come on!'

'Where?' said Pooh.

'Anywhere,' said Christopher Robin.

The House at Pooh Corner

Bibliography

A. A. Milne

These are the works of A. A. Milne published during his lifetime, with the date of first publication. Almost all were published both in London and New York.

Lovers in London, a novel, 1905
The Day's Play, pieces from *Punch*, 1910
The Holiday Round, pieces from *Punch*, 1912
Once a Week, pieces from *Punch*, 1914
Happy Days, pieces from *Punch*, 1915
Once on a Time, a story, 1917
Not That It Matters, essays, 1919
First Plays (*Wurzel-Flummery*; *The Lucky One*; *The Boy Comes Home*; *Belinda*; *The Red Feathers*), 1919
If I May, essays, 1920
Second Plays (*Make-Believe*; *Mr Pim Passes By*; *The Camberley Triangle*; *The Romantic Age*; *The Stepmother*), 1921
Mr Pim, a novel, 1921
The Sunny Side, sketches and verse, 1921
The Red House Mystery, a detective story, 1922
Three Plays (*The Dover Road*; *The Truth About Blayds*; *The Great Broxopp*), 1922
Success, a play, 1923
The Man in the Bowler Hat, a play, 1923
When We Were Very Young, poems for children, 1924
A Gallery of Children, stories for children, 1925
For the Luncheon Interval: Cricket and Other Verses, 1925

Four plays (*To Have The Honour* or *Meet the Prince*; *Ariadne*;
    Portrait of a Gentleman in Slippers; *Success*), 1926
Miss Marlow at Play, a play, 1926
Winnie-the-Pooh, 1926
Now We Are Six, poems for children, 1927
The House at Pooh Corner, 1928
The Ivory Door, a play, 1928
The Ascent of Man, an essay, 1928
By Way of Introduction, essays, 1929
The Secret and Other Stories, 1929
Those Were the Days, pieces from *Punch*, 1929
Toad of Toad Hall, a play, 1929
The Fourth Wall or *The Perfect Alibi,* a play, 1929
Michael and Mary, a play, 1930
When I Was Very Young, autobiographical sketch, 1930
Two People, a novel, 1931
Four plays (*Michael and Mary*; *Meet the Prince* or *To Have
    The Honour*; *The Fourth Wall* or *The Perfect Alibi*; *Portrait
    of a Gentleman in Slippers*), 1932
Four Days' Wonder, a novel, 1933
Peace with Honour, 1934
More Plays (*The Ivory Door*; *The Fourth Wall*; *Other People's
    Lives*), 1935
Miss Elizabeth Bennet, a play, 1936
Four Plays (*To Have the Honour*; *Belinda*; *The Dover Road*;
    Mr Pim Passes By), 1939
It's Too Late Now or *Autobiography*, 1939
Behind the Lines, verse, 1940
War with Honour, 1940
The Pocket Milne, 1941
The Ugly Duckling, a play, 1941
Chloe Marr, a novel, 1946
Birthday Party and Other Stories, 1948
A Table Near the Band, short stories, 1950
Before the Flood, a play, 1951
Year In, Year Out, essays, 1952

Prince Rabbit and the Princess Who Could Not Laugh, two stories for children, illustrated by Mary Shepard, were published in 1966. In 2024, Farrago, an imprint of Duckworth Books, published *The Complete Stories of A. A. Milne*, introduced by Gyles Brandreth and including previously uncollected material. In 2024 Farrago also published *The Rabbits*, featuring pieces that had first appeared in *Punch* between 1909 and 1914, and reissued his four full-length novels and his autobiography.

Books by Christopher Milne

The Enchanted Places, 1974
The Path Through the Trees, 1979
The Hollow on the Hill, 1982
The Open Garden, 1988
Beyond the World of Pooh, Selections from the Memoirs of Christopher Milne, edited by A. R. Melrose, with an introduction by Lesley Milne, was published in 2000.

Bibliography

Adlard, John, *Owen Seaman His Life and Work*, 1977
Barrie, J. M., *Peter Pan and Wendy*, 1911
Birkin, Andrew, *J. M. Barrie and the Lost Boys*, 1979
Brands, H. W., *T. R. The Last Romantic*, 1997
Burnett, Frances Hodgson, *Little Lord Fauntleroy*, 1886
Burnett, Frances Hodgson, *The Secret Garden*, 1911
Burnett, Vivian, *The Romantick Lady (Frances Hodgson Burnett): the Life Story of an Imagination*, 1927
Carpenter, Humphrey, *Secret Gardens, The Golden Age of Children's Literature*, 1985
Clark Ashby, Elizabeth, *The Miniature Library of Queen Mary's Dolls' House*, 2024

Crews, Frederick C., *The Pooh Perplex*, 1964

Darlington, W. A., *I Do What I Like*, 1947

Donaldson, Frances, *P. G. Wodehouse*, 1983

Grahame, Kenneth, *The Wind in the Willows*, 1908

Hoff, Benjamin, *The Tao of Pooh*, 1982

Lucas, Audrey, *E. V. Lucas: A Portrait*, 1939

Lucas, E. V., *Reading, Writing, Remembering*, 1932

Mackail, Denis, *Story of JMB*, 1941

Mackenzie, Compton, *Literature in My Time*, 1933

Mackenzie, Norman and Jean, *The Time Traveller: The Life of H. G. Wells*, 1973

Muggeridge, Malcolm, *The Green Stick*, 1972

Playfair, Giles, *My Father's Son*, 1937

Price, R. G. G., *The History of Punch*, 1951

Shea, Sarah E., and others, 'Pathology in the Hundred Acre Wood: A Neurodevelopmental Perspective on A. A. Milne.' *Canadian Medical Association Journal*, 2000

Shepard, E. H., *The Pooh Sketchbook*, edited by Brian Sibley, 1982

Sibley, Brian, *A. A. Milne: A Handlist of His Writings for Children*, 1976

Sibley, Brian, *Three Cheers for Pooh*, 2001

Sproat, Iain, *Wodehouse at War*, 1981

Stoycheva, Valentina, 'What Winnie the Pooh Can Teach Us About PTSD'. *Psychology Today*, 2019

Thwaite, Ann, *A. A. Milne: His Life*, 1990

Thwaite, Ann, *Goodbye Christopher Robin*, 2017

Usborne, Richard, *Wodehouse at Work to the End*, 1976

Vanbrugh, Irene, *To Tell My Story*, 1948

Wells, H. G., *Experiment in Autobiography*, 1934

Wullschläger, Jackie, *Inventing Wonderland*, 1995

Acknowledgements

'If anyone wants to clap,' said Eeyore, 'now is the time to do it.'

This book has come about because, half a century ago, in the mid-1970s, my wife and I started having children. Of course, I was introduced to A. A. Milne's work by my own parents long before that, in the 1950s, when I was a little boy being brought up in London, not far from where the Milnes had lived in the 1920s when A. A. Milne was writing his children's books. But it was only when Michèle's and my three children came along and we began reading Milne's poems and stories to them that I realized what an extraordinary writer Milne was – and is. To Benet, Saethryd and Aphra, night after night, between the late 1970s and the mid-1980s, in turn, out loud (and, I fear, *con brio*) I read *When We Were Very Young* and *Now We Are Six*. I think I liked the verses even more than they did.

At the time I was working in the theatre (I produced three plays in the West End in the 1970s: one won what is now called an Olivier Award) and I got it into my head that Milne's poems could form the basis of a musical revue – something along the lines of *Side by Side by Sondheim* (a hit in 1976) and possibly to be called *Half-way Down the Stairs*. I knew H. Fraser-Simson had composed music for some of Milne's verses, but not for all. I telephoned my friend, the actor Christopher Biggins, who had played Winnie-the-Pooh on stage, to ask his advice. Biggins suggested I call Julian Slade (1930–2006) who had been responsible for the music when Biggins played Pooh. I did just that – excited to do so, because *Salad Days*, *Free as Air* and *Follow That Girl* (all written and composed by Julian Slade with Dorothy Reynolds) were three of the favourite musicals of my boyhood.

I met up with Julian (then about fifty and living in the basement of his mother's house in Kensington) and, at once, we became firm friends and close collaborators. Quickly, my idea of a revue based around Milne's children's verses evolved into something much more ambitious: a full-scale play with music about the life and times – triumphs and tribulations – of A. A. Milne: son, husband, father, writer, soldier and creator of Winnie-the-Pooh. Julian had known Daphne Milne (she may, I think, have been a little like Julian's mother) and he knew Christopher Milne – knew him and liked him. More to the point, Christopher knew and liked Julian.

It is because of Julian Slade that I got to know Christopher Milne – and because Christopher was comfortable with Julian, by proxy he became comfortable with me. Christopher was a lovely man, shy by nature, instinctively reticent, but with us, talking about himself, his parents and Pooh, he was open and easy. He talked to us at length about every aspect of his and his family's life. Whatever question we asked, he did his best to answer, and he asked for nothing in return. He simply wished us the best of luck with our endeavours and when we sent him our final script, generously told us that we seemed to have got it all 'about right'. Our play included all the principal characters that feature in this book – JV and Alan and Ken and Daphne and Christopher

Robin, and 'Nou' the Nanny and Tasker, the gardener, too – and the story it told is essentially the story I have told here.

So, beyond Biggins and Julian Slade, my main acknowledgement must be to Christopher Milne. He has been my principal source, along with his beautifully written published memoirs, combined with his father's autobiography, *It's Too Late Now*, published in 1939, and A. A. Milne's multitude of published works, almost all of which Julian and I worked our way through very happily over several years. (I have re-read many of the *Punch* pieces and all of the novels more recently. I really love the novels.)

Our play did not make it to the stage until 1986. It was commissioned by Guy Woolfenden (for many years the composer and musical director at the Royal Shakespeare Company) when he was artistic director of the Cambridge Music Festival and *Now We Are Sixty* opened at the Cambridge Arts Theatre on 22 July 1986, directed by James Roose-Evans, with choreography by Geraldine Stephenson and musical direction by Stefan Bednarczyk. Ian Gelder played Alan, Rosalind Ayres was Daphne, Peter Bayliss was JV, Allan Corduner Ken, with Sarah Crowden as Nou, Aled Jones as Christopher Robin, and Julian Firth as a naïve young man who comes to Cotchford Farm to interview A. A. Milne as the author approaches his sixtieth birthday. (When the play was revived at the King's Head Theatre, Andrew C. Wadsworth played Alan and Russell Grant was JV.)

I am indebted to everyone involved in the production of the play. Together we talked at length about Milne, the nature of the man and the nature of his genius. Through writing the show, I was lucky enough to meet a range of people who had known Milne, from Dadie Rylands, the Cambridge academic who as a young man had known all the Bloomsbury Group, to Richard Goolden, so long associated with the part of Mole in *Wind in the Willows*. I was also lucky to have as friends two people with a special interest in Milne's work and life: the writer Humphrey Carpenter (author, with his wife, Mari Prichard, of *The Oxford Companion to Children's Literature*) and the true Pooh and Milne authority, the broadcaster and author, Brian Sibley. His book, *Three Cheers for Pooh*, is a masterly 'Celebration of the Best Bear in All the World.'

Equally masterly, and even more magisterial is Dr Ann Thwaite's 1990 biography, *A. A. Milne: His Life*. It is 'the' Milne biography and I know that Christopher Milne read it with real admiration and respect. I am indebted to Dr Thwaite for her work and for her kindness (she entertained me and my wife to tea as I was embarking on this book) and for giving all her working papers to the Harry Ransom Center at the University of Texas, where I was able both to read them and to listen to the audio tapes of her interviews with members of Ken's and Barry's families and with people who had known the Milnes and worked for them at Cotchford Farm during Alan's final illness.

As well as the Thwaite papers, the Harry Ransom Center holds the major archive of Milne material – correspondence, letters, postcards, bills, contracts, manuscripts, first editions – and Michèle and I were allowed free rein to study and copy whatever we found there. We were allowed to photograph hundreds of pages of material with my iPhone, which was a necessary blessing. Back home, on the phone I could enlarge each page, and begin to decipher Milne's almost indecipherable handwriting.

I am hugely indebted to Dr Eric Colleary, Cline Curator of Theatre and Performing Arts at the Harry Ransom

Center, and to his friendly colleagues, who checked us into and out of the library there every day during our visit. It would not have been possible to write this book without their help. And our time in Texas was hugely enhanced by the companionship and assistance of our friend Frank Gallagher, artist, story-teller and Mark Twain lookalike, who was able to join us and help us in our researches thanks to the generosity of his and our friend Joan Winchell, noted patron of the arts in general and patron of the Oscar Wilde Society in particular.

In New York, we made good friends with Anthony W. Marx, President of the New York Public Library and his colleagues, Dr Brent Reidy, Andrew W. Mellon Director of the Research Libraries; Dr Julie Golia, Charles J. Liebman, Curator of Manuscripts, Archives and Rare Books; and Iris Weinshall, the Library's Chief Financial Officer and Treasurer. I am grateful to Jane D. Hartley, United States ambassador to the United Kingdom, 2022–25, for introducing me to Tony Marx at the NYPL.

At the Royal Library at Windsor Castle, we have been brilliantly looked after by Dr Stella Panayotova, Royal Librarian and Deputy Keeper of the Royal Archives, and her colleague, Elizabeth Clark Ashby, Curator of Books and Manuscripts, Royal Collection Trust. At the Garrick Club in London, the librarians Moira Goff and Carmen Holdsworth-Delgado generously shared the Club's Milne material with us. Nigel Everett and Robert Whelan at the Theatre Royal, Haymarket, where five of Milne's plays were first presented, have also been wonderfully helpful. I also owe a huge debt of gratitude to the Pooh Corner Museum in Hartfield, where Neil and Sam Reed and Harriet Berry were so generous with their time and expertise in sourcing images from their astonishing collection. Special thanks must also go to Sara Stapley for her permission to use the picture of Christopher Robin in the army and for her valuable insights on the Milne family.

Perhaps it is because of the good nature of Pooh, but wherever we have been working on the book – in Jamaica, New York, Texas, London and Sussex, from Brown's Hotel to the Ashdown Forest – we have been blessed with a warm and helpful welcome. I keep saying 'we' because on all my travels I have been accompanied by my wife, Michèle, who has been my collaborator and good companion since we first met on 6 June 1968. Without her, her forbearance, patience and encouragement, there would have been no book.

My grateful thanks go, too, to our three children and to many friends for their kindness and encouragement while I have been working on this project, notably: James Albrecht, Stefan Bednarczyk, Susan Bowles, Finola Burrell, Selina Cadell, Dame Judi Dench, Jochen and Jutta Frank, Lord (Richard) Harries of Pentegarth, Jason Higgins, Merlin Holland, Dame Joanna Lumley, Marta Rucinska, Venetia Vyvyan, Jane Woolfenden and Rebecca Croft-Sharland Cadell. Someone I have not met and only know online, is a literary blogger called Claire who, at thecaptivereader.com, has posted a range of illuminating essays about the works of A. A. Milne, which I have both enjoyed and benefitted from.

My literary agent is my friend Jonathan Lloyd of Curtis Brown – the firm, founded in 1899 by Albert Curtis Brown, that has long looked after A. A. Milne and his Estate. Among the team at Curtis Brown I am especially grateful to Becky Brown, Stephanie Thwaites, Norah Perkins, Lily Kovacs and Rachel Goldblatt. My thanks, too, to Nigel Urwin, trustee of the C. R. Milne Estate.

ACKNOWLEDGEMENTS

The idea of writing the book was suggested to me by my friend and publisher at Penguin Michael Joseph, Dan Bunyard. We have created five books together and they have only come about because of his creative skill and encouragement. I am hugely indebted, too, to my editor, Emma Henderson, and to my friend Beatrix McIntyre, Senior Editorial Manager at Michael Joseph, for her dedication, kindness and attention to detail.

As every author knows, it takes a village to publish a book and the Michael Joseph village is an especially happy one, led by Louise Moore, whose colleagues involved in this project have included Stuart Brown (who designed the picture plates), Lee Motley (who designed the cover), Alice Chandler (picture researcher), Hannah Mockett (who helped secure the text permissions), Christina Ellicot, Rachel Myers and Kelly Mason (the principal Sales Directors for the book), Clare Parker and Gaby Young (publicity), Vicky Photiou (Marketing Director), Tanuja Shelar (Marketing Manager), and Sarah Scarlett (Rights). I am also grateful to Jill Cole for reading the proofs and to Catherine Hookway for supplying the index.

My grateful thanks, too, go to my American publisher, the inspiring Michael Flamini at St Martin's Press, and to my US editor, Claire Cheek.

While writing this book, I have also been recording my twice-weekly podcast, *Rosebud*. I am proud to say it is a multi-million-download podcast, produced by my friend Harriet Jaine. It is so successful because our guests include famous and interesting people: prime ministers, Oscar winners, Nobel laureates, billionaires, Olympic champions, scientists, celebrities, writers, artists, eccentrics – all sorts. The first question I ask every guest is: 'What is your very first memory?' Together we then begin to unpack and unpick their childhood. What *Rosebud* and this book have taught me is that, for almost everybody, childhood is the key to everything. Truly, a childhood lasts a lifetime.

Picture credits

Inset 1: Page 1: With kind permission of Pooh Corner Museum, Hartfield; **Page 3:** P. G. Wodehouse: © Bettmann via Getty; J. M. Barrie: © Hulton Archive/Stringer via Getty; E. H. Shepard: with kind permission of Pooh Corner Museum, Hartfield; **Pages 4–5:** © Punch Cartoon Library/Topfoto; the *Evening News*: © dmg media licensing; **Pages 6–7:** Christopher Robin and A. A. Milne: © PA Images/Alamy Stock Photo; Christopher Robin and Daphne, at London Zoo and in Pooh's House: all with kind permission of Brian Sibley; Christopher Robin and Daphne portrait: photograph by Madame Yevonde, with kind permission of Pooh Corner Museum, Hartfield; **Page 8:** photograph by Marcus Adams © Camera Press London

Inset 2: Page 1: © National Portrait Gallery, London; **Pages 2–3:** Cotchford Farm, 1926: with kind permission of Brian Sibley; letter: with kind permission of Harry Ransom Center, The University of Texas at Austin; holiday photos: with kind permission of Pooh Corner Museum, Hartfield; **Pages 4–5:** Elmer Rice: photograph by Maurice Goldberg/Condé Nast via Getty Images; Leonora Corbett: photograph by Culture Club Getty Images; letter: with kind permission of Harry Ransom Center, The University of Texas at Austin; book cover of 1944 US edition: The Frank Gallagher Picture & Print Collection, by kind permission of Frank Gallagher; **Pages 6–7:** Christopher Robin in British Army: with kind permission of Sara Stapley; Christopher Robin and Lesley de Sélincourt: ANL/Shutterstock.

Text permissions

Quotations from the following are reproduced with permissions from Curtis Brown Group Ltd on behalf of The Pooh Properties Trust:

Winnie-the-Pooh by A.A. Milne
Copyright © Pooh Properties Trust 1926

The House at Pooh Corner by A.A. Milne
Copyright © Pooh Properties Trust 1928

Now We Are Six by A.A. Milne
Copyright © Pooh Properties Trust 1927

When We Were Very Young by A.A. Milne
Copyright © Pooh Properties Trust 1924

Quotations from the following are reproduced with permissions from Curtis Brown Group Ltd on behalf of The Estate of the Late Lesley Milne Limited:

'Once A Week' by A.A. Milne
Copyright © The Estate of the Late Lesley Milne Limited 1920

'Two People' by A.A. Milne
Copyright © The Estate of the Late Lesley Milne Limited 1931

Index

'Oh, Bear!' said Christopher Robin. 'How I do love you!'
    'So do I,' said Pooh.

Winnie-the-Pooh

Piglet was comforted by this, and in a little while they were knocking and ringing very cheerfully at Owl's door.

"Hallo, Owl," said Pooh. "I hope we're not too late for — I mean, how are you, Owl? Piglet and I just came to see if you were in, because it's Thursday."

"Sit down Pooh, sit down, Piglet," said Owl kindly. "Make yourselves comfortable."

They thanked him, and made themselves as comfortable as they could.

"Because, you see, Owl," said Pooh, "we've been hurrying, so as to be in time for — so as to see you before we went away again."

Owl nodded solemnly.

"Correct me if I am wrong," he said, "but am I right in supposing that it is a very Blusterous day outside?"

"Very," said Piglet, who was quietly thawing his ears, and wishing that he was safely back in his own house.

"I thought so," said Owl. "It was on just such a Blusterous day as this that my Uncle Robert, a portrait of whom you see upon the wall on your right, Piglet, while returning in the late forenoon from a — what's that?

There was a loud cracking noise.

"Look out!" cried Pooh. "Mind the clock! Out of the way, Piglet! Piglet, I'm falling on you!"

"Help!" cried Piglet.

Pooh's side of the room was slowly tilting upwards and his chair began sliding down on Piglet's. The clock slithered gently along the mantelpiece, collecting vases on the way, until they all crashed together on to what had been the floor, but was now trying to see what it looked like as a wall. Uncle Robert, who was going to be the new hearth-rug, and was bringing the rest of his wall with him as carpet, met Piglet's chair just as Piglet was expecting to leave it, and for a little while it became very difficult to remember which was really the north. Then there was another loud crack ... Owl's room collected itself feverishly ... and there was silence.

*   *   *   *   *